'This volume sets out the thinking an
university-wide initiative and offers case
central message is surely twofold: both t
a liberating experience and that, with
institutional project, universities can lib
practices still further. This is an exen
much to dwell on to all interested in advancing university education.'

**Ronald Barnett, Emeritus Professor of Higher Education,
University College London Institute of Education**

'The Connected Curriculum initiative at UCL has rightly attracted
attention for its innovative approach to a researched-informed
undergraduate education. This new collection enlarges on the theory
and practice of the Connected Curriculum and provides the sector with
examples of the highest-quality pedagogical endeavours.'

**Professor Jacqueline Labbe, Pro Vice-Chancellor (Academic),
De Montfort University**

'As OfS and UKRI take separate paths, this is an especially
appropriate moment to encapsulate the synergy between education
and research. As we are required to demonstrate value for money for
student fees, it is vital that we can articulate the benefits to be gained from
learning in a research-rich environment. This volume is, therefore, both
timely and welcome in bringing to a wider audience the context for and
explanation of UCL's Connected Curriculum and, vitally, in Part Two a
series of invaluable case studies of the theory in practice. This will prove
to be an invaluable resource for research-intensive higher education.'

**Timothy A. Quine, Professor of Earth Surface Science,
Deputy Vice-Chancellor (Education) University of Exeter**

'For some years now, UCL has been leading the way in rethinking
teaching and learning in higher education, drawing upon the university's
formidable research base in technology-enhanced learning, assessment
for learning, improving learner outcomes, research-led teaching and
much more. Sector-leading initiatives, such as the Connected Curriculum
project, have taken this expertise into the heart of UCL's teaching
delivery. This collection of essays is an admirable testament to the
university's ambition to foster innovative, evidence-based and thoughtful
approaches to teaching and learning. There is much to learn from here.'

**Professor Karen O'Brien, Head of the Humanities Division,
University of Oxford**

Teaching and Learning in Higher Education

Teaching and Learning in Higher Education

Perspectives from UCL

Edited by Jason P. Davies and Norbert Pachler

First published in 2018 by the UCL Institute of Education Press, University College London, 20 Bedford Way, London WC1H 0AL

www.ucl-ioe-press.com

© Jason P. Davies and Norbert Pachler 2018

British Library Cataloguing in Publication Data:
A catalogue record for this publication is available from the British Library

ISBNs
978-1-78277-255-2 (paperback)
978-1-78277-256-9 (PDF eBook)

Typeset by Quadrant Infotech (India) Pvt Ltd
Printed by CPI Group (UK) Ltd, Croydon, CR0 4YY
Cover image © UCL Digital Media 2018, photographer: Mary Hinkley

Contents

List of figures and tables

About the contributors

Paul Bartlett is a Principal Teaching Fellow within the UCL Department of Physics and Astronomy. He has experience of education and training in the public, private and university contexts where he has focused on practical skills acquisition for trainees and students.

Chris Blackman is a Senior Lecturer in Inorganic Chemistry at UCL. He has a particular interest in the use of e-learning resources to support the teaching of practical chemistry.

Nicole Blum is a Senior Lecturer in the Development Education Research Centre at UCL Institute of Education. Her research interests include pedagogy and learning in development education, internationalization and global perspectives in higher education, the ethnography of education, education for sustainability, and climate change.

Douglas Bourn is Co-Director of Development Education Research Centre at UCL Institute of Education and author of numerous books and articles on the themes of development education, global perspectives in higher education, global learning and global citizenship education.

Amanda Cain is a Senior Teaching Fellow in the Department of Structural and Molecular Biology at UCL. In addition to developing methods for research-led teaching, she has an interest in increasing the numerical fluency of UCL students and finding new and innovative ways to improve their experience.

Mark Carnall is the Collections Manager (Life Collections) at the Oxford University Museum of Natural History. His wide interests include digitization and 3D printing in museums. He has previously worked in a range of contexts to support public engagement with museum collections.

Helen J. Chatterjee is a Professor of Biology at UCL Biosciences and Head of Research and Teaching at UCL Culture. She has a particular research interest in the value of cultural encounters to health, well-being and education.

Jason P. Davies is a Senior Teaching Fellow in the UCL Arena Centre for Research-based Education. He is particularly interested in developing inclusive education in higher education, interdisciplinarity and ethnographic approaches to learning and university culture.

Rosalind Duhs was founding Director of UCL Arena (2014–16). Her PhD was a comparative study of academic staff learning to teach in research-intensive universities in England and Sweden. Her interest in educational development has led to accreditor and consultancy work for Advance HE and she continues to contribute to UCL projects.

Dilly Fung is an international champion of research-based education and the architect of UCL's research-based education strategy, Connected Curriculum. She will become Pro-Director (Education) at the LSE in July 2018, and was previously a Professor of Higher Education Development and Academic Director of the UCL Arena Centre for Research-based Education.

Carl Gombrich is Programme Director of the interdisciplinary undergraduate Arts and Sciences BASc at UCL. He is a regular speaker and writer on matters concerning interdisciplinary undergraduate education and was a member of the British Academy's Working Group on Interdisciplinarity.

Lesley Gourlay is Head of the Department of Culture, Communication and Media and a Reader in Education and Technology at UCL Institute of Education. She works predominantly on posthuman theory, and the digital and textual practices in higher education.

Leonie Hannan is a Research Fellow at the School of History, Anthropology, Philosophy and Politics, Queen's University Belfast. She is a social and cultural historian with a particular interest in the value of heritage objects in teaching and learning contexts.

Gwyneth Hughes is a Reader in Higher Education at UCL Institute of Education. She has published widely on learning and teaching in higher education, particularly on the theme of ipsative assessment.

Tansy Jessop is a Professor of Research Informed Teaching at Southampton Solent University. She leads the TESTA project on programme assessment and feedback and has published variously on assessment and feedback, learning spaces, narrative methods and social justice in education.

Thomas Kador is a Senior Teaching Fellow at UCL Culture and for the Arts & Sciences (BASc) programme. His interests include heritage pedagogics, object-based learning, everyday practice and social change, as well as public and community-based approaches to heritage.

Jonathan Kendall is a Senior Teaching Fellow at the Bartlett School of Architecture, UCL, where he has taught since 1999, specializing in urban design. He combines teaching with professional practice, and is Partner and Director of Urban Design at Fletcher Priest Architects.

Monika Kraska is a doctoral candidate at UCL Institute of Education within the Development Education Research Centre. She is interested in internationalization and global citizenship within higher education.

Jenny Marie is a Principal Teaching Fellow at the UCL Arena Centre for Research-based Education. She has been working in academic development for more than ten years and has led UCL ChangeMakers since 2015.

Teresa McConlogue is a Principal Teaching Fellow at the UCL Arena Centre for Research-based Education. She has worked in the UK and internationally to support staff and students to develop higher education. Her main focus has recently been on assessment practices and inclusive education.

Ruth Morgan is a Professor of Crime and Forensic Science, in the UCL Department of Security and Crime Science, and Director of UCL Centre for the Forensic Sciences. Her chief research interest is the interpretation of forensic science evidence, and how interdisciplinary approaches from the sciences, social science and humanities can address this complex challenge.

Emma Newall is a Lecturer in Science Education at UCL Institute of Education. She has been working in STEM enrichment and education since 2003, with a particular interest in research-based learning.

Julianne Nyhan is a Senior Lecturer in UCL's Digital Information Studies. She has a broad interest in the Digital Humanities and its history, and in particular the overlooked non-canonical and oral aspects of the field's emergence.

Martin Oliver is a Professor of Education and Technology at the UCL Institute of Education. His research focuses on higher education, including areas such as the curriculum, doctoral study and students' experiences.

Norbert Pachler is a Professor of Teaching and Learning and Pro-Director: Teaching, Quality and Learning Innovation at the UCL Institute of Education. He is also Pro-Vice-Provost: Education at UCL with responsibility for e-learning and online learning. He has a particular academic interest in teacher education and development, technology-enhanced learning and foreign language education.

Caroline Pelletier is a Reader in Culture and Communications in the Department of Culture, Communication and Media at UCL Institute of Education. Her research explores the significance of technology for teaching, learning and knowledge.

Bahijja Tolulope Raimi-Abraham is a Lecturer in Pharmaceutics at King's College London. During the time of her Nuffield Research Placement she was also an Engineering and Physical Sciences Research Council-funded Postdoctoral Research Associate at UCL.

Kerstin Sailer is Reader in Social and Spatial Networks at UCL's Bartlett School of Architecture. Her research interests lie in the interplay between complex buildings and social behaviours. For the Master's course 'Space Syntax: Architecture and Cities' she has developed interactive and iterative methods of teaching academic writing to students, including blogs.

Matthew Seren Smith is the Learning Technologist for UCL's Faculty of Engineering. He advises academics and students on technology use in education. He is interested in how the two intersect and ways in which to better understand this relationship.

Melissa Terras is a Professor of Digital Cultural Heritage at Edinburgh University, the Director of Digital Scholarship in the College of Arts, Humanities and Social Sciences, and Honorary Professor of Digital Humanities at UCL. Her research focuses on the use of computational techniques to enable research in the arts, humanities, and wider cultural heritage and information environment that would otherwise be impossible.

Keith Turner is CEO of Learnexx3D Virtual Labs. He is an entrepreneurial business and software products manager with over 20 years' executive level experience in founding, funding, developing, restructuring and selling companies.

Anne Vanhoestenberghe is an Associate Professor with the Aspire Centre for Rehabilitation Engineering and Assistive Technology at UCL. She leads Medical Engineering courses for undergraduate and postgraduate programmes.

Sarah Warnes is a Senior Teaching Fellow at the UCL School of Management. Since entering higher education in 2007, Sarah has been committed to developing her teaching practice, always looking for new and effective ways to inspire students to actively learn.

Andrew Wills is a Professor in Physical Chemistry at UCL and a member of the Royal Society of Chemistry's Education Division Council. He has a broad interest in bringing innovations into the support and pedagogy of university students.

Acknowledgements

We would like to thank everyone who helped to make this book happen. It is hard to do justice to them all. We are particularly grateful to Nicky Platt and Jonathan Dore at the UCL IOE Press for their forbearance.

Many of the initiatives described in the book are part of a larger community deeply committed to student learning at an institution with an education strategy explicitly focusing on the nexus between research and teaching and their parity. We owe that strategy to the support of the Provost, Michael Arthur, and the Vice-Provost (Education & Student Affairs), Anthony Smith.

We also want give a special acknowledgement to students past and present; they might be surprised how much we learn from them as we strive to improve their learning experience.

Our final debt of gratitude must go to our colleagues in the UCL Arena Centre for Research-based Education, and the UCL Institute of Education and their commitment to education.

Introduction

Jason P. Davies and Norbert Pachler

In recent months and indeed years there has been much debate about teaching excellence in higher education in the UK specialist press, as well as more widely, with a focus on the 'undergraduate student experience'. The principal driver of this has been the National Student Survey,[1] which began in 2005. More recently, the UK government launched the Teaching Excellence Framework (TEF) (BIS, 2016), which is based on a 'basket' of different metrics covering the categories of teaching quality, learning environment, student outcomes and learning gain, as well as narrative statements. These are, it is claimed, intended to inform student/applicant choice, raise the profile and value of teaching, recognize and reward excellence in teaching, as well as meet the needs of employers. The first results were published in June 2017 (BIS and Johnson, 2017) and have led to the award of gold, silver and bronze ratings for all those institutions that participated. There continues to be much debate about the extent to which the methodology chosen and the metrics informing them really inform us about the actual quality and nature of teaching taking place in universities, as they are based on student satisfaction, retention and employment. For a detailed account of the TEF, see for example Wonkhe (n.d.), which provides in-depth coverage and analysis of higher education policy.

The TEF is, of course, not the first policy initiative aimed at improving the quality of teaching and learning in higher education in the UK, but it is arguably the most significant to date. Others include the inauguration of the Institute for Learning and Teaching in Higher Education (ILTHE) as one outcome of the influential Dearing Report in the late 1990s, which later became the Higher Education Academy (HEA)[2] and which readers may know in particular for its many publications and surveys – among them the Postgraduate Taught Experience Survey (PTES)[3] – as well as its UK Professional Standards Framework and related fellowship scheme of professional recognition. Yet another initiative was the Centres for Excellence in Teaching and Learning (CETLs) in the second half of the 2000s. There were many more examples, too numerous to be covered here. The introduction and escalation of student fees over recent years have also led to a far more focused scrutiny of education.

These 'high-level' prompts have led to many institutions formulating strategies and initiatives that seek to cultivate a more distinctive kind of experience of higher education, and many of these find their place in the branding and publicity materials on each of their websites. It is not, however, always easy to get a sense of what is happening 'on the ground' as those responsible for providing education rethink how they engage the next generation with their subjects. Education is of course a subject in its own right, but it is not always easy for those outside the field to get a sense of what higher education learning is for those involved, in the sense of how students are learning and why that learning has been framed in a particular way.

The examples presented in this book are grounded in teaching at University College London (UCL), London's world-leading multidisciplinary and predominantly postgraduate university which, in pedagogical terms, has become increasingly well known for its Connected Curriculum initiative,[4] which offers a distinctive approach to education focused on integrating research and education through six dimensions of connectivity. A great deal has already been published on this in a short space of time as the initiative gathers pace: Fung (2017) explains the rationale in full, and both Carnell and Fung (2017) and Tong *et al.* (2018) present a fuller range of detailed examples. It has traditionally been assumed that undergraduate students are simply not ready or equipped to do 'real' research, and that they are therefore in the position of being passive recipients to be trained in how 'we' do things. But enough groundbreaking academics have found ways to involve students in actual research to the point that it is not just instinctively more plausible, but there are also a host of examples across subjects where it is actually being done.

This profound reconsideration of the university curriculum towards 'research-based education' (as it is often known) has also seen an institutional commitment to a range of other initiatives in the UCL2034 strategy,[5] including staff development and recognition of teaching, UCL ChangeMakers and (through Connected Curriculum) Liberating the Curriculum, each of which has its own chapter here. There are also longer-standing issues in higher education such as the relationship of education and research, modularization, assessment, globalization and interdisciplinarity. This list is not exhaustive, but it represents a broad spread of the factors that have led teachers and those supporting learning to rethink how they work over the last generation or so.

In this book, then, we 'merely' seek to provide an opportunity for interested parties such as practitioners and students, as well as the wider public, to explore some examples and approaches to teaching and learning in and across different disciplines from the perspective of a university intent on affording consideration of education the importance it deserves. The opening chapters are written to give accessible explanations of the broader trends and initiatives undertaken at UCL, and in higher education in general, and are intended to give just enough of the general picture to inform the actual case studies in Part Two.

In so doing, we deliberately neither make explicit use of theoretical/ contextual frames, nor seek to categorize, analyse or critique the practical approaches presented. Instead, we intend to present some examples of practice with a certain degree of immediacy, in the hope they speak directly to the reader and convey some of the enthusiasm for, interest in and commitment to the student experience and the specialist discipline in which they are situated.

The brief editorial introduction to each chapter (in grey boxes) outlines the relevant background, context and related initiatives. The contributions to this book have not been written specifically to exemplify the Connected Curriculum initiative, but rather to sit alongside it. These perspectives emerge from UCL's annual Teaching and Learning Conference (recently re-launched as the UCL Education Conference), in recognition of the importance of a holistic approach to the student experience, as well as the UCL Provost's Teaching Awards (now the UCL Education Awards) and Student Choice Teaching Awards, which recognize and reward UCL colleagues who are making outstanding contributions to the learning experience and success of students. Each draws attention to the specific considerations from Part One that are appropriate to their own contribution.

We hope, through our modest offering, to contribute to the debate about the quality of teaching and learning by showcasing some examples of how colleagues at UCL seek to engage students in their learning.

Notes

[1] www.thestudentsurvey.com

[2] www.heacademy.ac.uk

[3] www.heacademy.ac.uk/institutions/surveys/postgraduate-taught-experience-survey

[4] www.ucl.ac.uk/teaching-learning/education-initiatives/connected-curriculum

[5] www.ucl.ac.uk/2034

References

BIS (Department for Business, Innovation and Skills) (2016) *Higher Education: Success as a knowledge economy – white paper*. Online. www.gov.uk/government/publications/higher-education-success-as-a-knowledge-economy-white-paper (accessed 5 July 2017).

BIS and Johnson, J. (2017) *Universities rated in Teaching Excellence Framework.* Online. www.gov.uk/government/news/universities-rated-in-teaching-excellence-framework (accessed 5 July 2017).

Carnell, B. and Fung, D. (eds) (2017) *Developing the Higher Education Curriculum: Research-based education in practice.* London: UCL Press.

Fung, D. (2017) *A Connected Curriculum for Higher Education.* London: UCL Press.

Tong, V.C.H., Standen, A. and Sotiriou, M. (eds) (2018) *Shaping Higher Education with Students: Ways to connect research and teaching.* London: UCL Press.

Wonkhe (n.d.) *Higher Education: Policy, people and politics.* Online. https://wonkhe.com (accessed 5 July 2016).

Part One

Position papers

1

This first part of the book sets out broad positions on key themes in higher education, to create a context for Part Two, which consists of case studies illustrating practice at a world-leading, research-rich London university.

The authors explain a range of initiatives and strategies that are responses to the kinds of high-level considerations mentioned in the Introduction. Some consider changes in the field of higher education such as the increased interest in research-based education or assessment; others consider particular initiatives that UCL has set up in recent years such as student partnership or efforts to make curriculum and pedagogy more inclusive. All of them are written by people who are heavily involved in taking general trends and thinking through how to effect change in practice.

Chapter 1

The context of the Connected Curriculum

Jason P. Davies and Dilly Fung[1]

This opening chapter sets a broad perspective on some of the issues facing higher education in general: what kinds of pedagogical problems are we trying to solve, and why? After introducing the key UCL strategy of the Connected Curriculum and research-based education, it touches on a number of overarching themes about learning. These include the ways that educators construct environments for students to learn *in*, how their engagement is critical (and can be squandered) and the way that in recent years, higher education has rethought the curriculum in an attempt to move its focus from the teacher to the learner. As soon as we start to think along these lines, other questions emerge that might loosely be called 'identity-related' as we realize that one way or another, we are shaping our graduates' whole perspectives in far more ways than might initially have been expected. The chapter gives an overview of some of the key approaches that characterize modern university education, and sets the scene for the chapters that follow. In particular, it seeks to show how we have reached a point where research-based education is not just plausible and achievable, but in fact desirable, as a way of bringing a set of strands together that have hitherto rarely been coherently woven.

Introduction

A key aspect of UCL's 2034 strategy[2] is the commitment to having research-based education – learning through research and enquiry – at the heart of its curriculum. This is formulated in the Connected Curriculum,[3] a framework for curriculum development, which has six dimensions:

- Students connect with researchers and with the institution's research
- A throughline of research activity is built into each programme
- Students make connections across subjects and out to the world
- Students connect academic learning with workplace learning

- Students learn to produce outputs – assessments directed at an audience
- Students connect with each other, across phases and with alumni.

The six dimensions all stem from the core principle: that students learn most effectively through actively undertaking research and enquiry. The emphasis here is on drawing students into a research and learning community that collectively pushes at the edge of knowledge.

The philosophical underpinnings of the Connected Curriculum framework and its relevance to higher education more broadly are explored in a new open-access monograph, *A Connected Curriculum for Higher Education* (Fung, 2017). Fung draws on the field of philosophical hermeneutics (Gadamer, 2004; Fairfield, 2012) to argue that at the core of 'good' education is the development of both individuals *and* society. This is achieved through critical dialogue, within and across established disciplines, which advances knowledge and its impact for good on the world. Fung argues that the recent separation of research and education in higher education, in both policy and practice, should be challenged. Critical dialogue and open-minded analysis of evidence are at the core of both research and student learning, connecting the two. She argues that the curriculum in higher education can also be more usefully seen as a conceptual whole rather than as a set of separate curricula. Advocating a more connected and coherent set of research and learning opportunities that cut across traditional 'teacher', 'learner' and 'researcher' roles, she provides a range of case study vignettes of current practice from universities around the world, showing how departments today are responding to this challenge in innovative ways.

Fung provides 20 key questions about existing programmes of study in higher education for departments to explore with their students (Fung, 2017: 146):

Dimensions	Key questions for departments and programme teams
Core principle Students learn through research and enquiry	1. Are students encountering specific questions addressed by researchers and learning to articulate their own research questions, at every level of study? 2. Can we adjust our teaching methods, student assessments and other aspects of departmental practice to prioritize engaging all students actively in research and critical enquiry?

Dimensions	Key questions for departments and programme teams
Dimension 1 Students connect with researchers and with the institution's research	3. Do students have regular opportunities to learn about the institution's research, and other current research relevant to their studies? 4. Are students meeting with researchers and engaging with their work, for example through group activities such as 'Meet the researcher'? 5. Are students exploring the intellectual, policy-related, practical and ethical challenges associated with current research, and recognizing their relevance to professional life more widely?
Dimension 2 A throughline of research activity is built into each programme	6. Is there a well-designed core sequence of modules, units and/or learning activities through which students steadily build their research skills and understandings, and is this explicit to students? 7. Are students explicitly challenged to make intellectual connections between different elements of their programme? 8. Can students have some flexibility and even take risks with their research-related activities, for example by working towards a Showcase Portfolio for which they can curate their best work?
Dimension 3 Students make connections across disciplines and out to the world	9. Is the programme of study structured so that students need to step outside their home discipline(s) and see through at least one other disciplinary lens? 10. Are students required to make explicit connections between disciplinary perspectives, for example by collaborating with students of other disciplines to analyse evidence and issues? 11. Through making interdisciplinary connections, are students challenged to address complex global challenges?

Dimensions	Key questions for departments and programme teams
Dimension 4 Students connect academic learning with workplace learning	12. Are all students on the programme(s) able to analyse the ways in which their academic learning is relevant to the world of work? 13. Do students have explicit opportunities to prepare for the workplace, for example through meeting alumni, shadowing, and work placements, and where appropriate through critiquing the notions of work and professionalism in society? 14. Can students articulate effectively the skills and knowledge they have developed through their research-related activities and through their wider studies and experiences, and showcase these to future employers?
Dimension 5 Students learn to produce outputs – assessments directed at an audience	15. Are some student assessments outward-facing, directed at an audience, thereby enabling them to connect with local and/or wider communities (whether online or face-to-face)? 16. Are student assessments across the programme suitably varied, enabling them to develop a range of skills including expertise in digital practices and communications? 17. Are students required to revisit and use feedback on their tasks, both formative and summative, in order to improve their work?
Dimension 6 Students connect with each other, across phases and with alumni	18. Do students have frequent opportunities to meet and participate in collaborative enquiry with one another in diverse groups? 19. Are they building connections with students in other year groups, for example through events or mentoring schemes? 20. Can students meet and learn from diverse alumni, and build a strong sense of belonging to an inclusive research and learning community?

As these questions suggest, the focus of the Connected Curriculum approach is on opening up thinking about curriculum design and promoting more creative and flexible ways of designing degree programmes. This includes motivating students to engage fully with their studies by enabling them to connect with local and wider communities. Undertaking enquiry-based activities appropriate for their discipline, students can present and explore their findings to interested parties beyond the university.

As Fung (2017) notes, the Connected Curriculum approach has quickly made an impact across the higher education sector – across the UK, Europe and beyond. Why is higher education, and UCL in particular, ready for such a strategy? How did we get to this point? And what do we hope to achieve?

Education for the future

Just over a century ago, in his *Democracy and Education* (1916), the philosopher of education John Dewey laid out his argument that complex societies, faced with the fact that individuals die but groups persist, must educate the young if they are to continue in any organized form and retain their accumulated specialist understanding. To do this they need to create a semi-artificial (educational) environment that systematically emphasizes what they wish to promote and plays down that which they do not. We do not control every aspect of how people respond, and we cannot ultimately *make* people learn what we wish them to, but we can create opportunities for them to learn and, by selecting environments and opportunities, steer them in the direction we wish them to go. He stressed this environment and set of opportunities should not become so artificial and disconnected that it became an arid set of disconnected and meaningless exercises, but there was an equal danger in making it so 'real' that it was impossible to guide what was being learnt. If it is to be a true bridge to the wider world rather than just another part of it, education *must* select elements to include from within that wider world. That selection requires deliberate prioritizing of certain aspects, and evasion of others. In other words, there is no 'neutral' education: whatever we choose to cultivate in our young will shape the future of our society.

Dewey also, almost hilariously from our perspective, noted that there was an enormous amount of knowledge to pass on to the next generation; he could probably never have imagined how much knowledge we have now. We passed the point long ago of being able to 'tell them everything' and need to switch our attention to equipping our students with the ability to find out what they need to understand and integrate this new knowledge themselves. An undergraduate degree must be expected to be the culmination of 'schooling', and to be a preparation for the wider world and a full transition to adult life, even if that is then postgraduate education.

Some decades later, another American, the maths teacher and educational reformer John Holt, in documenting *How Children Fail*, told a story from James Herndon's *How to Survive in Your Native Land* (1971) about 'the dumbest kid in the dumb class'. Jim came across his teenage pupil at a bowling alley where he efficiently performed a complex set of counting tasks, keeping score of two lanes simultaneously (Holt, 1984: 175). The astonished teacher gave the boy bowling-based maths problems at school, but the teenager, who could solve them effortlessly at work, gave answers that were 'not only wrong but absurd'. Dewey's warning about keeping an artificial teaching environment still meaningful had not been heeded: too far divorced from a 'real' context, the school lessons had no meaning for this lad, and he did not even *expect* them to make any sense. The only sane response for the teenager was to get rid of this endless series of strange questions and impossible dilemmas by giving an answer – *any* answer – and enjoying the short-lived relief that the ball was, at least temporarily, back in the teacher's court.

Holt goes on to ask, 'how can we tell whether children understand something or not?' and notes that as a student, he got respectable grades but 'didn't have the faintest idea of what the course was about' (ibid.: 176). He continues that 'a field of knowledge … is a territory, and knowing it is … a matter of knowing how the items relate to, compare with, and fit in with each other' (ibid.: 179). Our final thought from Holt is his observation that it is much better for his young students to discover the basic properties of numbers for themselves, and by experience (ibid.: 200).

Though both writers were referring principally to children, a lot of their thoughts also apply to young adults, i.e. most university undergraduates. Both stress the absolute necessity of understanding as requiring meaning that depends on students establishing their own relationship with the wider world, not a second-hand surrogate from a teacher's description. In other words, they highlight the need to create a learning environment that manages to constrain meaning and connections to manageable levels, but does not stifle all the life and relevance out of the learning, and allows students to find their own way. Isolated and apparently arbitrary tests, equations and facts make real understanding impossible.

The third aspect of twentieth-century thinking to note here, roughly halfway between Dewey and Holt, is the idea of 'zones of proximal development' put forward by Lev Vygotsky (Daniels, 2005; Yasnitsky *et al.*,

2014). This idea essentially stresses that children (and, in our experience, adults) learn when a new idea is adjacent to their existing understanding, rather than being an entirely new set of ideas that arrives fully formed: advanced driving techniques are unlikely to be things you can pick up in the first or second lesson. Instead, the right kinds of opportunities must be arranged so that students are presented with chances to learn things that are genuinely new but sufficiently close to their existing understanding for that learning to be assimilated. You might say new learning has to be the right size to chew on.

These ideas seem fairly simple and obvious: society and knowledge are too complex to take in just as you go along, so we need carefully constructed educational environments and curricula if people are to understand rather than simply learn to repeat what they think are the right answers to pass exams. Furthermore, learning involves each and every person being able to discover facts for themselves. However, these thinkers were writing against a set of assumptions that are still common: for instance, the 'obvious' idea that one person explaining something to an audience is the same as the listeners understanding. In universities in particular, there is a sense that there is a huge amount to be learnt (because knowledge keeps expanding) and that, while undergraduate degrees have generally been organized to be manageable, the material to be learnt has often been the driving factor: the person with all the power has therefore usually been the teacher presenting the information rather than the learner actively putting their own learning together.

The emergence of 'the learner'

Somewhere between the late 1980s and early 1990s, universities began to pay attention to a range of ideas (inspired by the traditions that drew on Dewey, Holt, Vygotsky and a host of other thinkers) that put far greater emphasis on the learner as opposed to the teacher or the material. This had largely originated from schools and the further education sector, with ideas arriving in a variety of forms, such as 'learning communities' and 'communities of practice' (Lave and Wenger, 1991) and 'learning by doing' (Gibbs, 1988). The phrase 'student-centred learning' also began to gain traction at this point (e.g. Barr and Tang, 1995).

The emphasis now came to be not so much on the presentation of material by a teacher but on its reception and acquisition by the learners. Learning occurs in many ways, and many contexts: sometimes it will happen straightforwardly in a lecture, but often facts only sink in during the re-reading of lecture notes, or when another student explains it, or when the essay actually has to be written and the knots untangled, and so on. By definition, there must be more ways and places to learn than there are to teach because one can learn in all teaching contexts, but the penny can drop in virtually *any* context, though usually either while actively engaging with something or thinking about it afterwards. A key aspect of 'constructivism' is thus that people learn what they do (and reflect on), not what they just hear about. Somewhere in the process of learning something, learners must 'construct' their own version, (re)building in their own understanding the insight that another has tried to convey.

Student-centred learning

These ideas are nowadays generally referred to collectively as 'student-centred learning' or 'active learning': one learns to interpet by interpreting; one learns to analyse by analysing; and so on. In this model of education, the teacher is more a facilitator and a reality check than a guardian of all the correct information: teaching becomes a matter of creating the right conditions for learning rather than directly passing on knowledge.

Constructive alignment

The next landmark in this brief overview is the introduction into higher education of 'constructive alignment', whereby instead of testing knowledge almost as an afterthought, the assessment is understood to be an act of learning. An authority on this approach is Biggs and Tang (2011). In the old 'finals' mode of assessment, an exam would typically test a partially predictable subset of topics, creating the conditions for all kinds of gambling and guesswork by students about exactly what to revise: they arrived with a certain, supposedly measurable, level of understanding and 'demonstrated' it in the exam. Even though there is an argument that exams focus students' minds, it nearly always tips into anxiety, which undermines the learning process. There was certainly little expectation that one could discover something or learn something new in the exam room: learning was over, it seems.

A curriculum that is constructively aligned, in contrast, articulates 'learning outcomes' and begins by designing an assessment method that reflects what the teachers want the students to learn. If we want them to learn to sit and write for three hours addressing clearly defined but fairly randomly assigned problems, then 'finals' is perfectly aligned with that; as a law lecturer once pointed out to one of the authors, this is a good description of what his graduates do for a living. For him, the exam is explicitly a learning environment, where students get (more) practice in an important and relevant skill. If people learn what they do, it is not a question of whether they learn something in an exam room, but a case of admitting that they are always learning something, even if it is 'just' to write quickly.

But for the most part, what we think they should learn is more varied, less narrowly time-pressured, and includes access to resources and one another; after all, this is how most things are done most of the time. The exam itself is not written under exam conditions but to a deadline known well in advance, with access to resources and critical review by colleagues.

Constructive alignment therefore brought our attention to designing a curriculum that persistently has the students doing activities directly involving what we wish them to learn. They should also be able to make mistakes, learn from one another, find out what they don't know (before it's too late), and so on. These activities will be actual practice for the final intended learning outcome; so, in a humanities degree for instance, discussion tutorials are perfectly aligned with the ultimate aim of building skills in interpretation.

As an approach, constructive alignment also invites evaluation by students, and information about how well the learning is going. This is more useful than their final results; students have a great deal of practice throughout their lives of passing exams by mimicking understanding, recognizing which formula to apply (without really understanding why), focusing on a teacher's favoured approach, and so on.

Modularization

Articulating distinctive learning outcomes allows for modularization, the breaking up of a degree course into fairly distinct and stand-alone units.[4] Entry requirements can be set – or every course would have to cater for beginners – and then learning outcomes specified. This puts teachers' attention on assessing only what has been addressed within that module, which makes possible the following. First, students on cross-disciplinary degrees can in theory realistically identify individual modules that fit with their overall interests, and not struggle or fail simply because there is an implicit assumption that they will already have completed other modules. A second area to which modularization is intended to bring greater clarity is the 'expected student workload'; a unit of credit can be equated to a set number of hours' learning, meaning that the workload for a degree is roughly comparable across an institution and between different ones. Though this is very difficult to get right (not least because people learn at different speeds), it is at least a commitment to manageable workloads for students.

It is not just students who are expected to benefit from modularization; it should also allow the institution itself to monitor what individual courses it is offering, and potentially allows for a greater focus of attention, resources and time than a more free-moving and unpredictable three years of study. Beyond the university, it provides information relevant to accrediting bodies (such as architectural associations or engineers' professional bodies) as well as external examiners checking that a particular course is comparable to the rest of the sector's provision.

Those, at least, are the aspirations: that students find their way through a set of carefully crafted educational environments, steadily and authentically accumulating the knowledge, skills and attributes that characterize a historian, an engineer, an architect, and so on.

There are, inevitably, drawbacks inherent in any system. Sidestepping the ever-present possibility that a good idea can be executed badly, modularization and close-knit organization can become too successful in identifying discrete areas of knowledge. Students, told explicitly what they will need to learn to 'pass the test' (and what that test includes), can become too narrowly focused on the intended learning outcomes. Rather than providing room to experiment and understand (particularly by making mistakes), the 'identification of what counts' approach invites an overly rigid focus on what teachers have specified. The advantage of the older, undefined, method was at least that students could not so easily identify 'what doesn't count' and strategically abandon it. It can also create a sense that anything not on the curriculum is not worth exploring, since it would otherwise surely be there.

Another disadvantage of organizing the curriculum into manageable chunks is that we can end up breaking it into separate parts instead. Learning, as the anecdote from Holt about bowling scores illustrates, is heavily contextual, with all sorts of subtle triggers to guide and shape responses. Teaching colleagues regularly report that students do not 'carry learning over' from one module to another, partly because we have created separate units.

A close focus on assessments and outcomes also threatens to go against the grain of group work: when each person is assessed individually, why should students work with anyone else? 'Student-centred', despite its aspirations, can sometimes limit what a teacher provides and work against learning: we can end up with too much fixity in intended outcomes, which becomes a straitjacket as we try to focus on creating learning opportunities. To put it another way, it is centred only on what sort of student we unconsciously assume is in front of us, and all too often that is an asocial efficient machine whose motivation is inherent, but which can break down, at which point we should 'motivate' them again with incentives and encouragement. Most of us have yet to meet this student in real life; ours tend to arrive with the distraction of 'lives'.

A further difficulty that is often overly minimized is that of reducing authority: the traditional image of the authoritative and powerful teacher at the front, having the last word on everything, is something that we have endeavoured to move away from. But there are limits on how far we can become less teacher-centred: it is easy to forget how powerful the figure of 'the marker' is. Teachers have rightly decentralized a lot of the authority in the room in recent decades and moved to a more supportive role (and have hopefully become more approachable in the process), but when it is still teachers who award marks, power is never entirely absent from the conversation. A student once said to one of us that if he was honest, he preferred it when teachers didn't 'try to be his friend' as it complicated the relationship and whatever mark he ultimately received from them became the defining characteristic of their relationship from the moment he received it. The more approachable the teacher, the more the disappointment if he did not get the mark he hoped for, and the more confused the relationship became for him.

What exactly are we trying to do?

Underlying this ongoing consideration of how we might teach (or rather, how students might learn) is the serious question of what exactly we are trying to do. What is a degree? Students are not 'consumers'.[5] It is not an apprenticeship, where one learns a craft, because a great number of our graduates will go on to do other things, and we aspire to prepare them for that. Nor is a university 'a gym', where the activities themselves are meaningless and only the outcomes matter: whatever they go on to do, what they learn at university is worth knowing in itself. Nor is it a 'contract' for a 'service', since they can fail even after paying their fees. It is, as Land puts it, 'a proper entity – itself, and not really like anything else' (2016: 14).

Most higher education teachers and professional staff would like graduates not just to have learnt (about) their subject but also to have glimpsed something at the heart of their academic discipline: Chemistry is more than the periodic table; language is more than grammar and vocabulary. Moreover, we are aware that attributes and behaviours cannot be limited to knowledge, but are linked to the practice and use of that knowledge. All the medical knowledge in the world does not equip someone for a laboratory or medical practice. As in every area of life, there are customs, unwritten rules, written rules, irrelevant rules, etiquette, and the simple fact of 'practice makes perfect' to consider, even if few would believe that perfection is attainable. These 'cultures' vary from one discipline to another. From the perspective that we are also teaching them skills and attributes, students are not 'learning a discipline', but are rather the newest members of the 'disciplinary community'. Just as we do not expect adolescents to have grasped everything that is required of experienced adults, we cannot expect students to be proficient from the day they arrive.

However, this awareness that they are new can become the less helpful insistence that they cannot yet appreciate or even begin to understand cutting-edge or subtle aspects of research – surely they must acquire a vast amount of preliminary knowledge before they can actually do any exploration or formulation of their own versions of events, experiments, and so on. The result is that they become disconnected from the subject that interested them in the first place, whether that was a love of literature, a fascination with landscapes, or a desire to make the world a better place. While trying to prepare them for the more arcane aspects of our subjects, we have sometimes fallen into habits that hindered our own efforts: students given only basic understanding would struggle to see the broader relevance of what they were doing. They would merely be doing exercises – the repetition of apparently meaningless tasks for the sake of it – rather than activities – learning by doing.

Disciplinary communities

Treating students as fledgling members of the disciplinary community leads to subtle but important changes in practice, and contributes a great deal more meaning to the same activities and what they learn.

For instance, it is generally accepted that 'feedback is not always acted upon', as Pitt and Norton (2017: 499) mildly put it. However, as that study and many others show, students often receive their feedback as evidence that they have not yet reached some mythical point of perfection. Showing students the process of peer review, where established academics have their papers rejected and/or returned decked with metaphorical red ink, can have a profound effect: feedback is not then some exercise visited upon them by a tutting and disapproving tutor, but rather something to get used to, a normal part of academic practice (and indeed something to be expected in most areas of life). It is not something anyone ever 'moves past': it is rather an engine of discovery and an important part of the real practice of being a fully fledged scientist, architect, engineer, or linguist, etc.

It is a similar story with other areas of academic research: even undertaking relatively small and apparently menial tasks can lend relevance or meaning, but there must be a chance to see the wider picture. Filling up test tubes is boring, but filling up test tubes that will actually be used in medical experiments and potentially save lives has meaning. This is emphatically not a call to have students do (all) the menial work, but it is a suggestion that students should get a taste of it, as well as being shown the rest of the project of which the test tube work forms a part. Nor does undergraduate work need to be menial at all: the philosopher of science Hasok Chang oversaw undergraduate research projects at UCL during the 2000s. He ingeniously had students inherit work from previous years' efforts, thus spreading the workload realistically and allowing students to get to grips with particular aspects of research one at a time while retaining a sense of being part of a bigger picture. Nor was it just a 'sense': over time, they produced a book (Chang and Jackson, 2007; Chang, 2005).

The issue of meaning and relevance across the silos of modules or any other organization of learning depends upon this sense of a bigger picture. Teachers in the hard sciences in particular often say that students require an enormous amount of background understanding before they can begin to undertake anything resembling 'original research', but treating students as members of an academic community invites us to show them the whole of academic practice, at least in glimpses, thereby undermining a sense that many students have that they can ever 'arrive' at some sort of 'final understanding' of their subject. Involvement in some kind of 'real' academic activity is always a possibility worth exploring and indeed students often do get a taste of this in a final-year project or dissertation. As more and more initiatives appear that refuse to assume that we should shield students from 'the hard stuff', the possibility of making research-based education a central part of the undergraduate experience starts to become genuine.

Student as teacher

Approaching the issue of learning from a different angle, the saying goes that the best way to learn something is to teach it. This aligns perfectly with the inescapable fact that the majority of our graduates will go on to present information, projects and findings of various kinds to an audience. Whether we are thinking about preparing them for the future, or even just learning while they are with us, their presenting ('teaching') is an invaluable opportunity. Traditionally they would submit work to be marked by one or two academics, an audience that it is rather limited and generally at least a little unnerving: then, their efforts were typically discarded after marking.

In our information-rich, media-savvy world, typing out an extended piece of work, which is then marked and consigned to literal or metaphorical landfill, seems rather uninspired. Borrowing the environmental engineering and ecology principle that 'waste is food' (i.e. food for something else; see, for example, Chiras, 2016: 142, 585), there seems no reason not to provide an opportunity to create actual artefacts, by which I mean videos, software, installations, reports of actual projects, histories of real communities, and so on. Now the sense of meaning and purpose is greatly enhanced: the audience in the students' minds while preparing their work is not just one or two markers whom they may or may not like or trust, but rather they are actually participating in their disciplinary community and the broader society that Dewey was so keen they should join. Why wait?

This has a bearing on a critical issue in education, the issue of motivation. The higher education community is very concerned about 'motivating students' (at the time of writing, Google Scholar returned over 250,000 results across subject areas for 'student motivation university'), but often does so without really thinking about more than the subject matter that they are already finding demotivating. While it is true that a great performer could make watching paint dry interesting, and a supernova could be made unimaginably dull, this puts too much emphasis on the teacher to be sustainable or fair. Crucially, this also often overlooks the fact that the students are already highly motivated, just not necessarily about what is in front of them, or in the form that it has come.

Who are these students?

Our students bring complex and unfinished identities into our teaching environments, as do those supporting their learning. They will continue to develop that identity through their academic work, making judgements and discoveries about what they care about and how they want to go about being part of it. Providing opportunities to do that actively can transform not just their learning, but also the subject itself. For instance, 'gender', which gained a foothold as 'Women's Studies' (or similar) in the Humanities and Social Sciences, transformed those fields. In pharmaceutical research, which tends to focus on 'rich people's diseases' (Fraser, 2014), students from developing societies have a great incentive to learn what they can about diseases affecting their own countries; '(Big D) Deaf' students will bring a new perspective to linguistics and related subjects (not to mention their peers).[6] More recently, Black Studies has come to the fore in the UK with campaigns such as 'Why is My Curriculum White?' and #WhiteCurriculum, reflected in UCL's 'Liberating the Curriculum' initiative.[7] Responding to such questions requires a rethink of what is important in a subject, what has been overlooked – and what has been systematically excluded. The dialogue is an enriching one, even if at times the incumbents find it difficult to address the concerns being put to them.

We should in no way assume that only minority or marginalized groups have interesting identities: as a young teacher, one of us was on the receiving end of an angry speech by a young woman from Yorkshire, furious that she was being expected to learn about the notion of 'class' as part of a history degree, because her father's lifelong work as a manual farmhand had made it possible for her to go to university, and therefore proved that that there was no such thing as 'class'. A whole seminar about class and identity could be built unpicking that moment, but the point is that we make assumptions at our peril. Furthermore, we should never assume that just because someone has a particular ethnic or religious background, they must be its ambassadors: they might have come to university intending to move past it, to become 'just' a scientist, architect, medic, and so on.

The point is that while motivation can be 'created' in students, we would be foolish not to provide a way for them to bring their existing motivations to bear, creating a synthesis of learning the subject with their own distinctive flavouring. It is no longer possible to learn everything about a subject, but if students can follow their interests to connect with the world more widely, they will find things to learn and explore that we have not thought of: this is the thinking behind Connected Curriculum and also UCL ChangeMakers.[8]

These rich lives

At graduation, the distinctive person who has been emerging all this time as a student is moving from the partially sheltered environment of education to represent themselves in the world. They may well have done far more at university than their academic studies: for some, roles like being president of the student film society will mean the academic work was a backdrop for their other interests, but either way, they are now expected to take first responsibility for their lives. By default, this means the world of work, which is even true of postgraduates. It means rather than fitting into a role to which they are more or less assigned, or perhaps 'guaranteed' is a better term, they must now negotiate and articulate who they are and who they might be in response to a particular environment. This is true not only of job applications and interviews, but also of the whole process of finding one's way through life. It will require more than presentation skills or CV writing: it calls for an engaged understanding, critique and assimilation of what that will entail, and they will benefit from having a good grip, not just on how to learn, but also how *they* learn.

This grasp of their own distinctiveness is worth little if it degenerates into a sense of their own specialness: everyone has to be distinctive for it to be of value. Few things in life are achieved alone, and grasp of the process of interaction is often the difference between a desultory result and one to be proud of.

This leads us back to assessment. Students make essays, reports, and so on, and the marker is the implied audience. But, as already mentioned, the audience or viewers are also involved in the composition process and must be factored in. Audience matters because to get our message across, we anticipate them in a million ways, adjusting our language, tone, sentence length, and so on. To misjudge this is, at worst, to waste everybody's time and as in every other area of life, we (can) learn from experience. To represent the same idea to different audiences and in different forms is to understand it more deeply, as we reflect on what is important and relevant to those audiences.

What if artefacts or objects submitted for assessment could be 'real' in the sense of being produced, not just as an anxious exercise to gain a mark, but as things in themselves? Assessment for a wider and more varied audience unleashes a level of interest that few markers can inspire: if the video you are producing will go on YouTube, you simply cannot approach it in the same way as if it is uploaded to a university virtual learning environment, never to be seen again. Once again, thinking education through takes us through 'getting across content' to 'cultivating the person'.

Universities have a key role to play in society as a whole: we live in interesting times and if our graduates are not ready to play a confident and capable role in shaping and reshaping our ever more complex society, then who is? If we wish our graduates to have a distinctive role that makes a university education worthwhile, we will hope for them to be key players, able to identify and champion relevant and important themes. They will need to bring together everything touched on here, and more. They will need support from those with experience to join or build networks in the wider world. This is not a vision of our graduates taking over the world for their own benefit and to further their own interests but rather to think beyond parochial issues, something each generation has to take on for itself.

Universities thus have a powerful impact in terms of what kind of teaching they offer, what attributes graduates might have, and what skills they bring to the wider world. As institutions, they have a very long perspective, shaped over a millennium, and to look long-term means to look more closely, and if universities are anything consistent over time, they are institutions where people look into things until they really understand them. This survey has endeavoured to bring together all the reasons why we have reached a point where research-based education can, and should, be the core of what we do as related aspects of teaching and research. In those senses, UCL's Connected Curriculum is an idea whose time has come, though it is not the only way to go about addressing the threads highlighted here. While it is designed to embrace a wide variety of other ideas, it is something that synthesizes a great range of what we now understand and value about teaching, learning and research as a field of activity in higher education.

Notes
[1] Addresses for correspondence: j.p.davies@ucl.ac.uk; dilly.fung@lse.ac.uk
[2] www.ucl.ac.uk/2034
[3] www.ucl.ac.uk/teaching-learning/education-initiatives/connected-curriculum
[4] Modularization is also discussed by Tansy Jessop and Gwyneth Hughes in Chapter 5.
[5] See Jenny Marie in Chapter 3.
[6] The Deaf community do not consider a lack of hearing to be significant: see https://en.wikipedia.org/wiki/Deaf_culture.
[7] Outlined in Chapter 7 by Teresa McConlogue.
[8] This is explained further by Jenny Marie in Chapter 3.

References
Barr, R.B. and Tang, J. (1995) 'From teaching to learning: A new paradigm for undergraduate education'. *Change: The Magazine of Higher Learning*, 27 (6), 13–25.

Biggs, J. and Tang, C. (2011) *Teaching for Quality Learning at University: What the student does.* 4th ed. Maidenhead: Society for Research into Higher Education and Open University Press.

Chang, H. (2005) 'Turning an undergraduate class into a professional research community'. *Teaching in Higher Education*, 10 (3), 387–94.

Chang, H. and Jackson, C. (eds) (2007) *An Element of Controversy: The life of chlorine in science, medicine, technology and war.* London: British Society for the History of Science.

Chiras, D.D. (2016) *Environmental Science.* 10th ed. Burlington, MA: Jones and Bartlett Learning.

Daniels, H. (ed.) (2005) *An Introduction to Vygotsky.* 2nd ed. London: Routledge.

Dewey, J. (1916) *Democracy and Education: An introduction to the philosophy of education.* New York: Macmillan.

Fairfield, P. (ed.) (2012) *Education, Dialogue and Hermeneutics.* London: Continuum.

Fraser, G. (2014) 'Big pharma has an interest in rich people being sick'. *The Guardian*, 17 October. Online. www.theguardian.com/commentisfree/belief/2014/oct/17/big-pharma-interest-rich-people-sick (accessed 13 March 2018).

Fung, D. (2017) *A Connected Curriculum for Higher Education*. London: UCL Press.

Gadamer, H.-G. (2004) *Truth and Method*. 2nd rev. ed. Trans. Weinsheimer, J. and Marshall, D.G. London: Continuum.

Gibbs, G. (1988) *Learning by Doing: A guide to teaching and learning methods*. London: Further Eucation Unit.

Herndon, J. (1971) *How to Survive in Your Native Land*. New York: Simon and Schuster.

Holt, J.C. (1984) *How Children Fail*. Harmondsworth: Penguin.

Land, R. (2016) 'Toil and trouble: Threshold concepts as a pedagogy of uncertainty'. In Land, R., Meyer, J.H.F. and Flanagan, M.T. (eds) *Threshold Concepts in Practice*. Rotterdam: Sense Publishers, 11–24.

Lave, J. and Wenger, E. (1991) *Situated Learning: Legitimate peripheral participation*. Cambridge: Cambridge University Press.

Pitt, E. and Norton, L. (2017) '"Now that's the feedback I want!": Students' reactions to feedback on graded work and what they do with it'. *Assessment and Evaluation in Higher Education*, 42 (4), 499–516.

Yasnitsky, A., van der Veer, R. and Ferrari, M. (eds) (2014) *The Cambridge Handbook of Cultural-Historical Psychology* (Cambridge Handbooks in Psychology). Cambridge: Cambridge University Press.

Chapter 2

The research–teaching nexus revisited

Martin Oliver and Lesley Gourlay[1]

Universities have a dual role: they are the key locations for research as well as higher education. These are obviously complementary in that students are learning in the environment where the latest discoveries are being made or discussed. However, the two make very different demands on staff attention, particularly since 1986 when the UK government linked funding directly with research outputs through the 'Research Excellence Framework' (as it is currently known). This effectively made teaching the lesser sibling of the two, and education suffered as a result. Furthermore, there is no guarantee that a successful researcher will make a successful teacher and vice versa, even though academia is full of people who do manage both. Gourlay and Oliver provide an overview of how this 'nexus' of research and teaching has been positioned in recent years, and the various ways that people have attempted to think through the relationship between the two. One result of these discussions and experimentation, as they explain, has been a significant expansion in what we understand 'education' (and particularly '*higher*' education) to be. Versions of 'research-based education' have been somewhere in the conversation for centuries, even if it has proven harder to implement than one might have thought.

Introduction

This chapter explores the idea of the research–teaching nexus, which provides the foundation for research-based approaches to education, such as UCL's Connected Curriculum.

Although this is an idea that can be traced back across two centuries, it remains controversial, and its feasibility is still questioned. However, research has developed an increasingly sophisticated account of the various strands that this 'nexus' consists of, and how students experience it. These strands will be reviewed to identify opportunities for building connections between research and teaching.

Research-based education

Many contemporary discussions of learning and teaching in higher education involve contrasting 'passive' or 'transmissive' approaches to teaching – such as lectures – with 'active' forms of learning, in which students are asked to make, do or perform in particular ways. Such discussions are well intentioned, reaching for an important principle – that learning involves more than simply receiving information – but unfortunately, these ideas of 'engagement' or 'participation' can be deeply ideological, and even naïve, where they ignore important but solitary or invisible activities that are vital to higher education, such as reading and thinking (Gourlay, 2015).

One challenge to these discussions is that they ignore what people actually do when they study, relying on preconceptions rather than evidence. What this suggests is that, if higher education is in any way about knowledge – about what it is, how it is made, what its limits are, whose ends it serves, and so on – then it is important that students come to understand the ways in which knowledge is produced, shared and defended. As Mary Henkel has argued, the value of research-informed teaching and learning arises from:

> a) the acquisition and critical appreciation of substantive knowledge in the context of assumptions that that knowledge is partial and in process of development and revision within a regulated environment;
>
> b) understanding of the processes through which that knowledge is acquired;
>
> c) learning the skills to practise 'disciplined inquiry' sanctioned by an epistemic community or institution. (Henkel, 2004: 29)

In other words, the value arises from learning how to *be* historians, chemists, linguists, and so on.

These principles are central to the idea of research-based education. Initiatives such as UCL's Connected Curriculum (Fung, 2017) promote the idea that students should learn not just by hearing about research, but by learning how to be researchers. This involves changing their relationship to disciplinary knowledge: they should, through their education, learn how to undertake research within their discipline themselves, and in so doing, develop a sense of their own identity as a researcher.

The Connected Curriculum consists of six dimensions, which are to be enacted by students learning through research and enquiry (Fung, 2017):

1. Students connect with researchers and with the institution's research
2. A throughline of research activity is built into each programme
3. Students make connections across subjects and out to the world
4. Students connect academic learning with workplace learning
5. Students learn to produce outputs – assessments directed at an audience
6. Students connect with each other, across phases and with alumni.

To understand what it is that this initiative is intended to achieve, and to make sense of why it was necessary to 'close the divide between teaching and research' (UCL, 2015) in the first place, it is helpful to place this discussion in a broader historical context. In particular, it is important to frame this in terms of the 'research–teaching nexus', which has come to stand as an important principle in determining the role of the university within society.

The history of the research–teaching nexus

The idea of the research–teaching nexus is commonly traced back to the work of Wilhelm von Humboldt in the early 1800s. When Humboldt was given responsibility for reforming Prussian education, he did so by reacting against the dominant, conservative model of universities. He believed that approaches in use at the time merely reproduced existing knowledge instead of helping students to learn how to discover it for themselves. His alternative to this took as its central principle the idea of students developing as independent researchers:

> Just as primary instruction makes the teacher possible, so he renders himself dispensable through schooling at the secondary level. The university teacher is thus no longer a teacher and the student is no longer a pupil. Instead the student conducts research on his own behalf and the professor supervises his research and supports him in it. (Humboldt, 1964)

This idea became influential in shaping 'research universities': institutions that marked themselves out through their active engagement with the discovery, not just the preservation, of knowledge. Although this view has persisted, and still influences contemporary debates, it has not done so without challenge. For example, as Halse *et al.* (2007: 727) describe, John Henry Newman proposed in his *Idea of a University* (1852) that the capacity to research and to teach were quite distinct and, indeed, 'not commonly found in the same person'. Nonetheless, Humboldt's vision was still argued to form an ideal for universities; it even influences contemporary discussions about the role of the university in society.

One place in which such arguments can be uncovered are discussions about the nature of scholarship. These can be exemplified by Boyer's framework (1990), which drew on a study of the activities of the professoriate to create an integrated model of academic practice. This model explicitly attempted to overcome the perceived structural divisions between research and teaching by offering a more nuanced, integrated account of different *forms* of scholarship. Boyer elaborated these as the scholarships of discovery, integration, application and teaching. This offered a far richer set of possibilities than the previous binary that set research against teaching and started to make the idea of a 'nexus' more meaningful. Previous research had tended to create a one-directional account of the relationship between research and practice: research happened first, and teaching about it happened later. Discussion of links between the two therefore focused on bringing research into the curriculum, rather than on bringing teaching into research. Boyer's account raised other possibilities, such as the idea that scholarly insights from teaching might generate research questions, or that the challenges of application might give rise to new discoveries. This interplay of possibilities started to describe the complexities that might shape a 'nexus', rather than simply characterizing this as a gateway or point of passage.

This move away from an 'either/or' account of the relationship between research and teaching proved strategically important. Clark (1997), for example, developed this idea in response to the 'incompatibility thesis', which proposed a zero-sum account of academic work by suggesting that time spent on research was necessarily taken away from teaching, and that, consequently, academics who do research were abandoning students. As an alternative, Clark developed the idea of the 'research–teaching–study nexus', based on the idea that some academic activities might be understood in several different ways:

> Research activity can and does serve as an important mode of teaching and a valuable means of learning. [...] In its strongest and most normative form the thesis becomes a claim that student involvement in research is an efficacious way to educate throughout the educational system and the great mass of students, as well as the elite performers, for the inquiring society into which we are rapidly moving. (Clark, 1997: 242)

While this account offered a more sophisticated model of the various relationships that might link research and teaching, it has only been partially successful in defending these. The idea that teaching and research are in some way intrinsically linked has come under increasing pressure from policy, funding and the demands of specialization. For example, developments in policy internationally focused on preparing students for work, or on the creation of educational and research markets, have made it hard to sustain connections between research and teaching (Zubrick *et al.*, 2001). Similarly, the selective investment of research funding in elite institutions – a move justified on the grounds of promoting international competitiveness – has led to associated questions about whether all undergraduates need to be taught in a research environment (Healey *et al.*, 2010).

As a consequence, whatever the ideal might be, at a practical level the current situation is such that many currently believe that research and teaching 'are not just distinct but incompatible in the working lives of today's academics' (Henkel, 2004: 20).

A lack of evidence

Part of the reason that the existence, let alone the value, of the research–teaching question continues to be queried is that it remains very difficult to provide evidence of its benefits. Neumann (1994), for example, reviewed work carried out over the previous decade, and concluded that this had failed to generate persuasive evidence of a link between research and teaching, let alone the benefits of that link. These studies were mostly surveys, and relied on self-reported accounts of work patterns in order to explore academics' work preferences, time usage and reward systems. However, surveys of students also failed to show any convincing evidence: it seemed that, at that point, students were either unaware of their teachers' research activities, or saw little relevance in them. Five years later, Brew (1999) similarly found little empirical evidence of such connections.

This paucity of evidence led Hattie and Marsh (1996: 533) to describe the research–teaching nexus as 'an enduring myth'. Rather than abandoning it, however, they challenged institutions to pursue 'improvement of the nexus between research and teaching ... to increase the circumstances in which teaching and research have occasion to meet'.

The situation seems to have changed very little in the following years. Focusing on a vocational university, Healey *et al.* (2010) found most students remained unaware of research at their institution throughout the course of their studies. Many students said they were disappointed about this, because they believed staff involvement in research would increase their understanding of the subject, and that teaching would be more effective if their lecturers involved them in aspects of the research process.

However, rather than concluding from these studies that the research–teaching nexus does not exist, researchers began to explore the possibility that it had not been adequately theorized. In other words, the difficulty in finding evidence for the existence or effects of the research–teaching nexus was at least in part due to the ongoing ambiguity of the term. Without specifying this idea in such a way that it can be made visible, it will remain impossible to study. For this reason, subsequent studies approached the topic differently, trying to explore different ways in which the nexus was understood and enacted, in order to develop a better theoretical account of this phenomenon.

Exploring the character of the research–teaching nexus

These new approaches to studying the research–teaching nexus involved documenting people's experiences of points of connection and looking closely at pedagogic practices that seemed to involve research in some way. In spite of the managerial pressures and resource constraints that contributed to separating these areas of academic work, work was undertaken that began to explore and document the wide range of relationships that connected research and teaching, including perceptions of the ways in which they could be integrated, or even have positive influences on each other (Coate *et al.*, 2001).

Henkel (2004), for example, explored the different ways in which people understood these connections, and drew four conclusions that helped to scope out an agenda for work in this area:

1. Although general belief in the research–teaching nexus was widespread, the term has been used inconsistently, making it hard to evidence.
2. There are disciplinary differences in the prevalence of this belief. These include differences in whether the nexus was seen as a pedagogic construct, or as part of academics' personal identity. There were also differences in whether it was seen as a one-way process (flowing from research to education) or a two-way process (in which education could also influence research).
3. These discussions were primarily teacher-focused.
4. One underlying motivation was that many academics were passionate about their subject. This passion was seen as driving both research and their commitment to the research–teaching nexus.

As a consequence of this refocusing, studies began to focus in closer detail on areas such as inquiry-based learning (e.g. Healey, 2005), which seemed to enact the kinds of pedagogy called for by Humboldt almost two centuries earlier. This more fine-grained work began to reveal the complex and often 'taken for granted' ways in which research and teaching were interlinked. Neumann, for example, developed an account that explained the research–teaching nexus in terms of:

> A multi-level relationship between teaching and research operating on three levels that have been termed:
>
> - Tangible: the transmission of knowledge and skills
> - Intangible: the transmission of approaches and attitudes to knowledge
> - Global: the direction given to course offerings by departmental research activity. (Neumann, 1994: 324)

Neumann's study of students' experiences managed to show some evidence for the existence of each of these areas. For example, tangible connections were visible where lecturers were working at the forefront of knowledge and shared this work in their teaching, as well as in lab-based courses where students tried out cutting-edge techniques of the kinds used in research projects. Intangible connections were frequently conveyed by means such as lecturers' enthusiasm for their subject, or through the pedagogy of courses that encouraged students to adopt a questioning, critical approach to their topics. The global nexus was visible in areas such as the range of topics on offer within a course, which reflected the expertise of appointed staff within a department.

Neumann also noted that the relative visibility of these different levels of relationship was influenced by several things, including the practices of the discipline; the year of study; and also the ability and motivation of the students, with those who were interested in further study or in becoming academics themselves showing most awareness of the links between research and teaching.

These observations helped to overturn some of the earlier scepticism about the research–teaching nexus. Clark, for example, had sought to locate the research–teaching–study nexus in the context of 'the advance laboratory (or seminar)' or dissertation work (Clark, 1997: 243); the possibility of finding this within undergraduate lectures, for example, was explicitly rejected. Neumann's work served to confirm the importance of laboratories and seminar work, but opened up the possibility that connections between research and teaching might be found even in initial undergraduate classes.

The influence of disciplines in shaping the relationship between research and teaching has become increasingly important in these studies. Griffiths (2004), for example, drew on work in the sociology of knowledge to argue that participation in research-based teaching is likely to be harder where the knowledge base is codified, largely uncontested and where programmes of inquiry take highly specialized forms; whereas it will be easier where the focus is on interpretation, where there are competing frameworks of understanding, and where multiple disciplines explore common problems within applied or vocational fields. However, although these characteristics might affect a student's opportunities to participate in research, they would have less influence on whether teachers present recent research, for example.

Healey (2005) similarly argued that there would be disciplinary variation, building his argument at least in part on an organizational or apprenticeship model:

> Undergraduate students are more likely to have opportunities to
> work as, for example, a research assistant on a research project
> in a biology laboratory, than to work alongside, say, an English
> professor interpreting a play. (Healey, 2005: 73)

Interestingly, however, Healey's conclusions here appear to contradict those drawn by Griffiths. Further empirical work would be needed to provide evidence about the relative availability of opportunities across different disciplines.

Studies of this kind have helped to move the debate around the research–teaching nexus beyond the simple binary of whether this does or does not exist in some measurable way, and towards more complex discussions about the qualities of various relationships. Accordingly, Griffiths classified different points of connection between research and teaching according to whether they were specific or diffuse in character; whether research was weakly or strongly embedded in teaching activities; and whether the relationships were unidirectional or two-way. On the basis of this, Griffiths developed four different models of connections between research and teaching:

- Research-led teaching, where the curriculum is structured around content that reflects the research interests of staff, and the emphasis is on understanding research findings rather than research processes

- Research-oriented teaching, in which the emphasis is on learning about research, with a focus on understanding the ethos and processes of knowledge production
- Research-based teaching, where the curriculum is largely enquiry-based, connections between teaching and research are two-way, and divisions between staff and students' roles are minimized
- Research-informed teaching, which has been referred to elsewhere as the scholarship of learning and teaching; here, irrespective of what is taught, the process of teaching is itself shaped by research evidence (for example, about effective pedagogy, or the processes of knowledge production).

Healey *et al.* (2010) later modified this, substituting 'research tutored' for research-informed. This development was based on the creation of a quadrant diagram, differentiating between (on one axis) an emphasis on research processes and an emphasis on research content; and (on the other axis) treating students as participants in research or as an audience for it (Healey, 2005). In this later terminology, research tutoring involves students learning about research findings through small group discussions with a teacher.

Whilst this finer-grained analysis gave cause for optimism about the existence of the research–teaching nexus, it simultaneously gave support to some of the critiques of this idea. The concerns voiced by Newman (1852), Hattie and Marsh (1996) or Henkel (2004) about incompatibilities between research and teaching could also be revisited using this framework. What this clarified was that although there may still be connections between research and teaching in a range of different contexts, the priorities of the institution, the influence of managerial policies and the levels of resourcing available to institutions could affect the quality of these connections in important ways.

Halse *et al.* (2007), for example, drew attention to Marginson's 'charmed circle' of resourcing. Within this charmed circle, established institutional research status attracts high-performing research staff and student applications, which in turn generate resources that support more research. Those outside the circle will always be in a deficit position, and will struggle to enter. The consequence, in terms of research–teaching connections, include fewer staff able to talk about leading research, less infrastructure that could support practice and engagement, and a different profile of student motivation, all of which make meaningful connections between research and teaching harder to establish.

Their research also served to demonstrate that connections between research and teaching cannot be taken for granted, but need support and encouragement. In their study, they reviewed the profiles of recipients of national teaching awards to explore the kinds of research–teaching relationship that they had created. In this study, they found there was no clear link between the institutional mission and the receipt of a national teaching award. They also found that the majority of winners were active researchers.

Material connections

The discussions of the research–teaching nexus above either focus on qualities such as motivation, or practices such as teaching. There is very little mention of the material cultures of research or teaching, apart from the discussion in some studies of lab work. This is surprising, given that the field of Science and Technology Studies has argued for several decades that knowledge generation is shaped both by social influences and material concerns (Latour, 2005). Ethnographies of laboratory work, for example, show how scientific knowledge, far from being purely something discussed in published work, only becomes credible because such writing follows from less visible work with tissue samples, chemicals, machines, print-outs, desks full of academic papers, rejected draft manuscripts, and so on (Latour and Woolgar, 1979). Similarly, Bowker and Star (2000) have shown that the importance of infrastructure is commonly overlooked, even though it shapes practice in profound ways.

These influences have begun to be explored in research on education:

> Humans, and what they take to be their learning and social processes, do not float, distinct, in container-like contexts of education, such as classrooms or community sites, that can be conceptualised and dismissed as simply a wash of material stuff and spaces. The things that assemble these contexts, and incidentally the actions and bodies including human ones that are part of these assemblages, are continuously acting upon each other to bring forth and distribute, as well as to obscure and deny, knowledge. (Fenwick *et al.*, 2011: vii)

In the context of higher education, this reframing of knowledge work has brought attention back to the value of campuses, and the way in which the co-location of learners, teachers, labs, classrooms, lecture theatres, libraries, and so on is important in making higher education practical (Cornford and Pollock, 2002).

There has been relatively little recognition of this within studies of the research–teaching nexus; where material considerations are mentioned, this is often only in passing. For example, Healey *et al.* (2010) identified a range of ways in which students became aware of staff research. Some of these were expressed in purely social terms – through guest lectures or research seminars, for example. However, some material connections were also identified, although the roles these played were not explored further. These points of connection included conventional outputs of research, such as journal articles and books, but also more mundane things such as notice boards and displays, where information about projects, seminars or publications might be provided.

However, work at UCL has explored these material cultures of research and teaching. Plewes and Issroff (2002), for example, explored the kinds of resources that were used as part of teaching practice. Their studies with medics revealed the importance of a wide range of material resources in their teaching, including 'potted specimens, x-ray displays, posters with clinical topics on, videos, plastic models, and then of course computers'. These resources are objects of analysis for researchers and professional practitioners: bringing them into an educational context allows students to rehearse those kinds of analysis in a supportive environment, gaining experience of the kinds of research practices valued in their discipline.

Subsequent work has shown the importance of material resources in a range of other disciplines, too. Learning how to handle objects is an important part of studying archaeology, for example (Sparks, 2010), and working with a specific set of skulls can provide important insights into concepts of phylogeny (Duhs, 2010). This has led to the development of a pedagogy of object-based learning, and a growing body of practical advice about how best to implement these kinds of approaches (e.g. Cain, 2010). Research has also shown that digital resources and services can also function in this way (Gourlay and Oliver, 2013). Students at UCL made extensive use of digital devices and services, many of which were also widely used by researchers. Some of these were ubiquitous but prosaic, for example office tools such as Microsoft Word or Google Docs, or search engines such as Google, but others were primarily academic, such as Google Scholar, Endnote or specialist social networking sites such as academia.edu or ResearchGate.

Taken together, these material and digital objects provide a new perspective on the research–teaching nexus, allowing points of connection to be identified by tracing the resources that cross between one set of practice and the other.

Conclusions

For an idea that has been advocated for over two centuries, it seems that research-based education has been surprisingly challenging to implement. However, part of the reason for this perception may be the lack of clarity about what research-based education consists of. This has made it difficult to provide convincing evidence one way or the other. Developing consensus around the idea of research-based education, including recognition of the sociomaterial elements of this work, may help to address this ambiguity.

Another part of the reason has been that policies and patterns of resourcing have separated out areas of academic work in order to render them transparent, accountable and manageable. At the individual level, teaching and research are often kept separate through organizational and institutional procedures, such as parallel processes for planning and rewarding activity. Institutionally, the pressures of market competition and limited resources are leading to greater specialization and differentiation. Under these circumstances, the problems of implementation become all too apparent.

However, another part of the difficulty is to do with the very general way in which these ideas have been discussed. At an abstract level, the research–teaching nexus has proved elusive; however, reframing this idea in terms of the people, things and places involved in teaching and research work has begun to show the rich web of connections that exist. Work remains to be done to explore the diversity of these connections more extensively, but focusing in on these fine-grained, day-to-day practices has already helped to develop approaches such as object-based learning that will create links between research and teaching.

Although it has taken much longer than Humboldt might have hoped, the principles of research-based education have been clearly laid out, as for example in the Connected Curriculum framework. The next steps will involve generating an evidence base that allows this idea to be interrogated critically, so that the qualities of different kinds of connection can be understood better. This will, in turn, enable the development of new pedagogic strategies that can be used to provide a better kind of research-based education for our students.

Notes

[1] Addresses for correspondence: martin.oliver@ucl.ac.uk; l.gourlay@ucl.ac.uk

References

Bowker, G.C. and Star, S.L. (2000) *Sorting Things Out: Classification and its consequences*. Cambridge, MA: MIT Press.

Boyer, E.L. (1990) *Scholarship Reconsidered: Priorities of the professoriate*. Princeton, NJ: Carnegie Foundation for the Advancement of Teaching.

Brew, A. (1999) 'Research and teaching: Changing relationships in a changing context'. *Studies in Higher Education*, 24 (3), 291–301.

Cain, J. (2010) 'Practical concerns when implementing object-based teaching in higher education'. *University Museums and Collections Journal*, 3, 197–201.

Clark, B.R. (1997) 'The modern integration of research activities with teaching and learning'. *Journal of Higher Education*, 68 (3), 241–55.

Coate, K., Barnett, R. and Williams, G. (2001) 'Relationships between teaching and research in higher education in England'. *Higher Education Quarterly*, 55 (2), 158–74.

Cornford, J. and Pollock, N. (2002) 'The university campus as a "resourceful constraint": Process and practice in the construction of the virtual university'. In Lea, M.R. and Nicoll, K. (eds) *Distributed Learning: Social and cultural approaches to practice*. London: RoutledgeFalmer, 170–81.

Duhs, R. (2010) 'Learning from university museums and collections in higher education: University College London (UCL)'. *University Museums and Collections Journal*, 3, 183–6.

Fenwick, T., Edwards, R. and Sawchuk, P. (2011) *Emerging Approaches to Educational Research: Tracing the sociomaterial*. London: Routledge.

Fung, D. (2017) *A Connected Curriculum for Higher Education*. London: UCL Press.

Gourlay, L. (2015) '"Student engagement" and the tyranny of participation'. *Teaching in Higher Education*, 20 (4), 402–11.

Gourlay, L. and Oliver, M. (2013) 'Beyond "the social": Digital literacies as sociomaterial practice'. In Goodfellow, R. and Lea, M.R. (eds) *Literacy in the Digital University: Critical perspectives on learning, scholarship, and technology*. London: Routledge, 79–94.

Griffiths, R. (2004) 'Knowledge production and the research–teaching nexus: The case of the built environment disciplines'. *Studies in Higher Education*, 29 (6), 709–26.

Halse, C., Deane, E., Hobson, J. and Jones, G. (2007) 'The research–teaching nexus: What do national teaching awards tell us?'. *Studies in Higher Education*, 32 (6), 727–46.

Hattie, J. and Marsh, H.W. (1996) 'The relationship between research and teaching: A meta-analysis'. *Review of Educational Research*, 66 (4), 507–42.

Healey, M. (2005) 'Linking research and teaching: Exploring disciplinary spaces and the role of inquiry-based learning'. In Barnett, R. (ed.) *Reshaping the University: New relationships between research, scholarship and teaching*. Maidenhead: Open University Press, 67–78.

Healey, M., Jordan, F., Pell, B. and Short, C. (2010) 'The research–teaching nexus: A case study of students' awareness, experiences and perceptions of research'. *Innovations in Education and Teaching International*, 47 (2), 235–46.

Henkel, M. (2004) 'Teaching and research: The idea of a nexus'. *Higher Education Management and Policy*, 16 (2), 19–30.

Humboldt, W. von (1964) 'Der Königsberger und der Litauische Schulplan'. In Flitner, A. and Giel, K. (eds) *Werke in fünf Bänden* (Vol. 4). Darmstadt: Wissenschaftliche Buchgesellschaft, 168–73.

Latour, B. (2005) *Reassembling the Social: An introduction to actor-network-theory*. Oxford: Oxford University Press.

Latour, B. and Woolgar, S. (1979) *Laboratory Life: The social construction of scientific facts*. Beverly Hills, CA: SAGE Publications.

Neumann, R. (1994) 'The teaching–research nexus: Applying a framework to university students' learning experiences'. *European Journal of Education*, 29 (3), 323–38.

Newman, J.H. (1852) *The Idea of a University*. London: Longmans, Green and Co.

Plewes, L. and Issroff, K. (2002) 'Academic staff attitudes towards the use and production of networked learning resources'. Paper presented at the 3rd Networked Learning Conference, University of Sheffield, 26–28 March 2002. Online. www.networkedlearningconference.org.uk/past/nlc2002/proceedings/papers/29.htm (accessed 13 March 2018).

Sparks, R.T. (2010) 'Object handling in the archaeology classroom: Strategies for success'. *University Museums and Collections Journal*, 3, 191–5.

University College London (UCL) (2015) *UCL 2034 Strategy*. Online. www.ucl.ac.uk/ucl-2034 (accessed 23 June 2015).

Zubrick, A., Reid, I. and Rossiter, P. (2001) *Strengthening the Nexus between Teaching and Research*. Canberra: Department of Education, Training and Youth Affairs.

Chapter 3

Students as partners

Jenny Marie[1]

If students can do research, then they are no longer mere consumers but 'full participants' in higher education. The logical extension of this is that students may well be able and well positioned to initiate changes to their curriculum and institution: they possess a perspective that staff simply cannot have. Jenny Marie's outline of the UCL ChangeMakers initiative documents the way that UCL has put students at the heart of the UCL 2034 vision and how her team have been supporting this (and even since the chapter was written, ChangeMakers has expanded further). Students can not only become the driving force for all kinds of changes, but those that do so also report a range of benefits, in their well-being, employability, attainment and confidence. Initiatives like ChangeMakers are a central aspect of the way that universities are not just responding to pedagogical understanding and needs, but also actively rethinking what the relationship between students, staff and institution is, and could be. Such changes are widespread as we all get to grips with much higher fees and different governance and funding regimes. Marie therefore considers some of the issues submerged in the many metaphors for being a student, challenging not only the widespread claim that students are now 'paying consumers' but also some of the reactions to that, such as treating students as 'experts' (in what it is to be a student).

Introduction

This chapter considers an institutional scheme to encourage students and staff to work in partnership on projects to enhance the student learning experience. The scheme exists in the context of the university's commitment to students becoming full partners in the future of the institution.

The concept of students as partners is a political one and I consider how this is positioned in opposition to the concept of students as consumers. Students as partners has benefits for staff, helping them to practise in ways that are meaningful and effective for student learning. It also has great benefits for students, improving attainment and well-being. Yet partnership work is not without its challenges, not least in terms of the students we reach, who we represent and the extent to which partnership is achieved.

Background to students as partners at UCL

UCL has placed students at the heart of its UCL 2034 vision.[2] It states that one of the university's objectives is to 'ensure that our students, at every level (UG, PGT and PGR),[3] feel that they are a key and integral part of our university community, and that their opinions and suggestions are valued and acted upon, as full partners in the future of UCL'.[4]

UCL ChangeMakers is UCL's flagship student engagement initiative and sets the tone for the relationship between staff and students in terms of the responsibility each has for education at UCL. It began in 2014/15 as a pilot, where students could propose and carry out their own educational enhancement project. That year we supported 24 students to carry out 10 projects.

A year later, we massively expanded the programme. We first brought staff educational enhancement projects under the same programme, changing the requirements for these such that they had to be conducted in partnership with students. Twenty-three projects initiated by staff were funded in this way and the number of student-initiated projects was expanded to 29. At the same time, we introduced a 'scholars' scheme, whereby students worked with departments with lower student satisfaction than the university mean to enhance their assessment and feedback practices. Twenty such projects were supported (Marie *et al.*, 2016; Marie and Azuma, 2018).

2016/17 saw a further diversification of the opportunities available, with the piloting of Annual Student Experience Review (ASER) facilitators, who worked with the Student Academic Representatives and staff of departments with lower student satisfaction to ensure strong student input into the department's annual development plan. It also saw the pilot of students acting as partners with staff to help them reflect on their practice and how it could be further enhanced, with students contributing through physical and virtual teaching observations and looking at an assignment brief.

Students as partners: The rationale

The development of global knowledge economies has led to students increasingly being thought of as consumers of knowledge (Boden and Epstein, 2006). The UK's National Student Survey, which final-year students complete, is becoming ever more important in the choices that students make about where to do their degree and will form an important part of the UK's Teaching Excellence Framework, though at the time of writing the details of the next TEF are undecided.

While a strong student voice can be seen as long overdue, the transactional model of student–university relationships is neither inevitable nor desirable. In the UK the National Union of Students is resisting this model, along with academics (Wenstone, 2012). Universities support students to learn – students cannot passively receive graduate knowledge, skills and attributes with no effort on their part other than payment of a fee. Students must invest more than just money to get the most out of their time at university. What they get in return should be better than an 'off the shelf' product – it should transform both their ways of thinking and their lives (Mezirow and Associates, 2000).

Universities should be actively working against the transactional model of education by educating our students about it and by providing environments in which students are treated as partners in their education rather than customers, so that they adopt this mindset. Change projects do just that. One of the students who completed a UCL ChangeMaker project in the first year was very explicit that doing the project had changed his relationship with UCL:

> I was content to be a consumer of education at UCL. Undertaking a ChangeMaker project has allowed me to conceive [of] myself in a producing role. (CALTADMIN, 2015b)

Students as partners can be a political concept, which challenges the influence of neoliberal politics in the higher education sector. However, regardless of the politics, there are great benefits in working with students as partners for both the students themselves and the work that is undertaken.

Benefits for students taking part

STUDENT ATTAINMENT

Student–staff partnerships have many benefits for students: not least because students who do not hold a transactional model of their relationship with university are likely to take responsibility for their own learning and thus have higher attainment rates.

The majority of the students who completed the 2015 UCL ChangeMakers evaluation (85 per cent, with a 33 per cent sample) said that it had improved their experience of being at UCL. They wrote that it did so by enhancing their sense of community and of being valued. These are indicators of their sense of belonging and, as one of our UCL ChangeMakers projects established (CALTADMIN, 2015c), as well as being a powerful good in its own right, particularly for student welfare, a sense of belonging is also a predictor of attainment. As one of our scholars wrote following their work with their department: 'I genuinely feel more involved with the department and my academic studies' (UCL ChangeMakers, 2016: 17).

While being involved in partnership work may take up students' time, it is thus still likely to benefit their attainment through preparing them to be active, responsible learners, increasing their sense of belonging and because completing a project develops a range of skills, such as project management, teamwork and communication, which are important not just for gaining employment but also in academia.

Improved attainment is also likely to be achieved due to the results of the project. In the first year of UCL ChangeMakers, students piloted oral language exchanges and anatomical drawing classes – which are likely to improve their academic work directly. They also devised a feedback rubric, identified overlaps in their course and persuaded staff to embed more Problem Based Learning (PBL) in their courses – all of which are likely to improve their and other students' grades.

WELL-BEING

Partnership work can also improve students' well-being in a number of ways. As discussed, students gain an increased sense of value and community. As one scholar wrote: 'It is a great way of getting to know the staff and students in the department and thereby creates a sense of community' (UCL ChangeMakers, 2016: 13).

Feeling comfortable with staff is important for students to be able to seek any help they need, if they face difficulties.

Well-being is strongly linked to a belief that one can improve one's life. I believe that UCL ChangeMakers does encourage this belief. As one student said:

> My view is that the ChangeMakers scheme is quite necessary and I cannot understand a university that would not have one because it encourages students to make a change or at least understand what changes can be made on their campus and their role in facilitating that change and it gives them the skills and the confidence that is needed to make change in the wider community. (CALTADMIN, 2015c)

By empowering students we teach them that they can make change in their courses and by extension their community and personal life. I remember just how liberating it was, the first time I realized that it is always possible for me to improve any situation that I am in, because I am a factor in that situation: if I can change nothing else I can change my attitude or behaviour. The quote also implies that undertaking enhancement projects helps students gain a sense of responsibility for making change. I think this comes from the increased sense of belonging and citizenship. UCL aspires to create 'global citizens'; undertaking a project can increase students' sense of belonging to a collective and thus of responsibility to it, be that their department, the institution, local community, humanity or the global ecosystem.

EMPLOYABILITY

Graduates with good attainment, well-being, a sense of responsibility and belief that they have the ability to make change for the better are clearly going to be attractive to employers.

Undertaking a change project provides an opportunity for students to develop a whole range of skills, such as time management, project management, leadership, teamwork, persuasion and managing change.

Students have also spoken about the insight that they have gained into the operation of the university. As one scholar wrote: 'What was really interesting for me was the fact that I was able to witness and directly participate in the internal workings of a university, in spite of being a student' (UCL ChangeMakers, 2016: 14).

An understanding of how organizations operate is likely to put the students in good stead. In some cases, the students learnt about how things operated in other departments and even got a sense of the national context.

Students also got to see things from different perspectives: 'UCL ChangeMakers scheme has provided me with the opportunity to see the situation both from a student's perspective [and] from that of the tutors'. (UCL ChangeMakers, 2016: 12).

The ability to see things from another's perspective is a key life skill, which will help with both their own well-being and their effectiveness as an agent of change in future work.

Benefits for enhancement projects

It is commonly argued that student participation in educational enhancement projects is likely to improve the project outcomes, as students know what it is like to experience the learning environment and practices that are being developed. As Cook-Sather *et al.* state:

> ... students are neither disciplinary nor pedagogical experts. Rather, their experience and expertise typically is in being a

student – something that many faculty have not been for many years. (Cook-Sather *et al.*, 2014: 15)

This is quite contrary to traditional identities at university, where the academics are the experts. However, it is in keeping with the movement that has been occurring for the last thirty years away from didactic teaching towards more facilitative and co-learning roles, founded on the andragogical principle that adult learners bring their own experiences to the learning process (Knowles, 1984).

As Cook-Sather *et al.* (2014: 16) state, students should be treated as 'legitimate informants on the student experience'. In other words, they are authorities in what it is like to learn as a student at this institution now. Their authority to speak about what it is like as a student from their experience of being a student obviously gets weaker as we think about students with whom they have less in common – either in terms of background or type of degree. This makes inclusivity in partnership work a key value (HEA, 2014), as otherwise we risk increasing the gap between students who are currently empowered by higher education institutions and those who are marginalized by our structures and processes.

This is one reason I think we might want to be cautious in describing students as experts in the student experience. They know about their own experience as a student, but not necessarily about that of all students. We should not overstate what they can be informative about, nor should we hand the label of 'expert' over to anyone who has experience of anything. To me, that seems the surest way of devaluing expertise, which is highly problematic in the current context in which precisely that value is being questioned (see, for example, White, 2016). Expertise can come from experience, but simply experiencing something is insufficient. To gain expertise one also needs to reflect on the experiences critically, to analyse them and test hypotheses about what they mean. Students are well placed to do this, but they do not do it automatically. This is one reason that UCL ChangeMakers emphasizes the importance of research in students' projects: in undertaking the projects, students can become experts, but they have not started off that way.

The authority students have to speak about what it is like to be a student at their institution today certainly commands a strong rationale for consulting students on changes and giving them an input on decision-making. At UCL we have a strong Student Academic Representative (StAR) system, which is based on just that. However, does this rationale constitute a case for involving students as active agents of change? I think a case can be made that any development project involves a number of decisions throughout its lifetime and that each of these should be informed by a student perspective. This is far more likely and feasible if students are on the project team. Students have a vested interest in the outcomes of the project as key stakeholders and a willingness to participate in them. Alongside the many benefits that students gain from participation, I think there is a strong rationale for their involvement.

The student perspective is often the one that is most neglected in educational development. However, it is not the only relevant perspective. In empowering students, we have to be careful not to alienate staff or cause them to feel that their expertise is being challenged.

THE IMPORTANCE OF STAFF

Partnership is important for ensuring that enhancement projects are as successful as possible. Staff ensure that students understand what can be done in the context of their university department. As one of our project students said of their experience:

> So we started with this very big idea ... and then slowly as we talked to various members of staff about it we realized that actually the project was going to be ... almost impossible ... Our staff partner ... was really helpful when we met up with him to ... talk about the hierarchy of UCL and how change happens within it and who to speak to and how different departments within UCL have different goals and visions. (CALTADMIN, 2015a)

When asked if they were confident that the change they had worked towards would take place, students tended to be more confident when it fitted into institutional strategy and work being taken forward by staff: '... because this idea coincides with both parties it makes [it] more likely that [the change] is going to happen' (CALTADMIN, 2015a).

A study of the impact of the pilot year UCL ChangeMakers projects a year on also revealed the importance of staff input into the projects for their medium-term success and sustainability (Marie and McGowan, 2017).

The challenges

WHO DO WE REACH?

If student change projects have such huge advantages why don't all universities have them? One of the major challenges for student partnership projects such as UCL ChangeMakers is reaching the students who are disengaged. They are the very students who could gain the most from UCL ChangeMakers, in terms of attainment, well-being and future employability. If we don't reach them we don't really create a community of which students are an integral part. The question therefore arises of how we ensure the inclusion of students who are currently excluded by our structures and processes in ways we may not be fully aware of.

It may seem a little banal to state, but it is important to take the time to listen. I suspect that we are told what some of the barriers are, but it is difficult and time-consuming for us to take them seriously and find ways to overcome them. Twice recently, students have told me that they would love to take part, but they are away on research trips. I managed to accommodate one. The other I could not, although I would have dearly loved to. Yet, I have not systematically considered whether taking part in UCL ChangeMakers conflicts with research students' study trips or excludes year abroad students. If we want to be inclusive, we need to identify the different ways in which we make it hard for some to participate and what we can possibly do to make it a little easier. By showing willingness to adapt, we make it far more likely that other students will draw other barriers and inhibitors to our attention.

The question of who we reach and how to engage them is being addressed by the sector through the Realising Engagement through Active Culture Transformation (REACT) project (REACT, n.d.). At UCL, we are using this as a framework to query whom we are reaching and to try to determine the barriers to student engagement.

WHAT DO WE SUPPORT?

UCL ChangeMakers has framed itself to be about developing students' learning experiences. In doing so, we have taken most political projects out of the equation. However, would we have supported a project such as the Post-Crash Economics Society (PCES, n.d.)? For those unaware of it, students at the University of Manchester campaigned for changes to the economics curriculum following a conference at the Bank of England in 2011, which considered whether undergraduate economics curricula were fit for purpose in light of the financial crisis beginning in 2008. The changes were strongly resisted by academic staff at the university, who were not experts in the alternative forms of economics that students wished to be taught.

At a meeting of the UCL ChangeMakers steering group we addressed the issue of the extent to which the projects can challenge departmental practice. Some were in favour of requiring departmental sign-off of student-initiated projects before they were accepted. This has the merit of ensuring that the department have some ownership of the project, which makes it more likely that the project will have a lasting impact on the student learning experience. Eventually we decided not to require departmental sign-off: the point of many of the projects is to persuade staff that they should change, by establishing the student demand and the pedagogic benefits of the proposed change.

So would we have supported the Post-Crash Economics Society? Possibly, but initiatives such as ours cannot afford to support projects that challenge the university in ways that could be perceived as unhelpful because we are not a separate entity in the way a student union is. The major concern that staff tend to have of UCL ChangeMakers is that students may make unhelpful or unnecessary suggestions for change.

Having said this, universities are becoming braver themselves. UCL has taken on the 'Why is My Curriculum White?' campaign (UCLTV, 2014) and is attempting to address it by liberating the curriculum through the Connected Curriculum initiative (see McConlogue, Chapter 7). One of the difficulties that academic staff face in providing an education that is not centred on white, Western, heterosexual males is that they are not experts on other traditions. They, like the economics academics in Manchester, have been educated in a tradition other than the one students are now demanding. Where initiatives such as UCL ChangeMakers can be helpful is in helping staff to meet the challenges that this poses. Students are likely to be as much experts in these traditions as staff – they can suggest what alternative texts could be and perhaps explain the cultural thinking and mindset behind them to staff. Staff then retain the disciplinary expertise by judging the merit of the suggestions in the disciplinary context.

How successful are we at partnership?

UCL ChangeMakers is still transitioning towards partnership. Our student-initiated projects are very much student-led. One of the students who had undertaken one of these came and spoke to me recently. She said that she had heard that UCL ChangeMakers was supposed to be about student–staff partnership and she wondered if she had done something wrong or somehow missed out, because her project had been mainly led by her and some other students. She said that she had had a fantastic experience carrying out the project and had not particularly felt the need for staff input. So does it matter that they are more student-led than student–staff partnership projects?

The Exeter 'Students as Change Agents' scheme is intended as students taking charge, determining the change project and conducting it. Dunne and Zandstra (2011) wrote of the importance of pushing past partnership, to students as change agents, because institutions tend to determine the boundaries for partnership work: they determine the projects and recruit students as partners to help them undertake them. Being knowledgeable about their learning experience, students are better placed to determine which projects are likely to have the biggest impact and be of most value to them. Staff may not value these and thus be less prepared to invest time and effort in conducting the project.

UCL ChangeMakers was, at least at its inception, modelled on the Exeter 'Students as Change Agents' scheme. It is clear that students gain enormously from the experience of undertaking the projects, as discussed, and the outcomes can be of very high quality. I do not mind if the projects are student-led but I do think we are missing a trick because the projects are likely to have less longevity, and one of our aims is to create a single learning community. We therefore need to find ways of supporting students to recruit staff on a partnership basis.

We have less data on the extent to which partnership has been achieved on the staff-initiated projects. We clearly have some examples where it worked well: one student on such a project wrote that while the staff set the parameters of the work, the students had the freedom to plan it as they wanted. On another the member of staff wrote:

> As I wanted this project to be as truly collaborative as possible I told the students from the outset that ... I have no template of how to approach them, but instead was hoping that they would work with me on designing our methodology. The other things that I did provide was a space to meet regularly ... and a selection of objects from the UCL Museums and Collections that the students could explore and use as inspiration/jumping off points for our project discussions. (UCL ChangeMakers, 2016: 40)

We do not know how widespread such success was and we created a barrier to stronger partnership by having separate application processes for student- and staff-initiated projects, because that discouraged collaborative project design. Some projects were nevertheless formed in partnership and I had numerous queries about which route they should apply through. We have therefore abolished the student-initiated and staff-initiated distinction on the scheme.

COST–VALUE RATIO

Students as change agent projects would become prohibitively expensive if scaled up to cover all development work. We had 72 projects in 2015/16, which is not far off one project per teaching department, and we struggled to support them all with one full-time manager and myself as a part-time director.

The value of the work can be strongly argued but it is harder to put into metrics. How many percentage points did doing a UCL ChangeMakers project add to a student's final degree mark? How much more did that person earn because they did a project? How much happier were they? Over time, we could perhaps measure the difference between the students who undertook one and those who did not – but depending upon how successful we are at being inclusive, we will have to factor in that these may have been the students who were already going to do well. Measurements of belonging and engagement are not (yet) standard practice. It is easier to invest in something that produces a demonstrable return, such as teacher training, library books, the university's virtual learning environment and more computers.

Projects such as this have to sell themselves on the values that they demonstrate to potential students and through publicizing the good work achieved through the projects supported. UCL ChangeMakers is an important part of the current UCL Education Strategy (UCL, 2016), so it has a few years' grace before the next one is formulated to demonstrate the real value it provides to the institution.

What next?

So what is next for UCL ChangeMakers? Each year we aim to innovate and try something new. In 2017 we trialled students conducting observations of staff. This is something that has been done successfully at the University of Lincoln, Edinburgh Napier University and the University of Roehampton (Huxham *et al.*, 2017; Peat, 2011) and at a number of universities in the USA. We have also obtained the funding to support a project in every department by 2019/20.

Where will we be by 2034? Will students be full partners in the future of the institution? I hope so, but what that would look like is less clear. I can see pieces of the picture: students participating in enhancement projects, quality assurance, consulting on the teaching practices of staff, helping to design curricula and being partners in the professional development of staff. What it would look like as an integrated whole, however, is unclear to me.

Perhaps that is the way it should be: sixteen years is a long time – I hope that the future of student partnership is more than I can currently imagine.

Notes
[1] Address for correspondence: j.marie@ucl.ac.uk
[2] www.ucl.ac.uk/2034
[3] That is, undergraduate, postgraduate taught and postgraduate research.
[4] www.ucl.ac.uk/2034

References

Boden, R. and Epstein, D. (2006) 'Managing the research imagination? Globalisation and research in higher education'. *Globalisation, Societies and Education*, 4 (2), 223–36.

CALTADMIN (2015a) *UCL ChangeMaker Projects: Module choice v2* [video]. Online. www.youtube.com/watch?v=Np-z75MJc1k&feature=youtu.be (accessed 9 July 2015).

CALTADMIN (2015b) *UCL ChangeMaker Projects: Second language learning with Skype* [video]. Online. www.youtube.com/watch?v=oSMHhHKrJfs&feature=youtu.be (accessed 21 July 2016).

CALTADMIN (2015c) *UCL ChangeMaker Projects: Student belonging v2* [video]. Online. www.youtube.com/watch?v=cK4cDEX9-Pw&feature=youtu.be (accessed 21 July 2016).

Cook-Sather, A., Bovill, C. and Felten, P. (2014) *Engaging Students as Partners in Learning and Teaching: A guide for faculty*. San Francisco: Jossey-Bass.

Dunne, E. and Zandstra, R. (2011) *Students as Change Agents: New ways of engaging with learning and teaching in higher education*. Bristol: ESCalate.

HEA (Higher Education Academy) (2014) *Framework for Partnership in Learning and Teaching in Higher Education*. York: Higher Education Academy. Online. www.heacademy.ac.uk/system/files/resources/hea_framework_for_partnership_in_learning_and_teaching.pdf (accessed 13 March 2018).

Huxham, M., Scoles, J., Green, U., Purves, S., Welsh, Z. and Gray, A. (2017) '"Observation has set in": Comparing students and peers as reviewers of teaching'. *Assessment & Evaluation in Higher Education*, 42 (6), 887–99.

Knowles, M.S. and Associates (1984) *Andragogy in Action: Applying modern principles of adult learning*. San Francisco: Jossey-Bass.

Marie, J., Arif, M. and Joshi, T. (2016) 'UCL ChangeMakers projects: Supporting staff/student partnership on educational enhancement projects'. *Student Engagement in Higher Education Journal*, 1 (1), 1–5.

Marie, J. and Azuma, F. (2018) 'UCL ChangeMakers scholars: Embedding staff/student partnerships into quality assurance mechanisms'. *Student Engagement in Higher Education Journal*.

Marie, J. and McGowan, S. (2017) 'Moving towards sustainable outcomes in student partnerships: Partnership values in the pilot year'. *International Journal for Students as Partners*, 1 (2). Online. https://mulpress.mcmaster.ca/ijsap/issue/view/318 (accessed 5 April 2018).

Mezirow, J. and Associates (2000) *Learning as Transformation: Critical perspectives on a theory in progress*. San Francisco: Jossey-Bass.

PCES (Post-Crash Economics Society) (n.d.) 'The University of Manchester Post-Crash Economics Society'. Online. www.post-crasheconomics.com/ (accessed 9 July 2015).

Peat, J. (2011) 'New to the field: Integrating the student voice into the PG Cert'. *Educational Developments*, 12 (4), 18–19.

REACT (Realising Engagement through Active Culture Transformation) (n.d.) 'Student engagement and the REACT project'. Online. www. studentengagement.ac.uk/newsite/ (accessed 13 March 2018).

UCL (University College London) (2016) *UCL Education Strategy 2016–21*. London: University College London. Online. www.ucl.ac.uk/teaching-learning/ sites/teaching-learning/files/migrated-files/ucl_education_strategy_june2017_ finalv2_web.pdf (accessed 6 April 2018).

UCL ChangeMakers (2016) *2015/16 UCL ChangeMakers Report*. London: University College London. Online. www.cnmd.ac.uk/changemakers/docs/ UCL_ChangeMakers_Report_2015-16.pdf (accessed 5 April 2018).

UCLTV (2014) *Why is My Curriculum White?* [video]. Online. www.youtube. com/watch?v=Dscx4h2l-Pk (accessed 9 July 2015).

Wenstone, R. (2012) *A Manifesto for Partnership*. London: National Union of Students. Online. www.nusconnect.org.uk/resources/a-manifesto-for-partnership/download_attachment (accessed 21 July 2016).

White, M. (2016) 'Should we listen to the experts on the EU referendum?'. *The Guardian*, 8 June. Online. www.theguardian.com/politics/blog/2016/jun/08/ experts-eu-referendum-michael-gove (accessed 4 January 2017).

Chapter 4

UCL Arena and staff development

Rosalind Duhs[1]

As already mentioned, education has been less of a priority for many universities in recent years as funding and status were linked to the Research Excellence Framework and its predecessors. It has therefore become all the more important to find ways to acknowledge and recognize those who teach or support learning, as well as giving them opportunities to develop their activities further; in research, there are well-established ways to do this (conferences, promotions, grants, and so on). Unlike schoolteachers, university teachers were not traditionally required to have a teaching qualification, though in recent years a condition of their probation has usually included all or part of a postgraduate certificate in higher education (or similar), a counterpart to the schoolteacher's PGCE (postgraduate certificate in education). In the last few years, the Higher Education Academy (HEA) has created a set of 'Fellowships' based on the 'professional standards framework' (PSF) where staff can get recognition for their teaching practice. The schemes that award this also create opportunities for enhancing support of learning. The phrase 'supporting learning' is chosen deliberately: students depend on a wide range of staff such as librarians, digital support workers, administrators and many others. HEA Fellowships therefore include ways for these important 'non-teaching' staff to get recognition for their work to make student learning easier (or even, in some cases, possible). UCL Arena, which has expanded substantially even in the time since this chapter was written, has been part of the transformation of the university from 'research-intensive' to 'research-rich', where the former term implies that education is less important, and the latter that it is on an equal footing with research.

This position paper, written from an insider perspective, provides an analytical account of UCL Arena, UCL's scheme for the continuing professional development (CPD) of staff who teach and support learning. Three levels are studied: individual, departmental/institutional and national. The personal experience and motivation of scheme participants are discussed in relation to the institutional context of UCL as a research-intensive university, drawing on data gathered at research-intensive universities in England and Sweden and relevant literature. National influences such as the current UK government's focus on notions of teaching excellence, and what that might mean, are also examined.

The insider perspective: A brief analysis

It would be disingenuous not to acknowledge my involvement with UCL Arena and its impact on this paper. As the founding director of the scheme, I cannot claim to be a dispassionate writer. However, I have used the rich evaluative data generated by the 'plan, do, review' cycle that underpins the operation of UCL Arena as well as my research into the development of academic staff as teachers to lend credence to this paper.

There is a wealth of literature on the risk of bias resulting from insider perspectives, as well as the potential for rich 'thick description' (Geertz, 1973). Prebble *et al*. point out that 'academic developers [studying] ... their own practice' call into question 'the acceptability of their claims' (2004: 25). Holligan and Wilson (2015) interrogate the intricacies of the reputational fragility of educational research and identify two ideal types of researcher: 'the "intellectual-academic", motivated primarily by the intellectual virtue of research excellence and accountability to the academic community and the "humanistic-professional", motivated by service to the wider community' (2015: 453). They argue that it is advantageous to combine the characteristics of these types. In this paper, my perspective resembles that of Holligan and Wilson's 'humanistic-professional' informants. My professional life is shaped by 'issues of social and educational justice' (ibid.: 470). These are reflected in my own experiences, especially 'a desire to make a positive difference to the lives of others' (ibid.). This is not at the expense of 'intellectual-academic' rigour, however. This position paper explains how UCL Arena combines academic rigour and humanistic professionalism.

UCL Arena has the potential to enable us to '... [achieve] a significant impact and positive social transformation through education' (ibid.). If we can help our students to become the best they can through effective approaches to inspiring them to learn, they will be able to 'contribute significantly to society' in line with UCL's 20-year strategy, 'UCL 2034'.[2]

This position paper is a narrative of educational work based on research and experience. I will start by explaining what UCL Arena is.

UCL Arena: An introduction

UCL Arena provides a range of opportunities for staff across UCL to enhance their roles in teaching and supporting learning.

The Arena team runs varied sessions for all UCL staff with education-related roles, such as lecturers and teaching fellows, as well as those who support learning in any way. Researchers, teaching administrators, e-learning facilitators, lab technicians and librarians provide valuable learning support. UCL Arena enables these key contributors to the educational attainment of students to gain recognition for their work.

Many Arena events are led by staff from across UCL who generously share their good practice with colleagues. There are also two non-award-bearing courses, Arena One for postgraduate teaching assistants (PGTAs) and Arena Two for lecturers and teaching fellows on probation. Participants go on to apply for UCL Arena/HEA Associate Fellowship (Arena One) and Fellowship (Arena Two) when they are ready. Fellowship is a probationary requirement for new lecturers and teaching fellows, while Associate Fellowship is optional for participants in Arena One.

The goal of Arena is to empower us all at UCL to do the best we can to enrich the educational experience of both students and staff by enhancing our ability to help students at UCL to learn and develop. Participants also gain recognition for their engagement in education through the UCL Arena Fellowship scheme. There are four awards: Associate Fellowship, Fellowship, Senior Fellowship and Principal Fellowship. The educational experience of applicants guides their choice of award. The scheme is accredited by the Higher Education Academy (HEA) so participants can apply for UCL Arena and HEA awards in parallel. All our activities are underpinned by the United Kingdom Professional Standards Framework for teaching and supporting learning in higher education (UKPSF) (HEA, 2011). This increases the coherence of provision and makes it easier for participants who are planning their fellowship applications to identify strands of education-related activity that they can develop. Enhancements of teaching and learning can be integrated into the case studies that are central to written applications. A multimedia option is also available.

The appeal of UCL Arena is strong. By July 2016, just over two years after the April 2014 launch of the scheme, more than 3,700 individuals had taken part in UCL Arena events and 444 had gained UCL Arena/HEA fellowships.

Focusing on education at UCL

The unprecedented focus on the development of education at UCL evidenced by the rapid growth of UCL Arena has been initiated by the President and Provost, Professor Michael Arthur. He has led by example, becoming a UCL Arena Principal Fellow in December 2015. In a blog published by the HEA, he commented: 'What better way to demonstrate my commitment to excellent teaching than by becoming an HEA Principal Fellow?' (Arthur, 2016). The Provost's enthusiasm has undoubtedly had a positive impact on the scheme.

However, UCL still has a long way to go in terms of attaining higher numbers of fellowships. Around 15 per cent of academic staff had fellowships at the end of 2014/15, about 4 per cent less than the Russell Group average. A concerted effort to catch up would be necessary if fellowships became a measure of 'teaching excellence'. However, we are making good progress. The number of fellowships gained at UCL in 2015/16 far exceed the Russell Group and higher education sector average (see Figure 4.1).

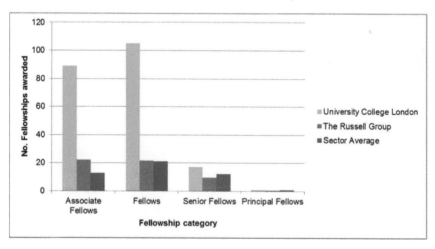

Figure 4.1: HEA Fellowship awarded by category through an accredited CPD scheme at UCL, 1 May 2015–30 April 2016

Source: HEA, 2016

It would be overly instrumental to focus only on the numbers of fellowships. The main purpose of UCL Arena is not the attainment of a key performance indicator (KPI), although this is important. The enrichment of the individual participant is paramount; any involvement with UCL Arena should be a positive, self-affirming experience, which empowers fellowship applicants to facilitate 'high quality student learning' (HEA, 2011).

A multiplicity of influences shape the experience of staff as they engage – or choose not to engage – in a scheme such as UCL Arena. I would now like to explore some of these influences. I will then explain how I have approached the design and management of the Arena streams of activity to maximize our chances of achieving our ambitious goals for the quality of provision, combining 'humanistic-professional' with 'intellectual-academic' (Holligan and Wilson, 2015) perspectives to underpin our work with UCL staff.

Developing as an educator in a research-intensive environment

Data gathered at research-intensive universities in England and Sweden in 2005 and followed up in 2014 inform this exploration. The initial data were gathered as follows: 26 visits to two universities for observation of courses and participants teaching; and 35 interviews with course participants, their mentors, and educational developers. A grounded theory approach was adopted; a detailed analysis of qualitative data generated theory. For the full text see Duhs, 2007. The substantive theory, based closely on the data that emerged, is relevant here. An overview is provided in Table 4.1 (Duhs, 2007: 159). The figure that summarizes the substantive theory is also included (Figure 4.2). The main themes derived from these data will be identified and explained briefly in relation to their relevance to UCL Arena.

This position paper focuses on three levels: the individual, the departmental/institutional and the national. On an individual level, learning about teaching and developing as a teacher can be an empowering experience, as we see from participant feedback on UCL Arena. However, as Figure 4.2 indicates, each individual encounters a unique intertwined network of contextual factors that impact on the experience of learning about education. It is essential to recognize these factors to mitigate any which might have a negative impact on teacher development and by extension fail to enhance student learning.

The perception of opposition between 'teacherliness' and the quest for academic prestige through research is fundamental. I will explain the concept of 'teacherliness' and analyse how it relates to a focus on research. I will then outline how UCL Arena is attempting to close the perceived chasm between research and education.

Teacherliness is a strongly values-based characteristic, defined as 'behaviour characteristic of and befitting a teacher: valuing devotion to teaching and student learning, sensitivity to the student experience, and motivation to learn about and develop teaching' (Duhs 2007, see Table 4.1). Intense teacherliness is widespread among UCL Arena participants who lead seminars, volunteer to join our Pool of Assessors of fellowship applications, and come repeatedly to our events. The concept of teacherliness applies to all activities that create a positive learning environment for students; teacherliness is often highly developed in staff in learning support roles who are sensitive to the student experience. How much space is there for teacherliness in a research-intensive university?

John Henry Newman saw the university as 'a place of teaching' and considered that 'to discover and to teach are distinct functions; they are also distinct gifts, and are not commonly found united in the same person' (Newman, 1852: xii). The complex relationship between research and teaching, addressed in more detail by Oliver and Gourlay in Chapter 2, is discussed by Trowler and Wareham (2007). Citing Rowland (2000: 1), they conclude that studies into the impact of research activity on teaching will 'state the obvious ... "some of the most inspiring teachers are able researchers, but not all; that some prominent researchers are good teachers, but not all."' (Trowler and Wareham, 2007). What incentives lead 'prominent researchers' to strive to become 'good teachers'?

Bourdieu's (1988) study, *Homo Academicus,* suggests that prestigious 'academic' capital can be built through administrative and non-research roles, but 'it always tends to appear ... as a substitute, or a consolation prize' (1988: 99). It is 'scientific' capital, 'founded on investment in the activity of research alone' (Grenfell, 2007: 123) that leads to 'external renown' (Bourdieu, 1988: 98). Bourdieu sees the male researcher as the norm. Although this is no longer the case, those who engage with teaching are generally more likely to be women. In June 2016, 70 per cent of UCL Arena Fellowships were held by women.

The tension between teaching and research is repeatedly raised in the literature on the development of education in research-intensive environments (Light and Calkins, 2015; Lucas, 2006; Malcolm, 2014). UCL Arena, working in synergy with the major UCL initiative of the Connected Curriculum (CC) (Fung, 2016), aims to knit these strands of academic work tightly together through student participation in active research-based learning. We are following the appealing Humboldtian idea of the 'unity of research and education' (Ricken, 2007: 489), whereby 'both teacher and student have their justification in the common pursuit of knowledge' (ibid.: 490).

It is our aim that staff should be strongly supported by UCL Arena as they develop inspiring research-based education. On a visit to UCL, Tony Harland, a pioneer in students' research-based learning (see his recent chapter: Harland, 2016), confirmed that staff research was enriched by enabling students to learn through research. Conversely, Elken and Wollscheid (2016) comment that their recent exhaustive literature review 'did not find existing studies of teaching–research links that show that traditional classroom teaching in general has a positive impact on research' (2016: 56). If we are to bring teaching and research together, we need to invite students to learn through discovery, extending learning spaces beyond 'traditional classroom teaching'. UCL Arena plays a central role in guiding and stimulating staff to create the powerful discovery-fuelled learning environments foregrounded in the CC. There are many examples of how staff and students are already engaging with the 'common pursuit of knowledge' at UCL as this volume illustrates (see also the UCL Teaching and Learning Portal, 2016).

But what of those who are not teacherly, those who may be so absorbed in their research and so uninterested in teaching that they have never even heard of UCL Arena? Returning to Figure 4.2, we now move from the individual perspective to the institutional and departmental ethos regarding teacherliness. These interlock to impact strongly on the propensity of each individual to engage with opportunities to develop education.

Research and education: Institutional and departmental influences

On an institutional level, a range of strategies provide UCL Arena with unprecedented backing to develop research-based education. The 'UCL 2034' vision foregrounds the aim of achieving 'the integration of research and education, underpinning an inspirational student experience'.[3] UCL Arena features in the UCL Education Strategy (UCL, 2016), which specifies:

1. The planned expansion of UCL Arena to underpin the development of research-based education at UCL (p. 8)
2. The establishment of a Digital Scholarship strand of UCL Arena (p. 18)
3. The review of the promotions process to include materials underpinned by UCL Arena (p. 23)
4. The importance of investment in UCL Arena to help UCL to achieve current ambitious educational goals (p. 23).

Table 4.1: Factors affecting courses and sessions on teaching at research-intensive universities

Factors which contribute to a favourable context for courses and sessions	Factors which affect courses and sessions	Factors which contribute to an unfavourable context for courses and sessions
Teacherliness: behaviour characteristic of and befitting a teacher: valuing devotion to teaching and student learning, sensitivity to the student experience, and motivation to learn about and develop teaching	Indeterminacy: vacillation as to what knowledge and form of delivery are appropriate for the teacher education of new academic staff	The primacy of research: the quest for the academic prestige accrued through successful research
Teacherliness leads to motivation to take part in courses; the emphasis on teaching is considered justified and is not contested	Educational developers find their role challenging and do not feel secure	Contestation and educational development: compulsion to participate and the imposition of top-down change promoting an unwelcome emphasis on teaching
Participants' enjoyment of the opportunity to meet colleagues from other disciplines and departments and learn from them	Course participants are exacting customers. It is difficult to meet their diverse needs	Participants' strong sense of disciplinary identity and the need to learn more about subject-related teaching
The allocation of adequate time for participation in courses		The intensity of academic work and the stressful context of the teacher education of academic staff; courses added to previous workload without the allocation of adequate time

Factors which contribute to a favourable context for courses and sessions	Factors which affect courses and sessions	Factors which contribute to an unfavourable context for courses and sessions
A departmental ethos which promotes and values teacherliness	Senior academic staff are uncertain about courses and the work of educational developers and Educational Development Units (EDUs)	A departmental ethos which promotes and values research at the expense of teacherliness
Timeliness of courses: new academic staff feel they are at the right stage of their early career to engage with and benefit from courses		New academic staff are compelled to attend courses while struggling to cope with a range of competing pressures
Intrinsically motivated participants who are engaged and show their appreciation of courses and sessions		Disgruntled 'strategic compliers' who make it plain that they are participating on sufferance and consider attendance a waste of time
Acknowledgement that participation in courses and sessions can lead to the development of teachers and teaching		Denial that courses/sessions can lead to the development of teachers and teaching

Source: Duhs, 2007: 159, Table 18

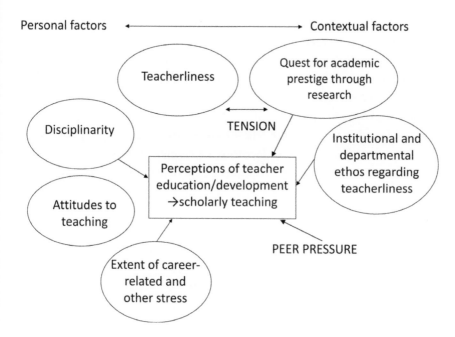

Personal factors ←——————————→ Contextual factors

Teacherliness

Quest for academic prestige through research

Disciplinarity

TENSION

Attitudes to teaching

Perceptions of teacher education/development →scholarly teaching

Institutional and departmental ethos regarding teacherliness

PEER PRESSURE

Extent of career-related and other stress

Figure 4.2: Contextual factors that impact on learning to teach in research-intensive environments

Despite these forceful indications of institutional support for UCL Arena, individuals who lack teacherly values may not be eager to join the UCL Arena community. It may be challenging to accept the increasing emphasis on education in UCL's research-intensive environment. The ethos in some departments may tend to lead staff to resist institutional initiatives to effect such groundbreaking cultural change. Any peer pressure to uphold a long-standing tradition of downplaying teacherliness in favour of dedication to research could be hard to withstand.

However, there is also an ethical imperative at play. Our educational role is a weighty responsibility. We can choose to be beneficent, to act in the best interests of the students we teach and provide them with the support they need to help them to learn and develop to reach their full potential. On the other hand, we can neglect through omission, doing the minimum, and ultimately through lack of engagement risk inadvertently doing harm to students by failing to provide them with the guidance they need. The ethics of teaching and learning offer stark ethical choices: engage and do good, fail to engage and risk doing harm. This ethical dimension of teaching and supporting learning is seldom considered, but the UKPSF highlights professional values including 'respect individual learners and diverse learning communities' (HEA, 2011, Professional Value 1). Those who gain UCL Arena/HEA Fellowships have evidenced their teacherliness, where relevant, inspired by their devotion to research in their discipline. They are required to show that they 'engage in continuing professional development in subjects/disciplines and their pedagogy, incorporating research, scholarship and the evaluation of professional practices' (ibid.: Area of Activity 5). The UKPSF is flexible enough to allow those who support learning to apply for fellowships. Staff in learning support roles may not teach in the sense of lecturing or running seminars, but they do have a significant impact on the student experience, through contact with students or colleagues.

UCL Arena: Guiding principles

It is essential for the UCL Arena team to provide a safe, welcoming space for the exploration of difficult issues in an open and informal way. We cannot ignore the pressures faced by academic staff who are required to bring in grant money and do cutting-edge research. But we can enable them to bring their research-related curiosity to UCL's teaching spaces, and invite them to apply their ingenuity to the creation of new ways of helping students to learn in their disciplines, in partnership with support staff.

A major obstacle to full participation in UCL Arena is lack of time. This can only be mitigated by departments with institutional backing. UCL is dynamic and compelling, and excels at engendering loyalty and motivating employees to give their best, often without counting the cost in terms of overtime. Problems arise when yet more is asked of hard-pressed staff, risking resentment and negative attitudes to what may be perceived as the extra burden of developing research-based education (see the factors in Table 4.1 and Figure 4.2).

On an institutional level, the UCL Education Strategy includes plans to integrate UCL Arena Fellowships into the promotions process as mentioned above. This will act as a strong incentive. UCL Arena also adopts several strategies to maximize the usefulness of participation. Our guiding principles combine the academic rigour and humanistic professionalism discussed by Holligan and Wilson (2015), academic rigour because our work is research-informed and humanistic professionalism because the UCL Arena team is sensitive to participants' contexts and requirements and aims to make a positive difference to the student experience.

First, every course and session is designed to create space to take account of participants' contexts and concerns. Facilitators take the time to explore what participants want from sessions and ensure that they leave with useful resources to increase the effectiveness of their teaching and learning support. The exploration of participants' aims may be done in advance of sessions on Moodle, UCL's virtual learning environment, for instance using 'hot questions' (see UCL Digital Education, 2016). This approach increases the relevance of session learning activities to participants.

Second, UCL Arena invites participants to contribute to sessions, sharing their perspectives and experience with others. This is vital as it shows respect for participants' considerable expertise and enriches sessions. Participants welcome the opportunity to find solutions to any teaching or learning support dilemmas with colleagues who may face similar issues. UCL Arena provides participants with the rare chance to interact with staff in other roles and disciplines, which they appreciate.

Third, UCL Arena facilitators are not prescriptive concerning teaching and supporting learning. They cannot be categorical because learning is unpredictable; it is contingent on a complex web of factors and varies according to discipline. It is essential to remember that: 'the relationship between what teachers do and what students learn is itself complex and contingent. It is dependent on many variables, change in any one of which may affect the student outcomes' (Prebble *et al.*, 2004: 11). There is no single best approach, but we can offer a menu of options and fruitful ways of developing research-based learning in partnership with participants.

Fourth, and very importantly, UCL Arena facilitators strive to follow the UKPSF (HEA, 2011) in their own work. A central aspect of this is Professional Value 3, 'Use evidence-informed approaches and the outcomes from research, scholarship and continuing professional development'. We avoid suggesting the adoption of new ways of stimulating student learning without searching the literature to see what has been done in higher education and studying impact. We cannot hope to bring about far-reaching change without supplying evidence to underpin our belief in the developments we recommend. We are benefiting from the expertise of the Institute of Education who have set up a library resource for participants as well as the UCL Arena Team.[4]

To summarize, we make sure what we do is relevant to participants, that we respect their expertise and experience, and invite them to contribute to sessions, and that our recommendations are evidence-based. We recognize that it is ultimately the responsibility of participants to decide how they want to apply UCL Arena learning, but we aim to initiate the development of enriching options. These guiding principles harmonize with appropriate theories of adult learning (for an overview, see Conlan *et al.*, 2003).

Gaining UCL Arena Fellowships

A highlight of UCL Arena is the celebration of fellowships at awards ceremonies. The sense of achievement among new fellows is palpable as it can be challenging to apply for recognition. Awards are of course individual, so applicants need to write case studies in the first person to make it clear what they have developed and achieved. The UKPSF requires evidence of effective approaches to teaching and/or supporting learning. To the modest, this may initially appear self-congratulatory, so support is needed to persuade applicants to provide an analytical account of their successes. Narratives of obstacles to student learning and how these were overcome with a rationale for solutions to problems make rich case studies.

What does the future hold for UCL Arena? The trajectory is positive, as indicated by Figure 4.3. National initiatives may well lead to a further growth in the number of fellowships. I will now focus on national level influences on the scheme.

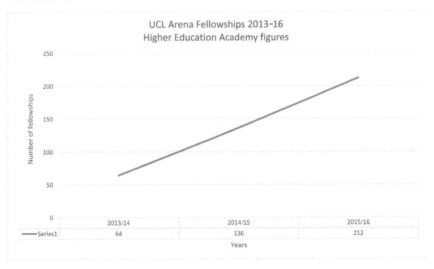

Figure 4.3: Fellowship awarded through UCL Arena

Source: HEA Arena Fellowship graph 2013–16

UCL Arena and national initiatives: The Teaching Excellence Framework

Current government goals in relation to university teaching are having a strong impact across the sector. In July 2016, Justine Greening, then Secretary of State for Education, introduced the second reading of the Higher Education and Research Bill by underlining the significance of her own university education: 'For me, the chance to go to university was absolutely pivotal to being able to make something of myself. ... I was the first person in my family to be able to go to university' (Greening, 2016). When Greening was at university, there were no tuition fees. The Higher Education and Research Bill proposes that universities with excellent teaching according to a set of metrics (to include student satisfaction, retention and graduate employability) will be able to raise undergraduate fees. The attainment of what is judged as teaching excellence is therefore related to the ability of universities to increase income, a strong incentive. The marketization of higher education through the shift of funding from the public to the private purse has created the 'student customer', whose status is arguably higher than ever before.

UCL is now in a strong position to meet the requirements of the Teaching Excellence Framework (TEF) following the recent growth of engagement with education. UCL Arena provides a springboard for the continuous development of teaching and learning in synergy with the Connected Curriculum and informed by the 'ChangeMakers' initiative (Marie, 2016, and Chapter 3 of this volume). ChangeMakers enables students to work in partnership with staff to enhance the student learning experience.

Summary and conclusions

This position paper has outlined the aims of UCL Arena in a research-intensive context. UCL's ambitious enterprise of embedding research-based education across the institution through the CC initiative in synergy with UCL Arena, including potential obstacles to universal engagement, has been explored. The ethical dimension of education was raised and the thinking behind the way the UCL Arena team designs learning opportunities for staff has been explained: the approach is participant-centred.

It is clear from the metrics that UCL Arena has been effective in attracting thousands to a range of events: by early 2017, over 500 individuals had gained fellowships since the April 2014 launch. The prospect of the TEF has increased the centrality of the educational mission, but this is not the only reason for the strong uptake of the opportunities offered by Arena. UCL Arena offers a forum for compelling dialogues about education, a safe space where challenges can be honestly disclosed and colleagues can collaborate creatively for realistic steps towards meeting them. Individuals who develop an application for a fellowship award derive a mosaic of benefits from the process: they appreciate what they have achieved through their teaching and support of learning, and are stimulated to think expansively so they can realize the full potential of their educational role.

Notes
[1] Address for correspondence: r.duhs@ucl.ac.uk
[2] www.ucl.ac.uk/2034
[3] www.ucl.ac.uk/2034
[4] http://libguides.ioe.ac.uk

References

Arthur, M. (2016) 'Talking teaching: Why I became an HEA Fellow'. *HEA Learning and Teaching Blog*, 6 January. Online. www.heacademy.ac.uk/blog/talking-teaching-why-i-became-hea-fellow-professor-michael-arthur (accessed 26 July 2016).

Bourdieu, P. (1988) *Homo Academicus*. Trans. Collier, P. Cambridge: Polity Press.

Conlan, J., Grabowski, S. and Smith, K. (2003) *Emerging Perspectives on Learning, Teaching, and Technology: Adult learning*. Online. https://openlibra.com/en/book/emerging-perspectives-on-learning-teaching-and-technology (accessed 4 April 2018).

Duhs, R.M. (2007) 'Developing Teaching and Learning in Higher Education: A comparative study of initial training to teach at university in England and Sweden'. Unpublished PhD thesis, Oxford Brookes University.

Elken, M. and Wollscheid, S. (2016) *The Relationship between Research and Education: Typologies and indicators: A literature review* (NIFU Report 2016:8). Oslo: Nordic Institute for Studies in Innovation, Research and Education. Online. https://brage.bibsys.no/xmlui/bitstream/handle/11250/2386141/NIFUreport2016-8.pdf?sequence=1&isAllowed=y (accessed 15 September 2016).

Fung, D. (2016) 'Connected Curriculum'. Online. http://discovery.ucl.ac.uk/1558776/1/A-Connected-Curriculum-for-Higher-Education.pdf (accessed 4 April 2018).

Geertz, C. (1973) 'Thick description: Towards an interpretive theory of culture'. In Geertz, C. *The Interpretation of Cultures: Selected essays*. New York: Basic Books, 3–30. Online. https://chairoflogicphiloscult.files.wordpress.com/2013/02/clifford-geertz-the-interpretation-of-cultures.pdf (accessed 4 April 2018).

Greening, J. (2016) Speech in House of Commons debate on the Higher Education and Research Bill, 19 July, vol. 613, col. 703. Online. https://hansard.parliament.uk/commons/2016-07-19/debates/3F059309-CBD8-4B30-A63C-562566715CF7/HigherEducationAndResearchBill (accessed 19 March 2018).

Grenfell, M.J. (2007) *Pierre Bourdieu: Education and training*. London: Continuum.

Harland, T. (2016) 'Deliberate subversion of time: Slow scholarship and learning through research'. In Trede, F. and McEwen, C. (eds) *Educating the Deliberate Professional: Preparing for future practices*. Cham: Springer, 175–88.

HEA (Higher Education Academy) (2011) *The UK Professional Standards Framework for Teaching and Supporting Learning in Higher Education*. York: Higher Education Academy. Online. www.heacademy.ac.uk/sites/default/files/downloads/ukpsf_2011_english.pdf (accessed 27 July 2016).

HEA (Higher Education Academy) (2016) *Annual Review of Accredited Continuing Professional Development (CPD) schemes 2016: University College London*. York: Higher Education Academy. Online. www.heacademy.ac.uk/ system/files/downloads/annual_review_of_accredited_cpd_schemes_2016_ guidance_notes.pdf (accessed 9 May 2018).

Holligan, C. and Wilson, M. (2015) 'Critical incidents as formative influences on the work of educational researchers: Understanding an insider perspective through narrative enquiry'. *British Journal of Sociology of Education*, 36 (3), 453–73.

Light, G. and Calkins, S. (2015) 'The experience of academic learning: Uneven conceptions of learning across research and teaching'. *Higher Education*, 69 (3), 345–59.

Lucas, L. (2006) *The Research Game in Academic Life*. Maidenhead: Open University Press.

Malcolm, M. (2014) 'A critical evaluation of recent progress in understanding the role of the research–teaching link in higher education'. *Higher Education*, 67 (3), 289–301.

Marie, J. (2016) 'UCL ChangeMakers'. Online. www.ucl.ac.uk/changemakers/ucl-changemakers-projects (accessed 4 April 2018).

Newman, J.H. (1852) *The Idea of a University*. London: Longmans, Green and Co.

Prebble, T., Hargraves, H., Leach, L., Naidoo, K., Suddaby, G. and Zepke, N. (2004) *Impact of Student Support Services and Academic Development Programmes on Student Outcomes in Undergraduate Tertiary Study: A synthesis of the research*. Wellington, NZ: Ministry of Education.

Ricken, N. (2007) 'The deliberate university: Remarks on the "idea of the university" from a perspective of knowledge'. *Studies in Philosophy and Education*, 26 (5), 481–98.

Rowland, S. (2000) *The Enquiring University Teacher*. Buckingham: Society for Research into Higher Education and Open University Press.

Trowler, P. and Wareham, T. (2007) *Tribes, Territories, Research and Teaching: Enhancing the "teaching–research nexus": Literature review*. York: Higher Education Academy. Online. www.heacademy.ac.uk/system/files/deliverable_1_ literature_review_13.9.7.pdf (accessed 10 September 2016).

UCL (University College London) (2016) *UCL Education Strategy 2016–21*. London: University College London. Online. www.ucl.ac.uk/teaching-learning/ education-strategy (accessed 4 April 2018).

UCL Digital Education (2016) *Moodle Resource Centre*. Online. https://wiki.ucl. ac.uk/pages/viewpage.action?pageId=23206399 (accessed 4 April 2018).

UCL Teaching and Learning Portal (2016) *Research-Based Learning: Case studies*. Online. www.ucl.ac.uk/teaching-learning/case-studies (accessed 4 April 2018).

Chapter 5

Beyond winners and losers in assessment and feedback

Tansy Jessop and Gwyneth Hughes[1]

This chapter introduces another key theme, that of assessment. For most, this triggers an image of students asking each other 'what mark did you get?' and such 'summative' assessment is often 'the important bit'. But as outlined in our opening chapter, high degrees of summative assessment distort learning, by introducing high-stakes and overly artificial and anxiety-inducing exercises that are far from being the best way of establishing what students understand and what they can do. This has often been exacerbated by modularization, where each module must be tested separately and the marks accumulated. Here, the authors think through some of the drawbacks of modularization, competition and, perhaps most importantly of all, the way that a focus on summative assessment undermines 'formative' assessment – the apparently simple process of working with students *during* the course to help them improve their understanding. In this chapter, and drawing on two different research projects, they outline and discuss various strategies for bringing students' attention back to their own learning through formative assessment. In particular, they consider how students' learning can be part of a dialogue with tutors centred on individual exploration and personal progress in understanding rather than being distracted by competition and endless rounds of summative assessment.

This chapter explores the relationship between findings from two assessment projects funded by the Higher Education Academy (HEA) and Joint Information Systems Committee (JISC) between 2009 and 2014 at two different universities. The projects were unrelated in design, approach and intention. Transforming the Experience of Students through Assessment (TESTA)[2] focused a wide-angled lens on modular degrees to gain a programme perspective of seven undergraduate programmes at four universities, while Assessment Careers examined the effectiveness of feedback on five postgraduate programmes at the then Institute of Education. The outcomes of both projects gave surprisingly similar interpretations of the problems with assessment and feedback. Modularization, already introduced in the opening chapter, limited students' capacities to use feedback and see connections across the whole programme of study because learning was compartmentalized; high levels of assessment fed a competitive culture; and disconnected and ineffective feedback impeded student learning. This chapter explores these problems, and demonstrates strategies and approaches that have worked to breach the walls of modular degrees and build a connected and meaningful experience where all students can achieve their 'personal best'.

The significance of assessment and feedback for student learning is well established in the literature. Ramsden (2003) goes as far as to say that 'from a student's point of view, assessment always defines the actual curriculum' (ibid.: 187). Gipps (1994) was the first to coin terms differentiating the measurement function of assessment ('Assessment of Learning') from its learning function ('Assessment for Learning'). More recently, Boud and Falchikov (2006) have extended these two functions of assessment to a third, related to developing graduate attributes and preparing students for the longer term in work settings. Feedback is equally prominent in the literature. Hattie and Timperley (2007) provide compelling evidence of the impact of feedback based on a meta-analysis of factors that contribute to learning, as do Black and Wiliam (1998). Their findings show that there are significant learning gains to be derived from formative feedback. Given the importance of assessment and feedback for student learning, this chapter re-emphasizes the importance of the assessment environment as the vital place for fostering student learning.

The measurement function of assessment tends to dominate in higher education: in curriculum design, assurance of standards, and the award of degrees (Boud, 2000). The task of ensuring that UK degrees are comparable and meet standards of quality is accomplished largely through assessment. Comparability and standardization are part of a 'scientific' paradigm that prizes objective, rational and measurable outcomes. The apparatus of quality assurance lends credence to the view that assessment is a logical science, with credits, word equivalence and review processes making assessment appear more linear and technical than it actually is (Knight, 2002). While quality apparatus such as moderation and external examining systems are held up as guardians of standards, anyone who has been involved in these processes appreciates their complex and fuzzy human dimensions (Bloxham, 2009). In our view, the technical–rational approach at the heart of quality assurance procedures is at odds with the more interpretive, relational and human dimensions of assessment and feedback. These dimensions are best cultivated in an assessment environment that nurtures learning, emphasizing formative tasks and formative feedback, which are often invisible in quality regimes (Jessop *et al.*, 2012).

Research has established that students learn best when teachers set challenging and high expectations (Chickering and Gamson, 1987; Gibbs and Simpson, 2004; Arum and Roksa, 2011). Creating an assessment environment that sets the bar high on challenge and student effort, and distributes that effort, is a vital component in student learning, often described as 'time on task' (Gibbs and Simpson, 2004). 'Final marks', or 'summative' assessment, designed to measure student achievement, is a poor vehicle for distributing student effort because it encourages instrumental behaviour and surface approaches to learning, particularly when assessment consists of small and frequent tasks (Harland *et al.*, 2015; Jessop and Tomas, 2017). Meaningful 'formative' assessment that connects concepts and problems, and leads into challenging summative tasks, is a more effective vehicle for engaging students in well-distributed intellectual endeavour (Jessop *et al.*, 2014). Students are more inclined to pay attention to and use formative feedback (Black and Wiliam, 1998), especially if it feeds forward to a more challenging summative task (Jessop *et al.*, 2014). Hughes (2011) has demonstrated the value of students attending to their own feedback in a connected cycle of comparing current with previous performance, with both formative and summative feedback engendering self-regulation where that connection is made explicit.

The TESTA project has shown that most degree programmes in the UK have high volumes of graded summative assessment, mainly designed to measure achievement, and low volumes of formative tasks designed to foster reflection and learning (Jessop *et al.*, 2014; Jessop and Tomas, 2017). High summative assessment loads reinforce grade-oriented and strategic behaviour among students, diverting attention away from formative tasks that have the freedom to be more playful, creative and open-ended. These patterns of assessment have evolved largely in response to modularization. Modular assessment favours a compartmentalized diet of assessment and feedback, with the feedback tending to remain within the confines of each module (Hughes *et al.*, 2015). These effects are compounded by the competitive framework within which summative assessment operates. In this environment, with few winners and many losers, not only do students behave strategically to gain marks at the expense of deep learning, but, worryingly, many students become demotivated and suffer from low self-esteem. TESTA has long advocated a rebalancing of summative and formative assessment as a means of engendering deep learning among students.

Using TESTA and research on ipsative assessment as part of a longitudinal assessment and feedback project Assessment Careers (Hughes *et al.*, 2013), this chapter makes a case for more personal, participatory and developmental approaches to assessment and feedback, built on dialogue (both 'inner' and 'outer' forms of dialogue). By definition 'ipsative assessment compares existing performance with previous performance' (Hughes, 2011: 353) and alternatives proposed in the chapter include more provisional, dialogic and relational forms of feedback that help students to recognize and improve upon their personal best. The failure of much feedback to help students grow in capability and self-knowledge arises from it being crafted by markers, and received by students, as the 'final word' on their abilities in alignment with research on fixed and growth mindsets (Dweck, 1999). Enabling students to view assessment as part of a developmental process requires alternatives to traditionally marked and technically accurate measurements of student achievement accompanied by feedback that implies fixed student capabilities. This approach will not easily be achieved within the narrow confines of modular curricula and necessitates a longitudinal and connected curriculum design, so that students have opportunities to demonstrate progress in key disciplinary skills and attributes (Hughes *et al.*, 2015).

Our chapter will begin by examining three problems in the assessment environment that prevent students from benefiting from assessment and feedback fully. These are the negative consequences of modularization, the low value assigned to formative assessment by both students and staff, and the competitive culture fostered by grades. It will then propose a philosophical shift in how to approach assessment and feedback, using ipsative assessment, which enables students to take the long view of their own progress. Finally, the chapter will provide strategies for connecting assessment and feedback across the curriculum using findings from TESTA and Assessment Careers. The relational and social constructivist paradigm informing the research on which the chapter is based suggests that motivation, reflection and collaboration are important ways of enhancing student engagement with assessment and feedback.

Methodology

The research data we use in this chapter are a combination of data collected on 73 degree programmes in 14 universities through the HEA-funded TESTA project, which spread beyond its original sample (Jessop *et al.*, 2014; Jessop and Tomas, 2017) and data collected as part of the JISC-funded Assessment Careers project. Data used in this chapter from both projects are textual data from focus groups and interviews with students in different universities, carried out between 2010 and 2016. The methodology is described in detail elsewhere (Hughes, 2011; Jessop *et al.*, 2014). Our main aim here is to discuss findings and implications and explore the intersection between findings from these two externally funded educational enhancement projects.

The trouble with assessment and feedback

Findings from the TESTA project (Jessop *et al.*, 2014; Jessop and Tomas, 2017) and from research on ipsative assessment (Hughes, 2011, 2014) provide evidence of flaws in the assessment environment. In this section, we explore three problematic features that inhibit student learning. The first is the modular structure of degree programmes and its consequences for slow, deep and connected learning; the second, the ambivalent value assigned to formative assessment by lecturers and students in the context of high-status and high-stakes summative assessment (Jessop *et al.*, 2012); and the third, the culture of competition, 'winner takes all' assessment, which freezes achievement and fosters fixed mindsets (Dweck, 2006; Hughes, 2014).

Unintended consequences of modularization

Modular degrees provide a framework in which defined knowledge areas are taught, usually over a time period of 12–15 weeks. Modules bear credits that students are required to accumulate over the course of an undergraduate or postgraduate degree through passing assessments. The key benefits of modularity are flexibility through the transferability of credits (to other universities or courses), and greater choice for students. Choice is a defining feature of many undergraduate degrees, particularly in the arts, humanities and social sciences. However, many universities promise more choice than they can offer, with choices constrained by timetabling, staffing and inadequate student numbers. Certain degrees do not lend themselves to student choice as the curriculum is partly determined by professional bodies, for example in medicine, law and engineering.

However, the benefits of choice, transferability and flexibility may be outweighed by the unintended negative consequences of modularization. Modular degrees lead to increased summative assessment loads as part of awarding transferable credits, with students completing between 33 and 48 summative assessments on average over the course of a three-year degree (Jessop and Tomas, 2017). The tendency on most modules is to include at least two assessment points, partly as a 'pedagogy of control' (Harland *et al.*, 2015), designed to ensure that students work hard at least twice in the semester. This assessment pattern is seen to avert the situation whereby students fail a module through failing a single assessment point. The compound effect of heavy assessment loads within short timescales is that students are more strategic and surface-oriented in their learning (Lizzio *et al.*, 2002; Harland *et al.*, 2015). In focus group data from the TESTA project, students describe the effects of focusing on summative assessment:

> A: A lot of people don't do wider reading. You just focus on your essay question.

> B: I always find myself going to the library and going 'These are the books related to this essay' and that's it. (UG students, Archaeology)

> If someone said, 'what did you learn on your degree?', I'd basically sum it up as saying I learnt what I needed to learn for assignments; I learnt what I learnt because I needed to complete an assignment, rather than I learnt because I was really interested in the whole thing. (UG student, English Language Studies)

Students report having content-heavy modules, possibly a further consequence of the compressed time frames and bounded knowledge within modular curriculum design. Heavy information loads compound the tendency for students to take a surface approach to learn the necessary facts to pass, with a resulting emphasis on 'knowing' in contrast to the slower and longer-term learning implied by 'acting' and 'being' (Barnett and Coate, 2005). If assessment is where student attention and effort intersect with the curriculum, the signs are that this is a fast and superficial affair, bounded in time, and lacking in the relational complexity that is a hallmark of higher-order thinking. Typical comments from students in TESTA focus groups exemplify the impact of content-heavy modules on their learning:

> The scope of information that you need to know for that module is huge … so you're having to revise everything – at the same time, you want to write an in-depth answer. (MSc student, Health discipline)

The strongest indication of the lack of connection between modules is in how students perceive their feedback. National Student Survey (NSS) scores evidence over a ten-year period that students score the items on assessment and feedback (Q. 5–9) at least 10 per cent lower than general scores on the quality of teaching, for example (Williams and Kane, 2009). Large-scale data from scores on the Assessment Experience Questionnaire (AEQ) V.3.3 used in the TESTA process indicate that students do not rate the quantity and quality of their feedback highly, nor do they find feedback useful, averaging between 3.00 and 4.00 on a 5-point Likert scale. The contrast between the espoused value of feedback in the literature (Hattie and Timperley, 2007; Black and Wiliam, 1998) and students' lived experience of it is telling. In TESTA focus groups, students provide insightful commentary on why they view feedback as a 'one-off' experience, often metaphorically deleting and discarding it. The connected, relational and iterative nature of feedback is interrupted within a modular system, as these comments demonstrate:

> It's difficult because your assignments are so detached from the next one you do for that subject. They don't relate to each other. (UG student, Education)

> Most of the time the feedback is just based on that piece of work so it is specific to the module and it doesn't really help. (UG student, Computer Science)

> Because they have to mark so many that our essay becomes lost in the sea that they have to mark. (UG student, Education)

Formative assessment is squeezed out

TESTA findings illustrate that modular degrees have impaired slow, deep and connected learning, through high summative diets, overloaded and content-heavy curricula, and disconnected feedback. These features of the assessment environment are compounded by the relative absence of true formative assessment, and its ambiguous status among both lecturers and students. True formative assessment is designed into the curriculum to engender learning from taking risks, being creative and collaborative, and meaningfully engaging with feedback from these tasks to refine and deepen understanding. At its most instrumental, formative assessment is a way of 'short-circuiting the randomness and inefficiency of trial-and-error learning' (Sadler, 1989: 120) through developing a deeper understanding of standards. In a broader sense, formative assessment is part of the process of learning through students' engagement, participation and production of work that elicits feedback, but is not finally judged.

The sheer volume of summative assessment squeezes out formative assessment as a meaningful pedagogic approach. The ratio of formative to summative is about 1:8 across a large number of undergraduate programmes (Jessop and Tomas, 2017). Formative is often patchily practised and weakly understood by lecturers, who struggle to engage students in anything other than 'dashing off' formative tasks, seeing them as slightly irrelevant to the main game of graded summative tasks. Students recognize the problem of competing agendas between summative and formative, evidenced in these focus group comments:

> What is the point of putting that much effort in when I have this much time to do an assessment that counts towards my degree? I find it really frustrating when people ask for ten-page reports and presentations which don't count and I am thinking why am I doing this?! It's brilliant practice but ... (UG student, Business and Management)

> It's a little bit pointless for me because I'd rather put all my energy and efforts into marked ones and get really high grades on them and not bother with the others. (UG student, Philosophy)

Academics indicate that they struggle to implement formative assessment because of its perceived low status, compared to summative tasks: 'The consequence of it not being officially part of the diet is that a hard core did it and no more' (Jessop *et al.*, 2012: 147). In general, students undertake very few formative tasks. Those who undertake it, see its value; those in the know are disappointed at its absence:

> It didn't actually count so that helped quite a lot because it was just a practice and didn't really matter what we did and we could learn from mistakes, so that was quite useful. (UG student, Media Studies)

> It was really useful. We were assessed on it but we weren't officially given a grade, but they did give us feedback on how we did. (UG student, American Studies)

> We don't [write formative essays], especially in the first year
> when we really don't have anything to do. The amount of
> times formative assignments could have taken place ... (UG
> student, History)

A culture of competition and ipsative assessment as an alternative

Much assessment in higher education, even with criterion referencing, is highly competitive. Although we could imagine a scenario in which all students meet the criteria to a high standard and obtain a high grade or mark, this is rare in practice and most courses expect a wide distribution of marks. Although publicly presenting class lists in order of attainment is not as commonly practised as it was in the past, students still know where they are in the hierarchy and compete with each other for top grades. There are winners and losers and many students know they are unlikely to be a winner. There may be variations between institutions and disciplines but what is happening here is that a student's performance is ultimately being compared to the highest possible standard.

Of course, we could argue that setting high standards and limiting the numbers who attain them pushes students to work hard. That may be so for some, but for others (possibly a majority) a continual string of mediocre or poor marks is demotivating. The psychologist Carol Dweck (1999) has argued that there are two responses to poor performance depending on a fixed or growth mindset. For those who have a fixed view of their own ability – and not a very high one – a poor performance confirms this and keeps self-esteem low. For those who have a growth mindset, a poor performance indicates that more work needs to be done and self-esteem can be maintained. But competitive assessment fits well with a fixed mindset – that the most able students get the best marks.

The culture of competition is reinforced by high summative and low formative assessment patterns. When external standards are the main focus of assessment and students are continually measured against the standards, they are very aware of how their own performance matches that of the top performers and this spawns competition with peers. However, competition is not the only way to motivate learners. Ipsative assessment, that is assessment based on an individual student's learning gain or a learning journey rather than final outcomes, provides a fresh approach to addressing the problems arising out of an overly competitive environment (Hughes, 2014). Hughes has argued that ipsative assessment empowers and encourages learners of all abilities to progress from wherever they are starting (ibid.). Measuring learning journeys or learning gain in this way is very different from measuring learning outcomes that are externally set for several reasons and has many potential advantages.

First, by contrast to a competitive assessment, in an ipsative assessment a student performance is compared to their own performances and so the standard can be set to be achievable for individuals. In other words, the goal is for a personal best not matching a cohort best. So, for an ipsative assessment with a realistic goal, success is within everyone's grasp. The emphasis here is on progress and this encourages a growth mindset that equates work and effort with a positive assessment result. The popularity of devices to monitor one's own performance in exercise, such as step counters, demonstrates the power of self-motivation through self-recording of progress against self-imposed targets. Of course, this assumes that everyone is capable of making some learning gain – but if not, the student is clearly in the wrong place or is going through a temporary bad patch, perhaps through illness, and in such cases a personal tutor can provide support.

A second difference between external standards-based and ipsative assessment is that ipsative assessment must take place over time. If there is not a sufficient interval between assessments, then it makes no sense to look at progress. This means that ipsative assessments require a cumulative curriculum design where assessments build on other assessments that test similar attributes, so that comparisons of performance can be made. An externally set assessment does not need to be spread out and can be a one-off performance such as an examination. However, cumulative and longitudinal assessments can also occur in a competitive assessment regime; for example, many programmes in higher education have course components that build up to contribute to a final mark or grade. The difference here is that ipsative assessments would focus on the progress between components and not only the outcome of each component. Some portfolios of professional practice demonstrate ipsative assessment when the student is graded for the learning journey as well as outcomes. However, in modular curricula the cumulative learning element may be confined to the module and not stretch across the whole programme as this is much more difficult to do (Hughes *et al.*, 2015). Unlike conventional assessment, ipsative assessment necessitates some form of recorded cumulative learning, which can make it more of a challenge to implement.

Third, there is much interest in self-regulated learning in higher education. Self-regulation is 'the purposive use of specific processes, strategies or responses by students to improve their academic achievement' (Zimmerman, 2001: 5). Assessment that focuses on learning and not only attainment – in other words, that is formative as well as summative – can support students in becoming self-regulated learners. However, feedback that is corrective and instructive – as when directed towards gaining the highest possible grade or mark – encourages dependency on the assessor rather than empowering students to plan making improvements for themselves. Meanwhile feedback that involves students in dialogue (Nicol, 2010) enables students to understand the learning requirements that are necessary for self-regulation better. Peer review where students are assessors provides students with the means to interrogate the assessment goals. In other words, students can learn more from giving rather than receiving feedback (Nicol *et al.*, 2014). But peer review and especially peer marking can run into difficulties when it is part of a competitive assessment regime. When students view the stakes as high, then the risk of peer assessment – that peers may not have enough expertise – causes concern. Ipsative processes with lower stakes readily support both feedback dialogue and peer review because the goal is developmental and not outcomes-driven and there is less of a worry about peers giving an unreliable result (Hughes, 2014).

Finally, we return to the problem of the student who fails to achieve a pass standard or fails to make progress. Without going into the complexities of the different ways in which failure can be managed, we could argue that the more information there is about how the student reached a point of failure, the better for deciding the next course of action. A student might fail to meet a standard, but ipsative information could show that the student has made progress and is on an upward trajectory and this might influence the next step. Viewing student learning trajectories in this way enables accurate identification of students who are not on the right learning path and need to transfer to another course, and distinguishes them from those who might do well with perseverance.

Strategies for improving assessment in higher education

In the next sections we present some examples of strategies to address assessment problems from two projects: Assessment Careers funded by JISC at what was then the Institute of Education, London; and TESTA, which was an HEA-funded project led by the University of Winchester.

Assessment Careers

Ipsative assessment is possibly practised informally in higher education but is very much under the radar. For example, students' formative assessment can build on previous work, and feedback can then emphasize the progress students have made since that previous work. Ipsative grading where a grade for progress contributes to summative assessment is more controversial because it might advantage weaker students who have further to travel, and challenge the monopoly of high grades enjoyed by the top performers. But the potential here for motivating all students, not only the high-flyers, and moving towards more equitable assessment practices, should not be ignored. There are case studies of ipsative assessment that demonstrate this potential (Hughes, 2017).

Cumulative feedback was explored in the Assessment Careers project at the UCL Institute of Education. The term 'assessment career' was used to capture the project's aim to explore how to engage all students in assessment and feedback longitudinally across a programme, using the concept of 'career' to capture the idea of student development over time. Baseline data indicated that assessment and feedback occurred in modules and that students did not make the best use of the feedback. The time and effort that staff put into feedback was therefore not efficient. Using five programmes for piloting new feedback practices, the project addressed several aspects of assessment to support a longitudinal and developmental approach to assessment: cumulative assessment, feedback dialogues and ipsative student progression decisions.

TESTA curriculum design strategies

At the Universities of Winchester, Dundee and Greenwich, evidence from TESTA has been incorporated into existing curriculum design processes, particularly the periodic review process. Programmes undergoing periodic review are required to participate in the TESTA process. Research data are collected using three methods. These are the TESTA audit of the planned curriculum; the Assessment Experience Questionnaire administered to final-year students; and student focus groups. These three sets of data are triangulated and crafted into a case study, which is discussed with the programme team in a generative conversation to enhance curriculum design. At this stage, teams view the whole assessment diet, and weigh up the balance of summative and formative, the sequence, balance and spread of different assessment types, with the outcomes they foresee over the three years of the degree. Some of the key decisions made by programmes include:

- Reducing the number of summative assessments
- Increasing meaningful formative tasks
- Developing multi-stage formative-summative tasks
- Mapping varieties of assessment
- Including more authentic and research-based tasks
- Designing and articulating connections between tasks across modules.

Using evidence from TESTA, course teams have redesigned assessment patterns to foster slow, deep and connected learning, through developing engaging and meaningful formative assessment, and by intentionally lengthening cycles of feedback that encourage student participation in the feedback process.

Both TESTA and Assessment Careers seek to address the three challenges of assessment identified earlier in the chapter, namely, the negative impacts of modular degrees on assessment, the low status of formative assessment and the competitive culture fostered by grades. There are similar themes across the two projects related to cumulative curriculum design, the emphasis on formative and developmental processes, and building strong connections across modules in feedback and assessment design.

Addressing the negative impacts of modularization

Strategies for connecting feedback across modules

Course teams in TESTA have developed inventive strategies for connecting feedback across tasks and modules so that students engage in a longer-term dialogue with their feedback, and improve their work on the basis of feedback. Subverting the one-off approach to feedback, and the grade-oriented notion that feedback is a postscript to the real thing, the grade, requires intentional strategies. The most powerful approach to making feedback connect with students over the long term is its relational and conversational framework (Nicol, 2010). Feedback that is didactic 'telling' or advising students is within the classic transmission model of education, which has few proven educational benefits. Contrastingly, feedback with questions that invite dialogue is more likely to trigger thinking and educational strides among students. Some of the strategies course teams have used to connect feedback on the basis of TESTA evidence include:

- Students identifying what areas they want feedback on, at the time of submission – feedback is then a response to student questions

- Requiring students to respond in writing to 'Ways to Improve', and append how they have addressed ways to improve in subsequent submission
- Using audio and screencast feedback to personalize and make feedback more conversational
- Synthesis activities encouraging students to reflect on individual feedback from a number of tasks to understand patterns in their work and address feedback.

FEEDBACK DIALOGUE

Transmission of feedback as a one-way process from assessor to student has been widely challenged and students do not learn to become self-reliant and self-judging if they only have access to feedback from an 'expert' (Molloy and Boud, 2013; Nicol, 2010). They may well ignore feedback or interpret it differently from what was intended (Price *et al.*, 2011). Students can gain insight into the frame of reference and how to interpret feedback if they take an active part in assessment as self-assessors or peer assessors. As part of the Assessment Careers project, students were encouraged by lecturers to ask for feedback and to reflect on their feedback as the start of a dialogue with an expert. Students were provided with space on assignment cover sheets both to request feedback and to reflect on how they had actioned previous feedback as in the TESTA project. A student commented:

> I like being able to ask the tutor quite directly the area that needs work and [what] to focus on. (MRes student)

And the form helped them look back at previous feedback and response to it:

> Particularly as I'd taken a long break between this and the previous module, so it actually made me go back and consider feedback from earlier assignments. (MA in Health Education student)

But not all students will have the capacity to self-assess or peer assess. Not all students understood the value of engaging with feedback:

> I didn't look at it until I had written the draft and was just about to submit, so I didn't spend time like thinking in detail when writing about what to ask the tutor. If I had, maybe I would have written more, so it was more like, at that moment of submitting, 'what am I thinking?', and I am not sure I could remember all the issues, so I just wrote what came to mind. (MRes student)

Guidance and support for self-assessment to build assessment literacy were recommendations that emerged from the Assessment Careers project.

FEEDBACK ANALYSIS BY A PROGRAMME TEAM

The Assessment Careers project initially involved five postgraduate Education programmes. For each programme current feedback practice was reviewed through developing a feedback analysis tool (Hughes *et al.*, 2015). The tool identified four key feedback types, each with a slightly different purpose for the student:

1. Praise
2. Ipsative feedback on progress (or lack of progress)
3. Critique
4. Asking questions.

Through counting written statements in each category for up to 20 pieces of marked work and averaging the number of comments in each category, a feedback profile for the programme was obtained. The profiles were very similar, with praise and critique predominating and with very little evidence of ipsative feedback. Asking questions did vary according to whether or not the intended purpose of the feedback was formative.

Although the method has flaws and only gives an approximate feedback profile, it has proved very valuable for staff development and for generating discussion about feedback practice. A tool such as this raises questions about whether or not students should be provided with explicit information on their progress during a programme of study to help them link action and effort with learning gains and thus develop a growth mindset. Assessors taking part in the project commented favourably on the analysis process, for example:

> Having categories for assessment (such as praise or advice for future assessments) was useful to the member of staff providing feedback – to identify what sort of balance of feedback types was being provided to students. (MA Health Promotion tutor)

One of the reasons why feedback does not often refer to progress is that it is difficult to judge progress when curricula consist of distinct units that do not have a common thread. This is especially problematic when units contain a body of knowledge or set of skills that are discrete. In a cumulative curriculum, knowledge from one unit is relevant for subsequent units so progress can be visible. Similarly, if skills build from one unit to the next, for example writing skills, then again progress can be visible and noted in feedback. Lack of curriculum coherence across a programme was identified as one of the key obstacles to using assessments that build skills and knowledge over time. Curriculum coherence requires team working, planning and transparency across modules so that the students' intended learning journey is visible and meaningful. While detailed and holistic curriculum planning will occur in some programmes, in many pressurized and/or fragmented higher education environments achieving curriculum coherence could be a serious challenge.

Rebalancing formative and summative assessment

The difficulty of rebalancing summative and formative assessment has several aspects. In twenty-first-century higher education, summative assessment has become a 'pedagogy of control' to ensure that students do at least two serious bouts of reading and work for each module in the midst of competing demands on their time (Harland *et al.*, 2015). Academics are reluctant to reduce summative assessment points if this further erodes student 'time on task'. This is a key reason for resistance to reducing summative assessment. For many academics reducing summative assessments to one per module is high-risk, as students have only one opportunity to demonstrate their capability, and may blow that opportunity. This is why TESTA advocates a rebalancing of summative and formative, as well-designed formative tasks help students to build capacity and knowledge in cumulative and connected ways, in line with the finding of Assessment Careers that students benefit from taking a long view of their learning journeys.

Developing meaningful and engaging formative assessment, which all students undertake, requires versatility and the ability to articulate a strong pedagogical rationale to students. The best ways of developing a strong culture of formative assessment involve a whole course team approach. Patchy formative assessment on a few modules will not encourage the pedagogic shift by students and staff to take formative tasks seriously. When formative tasks are designed as a programme strategy, in a co-ordinated and shared approach, this encourages students to see learning as a process fed by cycles of formative feedback. Strategies that have been effective include:

- Aligning formative with summative tasks in multi-stage cycles
- Feedback from formative tasks feeding forward to summative tasks
- Public domain tasks
- Authentic real-world tasks linked to own previous experience
- Research-based tasks.

Here are two examples of effective formative design developed in response to TESTA discussions.

Research-based formative

The BA (Hons) Film and TV at Southampton Solent University reduced the number of summative assessment points over the course of an undergraduate degree from 33 to 24. Simultaneously, it increased the number of required formative tasks from 18 to 30. A formative task was introduced in the second year (Level 5) to build student research capabilities for the final-year dissertation. Students were asked to find four sources linked to an area of study and to justify their choices within a seminar – the sources needed to include (a) a book, (b) a chapter, (c) a journal article, (d) a popular culture media article. The seminar group reached consensus on the best sources through discussion. The purpose of the formative activity was partly to develop student confidence at searching, researching and evaluating sources, in preparation for the research proposal and annotated bibliographies leading to the final-year dissertation.

Authentic assessment task using blogging

In response to the problem of the 'silent seminar', where students have evidently not completed academic readings, several TESTA programmes have implemented blogging on live sites (WordPress or Blogger). Blogging encourages communities of students to produce personal responses to readings and to comment on the posts of their peers. The real-world digital dimensions, conversational tone, and incentive to write for others about academic ideas all have power in fostering formative writing. Linking students' production of academic thoughts and threads on blogs to a synthesis task in the summative assessment lends further value and credence to undertaking formative blogging (Barlow and Jessop, 2016).

Tackling competition and learner demotivation through ipsative progression decisions

A sixth programme in the Assessment Careers project, a taught postgraduate research programme, joined the project towards the end and built on the ideas of ipsative feedback, cumulative curricula and self-feedback (Hughes *et al.*, 2017). Students used the reflective assignment cover sheets and drew upon these for an assessed portfolio that brought together all their work from three taught modules. A portfolio pass was a requirement for progression to the thesis stage of the programme where students become independent researchers working with a supervisor as they would for a traditional PhD. The programme leader was able to use these reflections as part of progression decisions for students who had not achieved the expected grades. Borderline or failing students who showed progress and engagement with feedback were recommended to progress to a thesis because they were on an upward learning trajectory. The emphasis on progress was motivating for these students.

Conclusion

This chapter has explored how assessment in higher education can be hampered by modularization, an over-use of summative assessment, and the competitive culture that stems from external standard-setting and use of assessment for selection. The negative consequences of modularization can be tempered by joining up curriculum units through student feedback dialogue and reflection. Ipsative assessment, where the focus is on a student's progress and learning gain, is an alternative that has much potential to reduce the excesses of competitive assessment and empower all learners, not just the high-flyers.

Both TESTA and Assessment Careers have shown the value of working with programme teams using research evidence and learning theories. Both projects have stimulated discussion and action to design coherent curricula that connect modular learning in a cumulative way. The promise of personal, dialogic and developmental feedback that encourages students to reflect over the long distance of their studies is at the heart of both enhancement projects. The TESTA project started with a question about the impact of modular degrees on student learning from assessment and feedback. In contrast, Assessment Careers began with questions about the impact of competitive forms of grading on student motivation and their learning journeys. From these different starting points, both projects reached similar conclusions about effective strategies to address systemic assessment problems.

There was inevitably resistance to fresh ideas uncovered during the projects. Changing assessment and feedback practice is by no means straightforward and may take many years (Hughes, 2014). Nevertheless, there has been uptake of the ideas by more enthusiasts and other initiatives and projects are pushing in this direction as higher education managers in the UK keep a watchful eye on National Student Survey scores for assessment and feedback. Systemic measures to embed changes that lead to more coherent and connected curriculum design have been put in place in an increasing number of universities through TESTA, and there is a growing community of academics across the sector who recognize the value of students achieving their 'personal best' through the work on ipsative assessment. Although there are challenges in changing assessment cultures, the rewards in motivation and learner empowerment make this a wholly worthwhile enterprise.

Notes

[1] Addresses for correspondence: tansy.jessop@solent.ac.uk; gwyneth.hughes@ucl.ac.uk
[2] www.testa.ac.uk

References

Arum, R. and Roksa, J. (2011) *Academically Adrift: Limited learning on college campuses*. Chicago: University of Chicago Press.

Barlow, A. and Jessop, T. (2016) '"You can't write a load of rubbish": Why blogging works as formative assessment'. Paper presented at the Staff and Educational Development Association (SEDA) Spring Teaching Learning and Assessment Conference, Edinburgh, 12–13 May 2016.

Barnett, R. and Coate, K. (2005) *Engaging the Curriculum in Higher Education*. Maidenhead: Society for Research into Higher Education and Open University Press.

Black, P. and Wiliam, D. (1998) 'Assessment and classroom learning'. *Assessment in Education: Principles, Policy and Practice*, 5 (1), 7–74.

Bloxham, S. (2009) 'Marking and moderation in the UK: False assumptions and wasted resources'. *Assessment and Evaluation in Higher Education*, 34 (2), 209–20.

Boud, D. (2000) 'Sustainable assessment: Rethinking assessment for the learning society'. *Studies in Continuing Education*, 22 (2), 151–67.

Boud, D. and Falchikov, N. (2006) 'Aligning assessment with long-term learning'. *Assessment and Evaluation in Higher Education*, 31 (4), 399–413.

Chickering, A.W. and Gamson, Z.F. (1987) 'Seven principles for good practice in undergraduate education'. *AAHE Bulletin*, 39 (7), 3–7.

Dweck, C.S. (1999) *Self-Theories: Their role in motivation, personality, and development*. Philadelphia: Psychology Press.

Dweck, C.S. (2006) *Mindset: The new psychology of success*. New York: Ballantine Books.

Gibbs, G. and Simpson, C. (2004) 'Conditions under which assessment supports students' learning'. *Learning and Teaching in Higher Education*, 1, 3–31.

Gipps, C.V. (1994) *Beyond Testing: Towards a theory of educational assessment*. London: Falmer Press.

Harland, T., McLean, A., Wass, R., Miller, E. and Sim, K.N. (2015) 'An assessment arms race and its fallout: High-stakes grading and the case for slow scholarship'. *Assessment and Evaluation in Higher Education*, 40 (4), 528–41.

Hattie, J. and Timperley, H. (2007) 'The power of feedback'. *Review of Educational Research*, 77 (1), 81–112.

Hughes, G. (2011) 'Towards a personal best: A case for introducing ipsative assessment in higher education'. *Studies in Higher Education*, 36 (3), 353–67.

Hughes, G. (2014) *Ipsative Assessment: Motivation through marking progress.* Basingstoke: Palgrave Macmillan.

Hughes, G. (ed.) (2017) *Ipsative Assessment and Personal Learning Gain: Exploring international case studies.* London: Palgrave Macmillan.

Hughes, G., Hawkes, D. and Neumann, T. (2017) 'Use of digital technology to capture and support student progress across a taught postgraduate programme'. In Hughes, G. (ed.) *Ipsative Assessment and Personal Learning Gain: Exploring international case studies.* London: Palgrave Macmillan, 105–28.

Hughes, G., Smith, H. and Creese, B. (2015) 'Not seeing the wood for the trees: Developing a feedback analysis tool to explore feed forward in modularised programmes'. *Assessment and Evaluation in Higher Education,* 40 (8), 1079–94.

Hughes, G., Smith, H. and Neumann, T. (2013) *Assessment Careers: Enhancing learning pathways through assessment: Final report.* Bristol: Joint Information Systems Committee. Online. http://jiscdesignstudio.pbworks.com/w/page/50671006/AssessmentCareersProject (accessed 7 April 2018).

Jessop, T., El Hakim, Y. and Gibbs, G. (2014) 'The whole is greater than the sum of its parts: A large-scale study of students' learning in response to different programme assessment patterns'. *Assessment and Evaluation in Higher Education,* 39 (1), 73–88.

Jessop, T., McNab, N. and Gubby, L. (2012) 'Mind the gap: An analysis of how quality assurance processes influence programme assessment patterns'. *Active Learning in Higher Education,* 13 (2), 143–54.

Jessop, T. and Tomas, C. (2017) 'The implications of programme assessment patterns for student learning'. *Assessment and Evaluation in Higher Education,* 42 (6), 990–9.

Knight, P.T. (2002) 'The Achilles' heel of quality: The assessment of student learning'. *Quality in Higher Education,* 8 (1), 107–15.

Lizzio, A., Wilson, K. and Simons, R. (2002) 'University students' perceptions of the learning environment and academic outcomes: Implications for theory and practice'. *Studies in Higher Education,* 27 (1), 27–52.

Molloy, E. and Boud, D. (2013) 'Changing conceptions of feedback'. In Boud, D. and Molloy, E. (eds) *Feedback in Higher and Professional Education: Understanding it and doing it well.* London: Routledge, 11–33.

Nicol, D. (2010) 'From monologue to dialogue: Improving written feedback processes in mass higher education'. *Assessment and Evaluation in Higher Education,* 35 (5), 501–17.

Nicol, D., Thomson, A. and Breslin, C. (2014) 'Rethinking feedback practices in higher education: A peer review perspective'. *Assessment and Evaluation in Higher Education,* 39 (1), 102–22.

Price, M., Carroll, J., O'Donovan, B. and Rust, C. (2011) 'If I was going there I wouldn't start from here: A critical commentary on current assessment practice'. *Assessment and Evaluation in Higher Education,* 36 (4), 479–92.

Ramsden, P. (2003) *Learning to Teach in Higher Education.* 2nd ed. London: RoutledgeFalmer.

Sadler, D.R. (1989) 'Formative assessment and the design of instructional systems'. *Instructional Science,* 18 (2), 119–44.

Williams, J. and Kane, D. (2009) 'Assessment and feedback: Institutional experiences of student feedback, 1996 to 2007'. *Higher Education Quarterly,* 63 (3), 264–86.

Zimmerman, B.J. (2001) 'Theories of self-regulated learning and academic achievement: An overview and analysis'. In Zimmerman, B.J. and Schunk, D.H. (eds) *Self-Regulated Learning and Academic Achievement: Theoretical perspectives.* 2nd ed. Mahwah: NJ: Lawrence Erlbaum Associates, 1–38.

Chapter 6

From internationalization to global citizenship: Dialogues in international higher education

Monika Kraska, Douglas Bourn and Nicole Blum[1]

As we consider assessment and, by implication, graduation, the question of what sort of graduate we are sending out into the world arises. A university education is not simply more stuff than A-level: it is, we hope, part of the transformation of a student into the adult they were always capable of being, realizing their potential. But as our opening chapter argued, there has to be a selection process for what is going to be emphasized: just being knowledgeable is a recipe for narrowness, and for our new graduate to be wrong-footed by a world that is far more complex than their university life prepared them for. Universities were 'global' long before almost any other ventures, with international collaboration on research going back centuries; our students come from all over the world, and our graduates go just about everywhere. We would be irresponsible not to consider how best to prepare them for that fact, but it is not straightforward – there are competing versions of what it is to be a 'global citizen', as this chapter explores.

Introduction

The term 'global citizenship' has become part of the vocabulary and policies of many higher education institutions (HEIs) around the world in the past decade. There are a number of reasons for this, including the pressure to 'internationalize', the need for universities to position themselves effectively within the global higher education marketplace, the need to look at what attributes graduates need to engage in societies and economies in the twenty-first century effectively, and a growing sense that universities have an increasingly broad, and global, social remit.

This chapter will review how the concept of global citizenship has evolved within higher education internationally, looking at both the debates around the terminology within the research literature, as well as its application within universities. It will also look specifically at examples of debates and practice within the training of professionals in health and engineering in the UK.

Linking internationalization and global citizenship

The relationships between globalization, internationalization and higher education have been a major topic of academic debate over the past decade. In response to both the economic and social pressures of globalization, universities now engage in a wide range of activities that aim to 'internationalize' their institutions, including recruitment of international students, internationalizing the curriculum and fostering cross-border research collaborations (Bourn, 2011: 568; see also Rumbley *et al.*, 2012).

Perhaps the most widely quoted and referred to definition of internationalization is by Knight (2012: 29) who calls for 'a process of integrating an international, intercultural, or global dimension in the purpose, function or delivery of postsecondary education'. This broad definition provides space for a diverse range of activities related to teaching and learning, student recruitment and research, and there has been significant debate about the most relevant forms that these initiatives should take.

For many academics and researchers, the focus of internationalization is most strongly linked to marketization, international competition and the recruitment and exchange of students (see Robson, 2011; Huisman and van der Wende, 2005; Takagi, 2012). However, there have also been attempts to conceptualize it alongside topics such as human rights, ethics and values, which can together form the 'foundation for a balanced and integrated university experience at the interface of global and local exposure' (Cross *et al.*, 2009, cited in Robson, 2011: 621). These debates pose significant questions about the broader purpose and role of higher education in an era of globalization.

The concept of global citizenship has emerged alongside these discussions of internationalization, and is often proposed as a way of equipping graduates to cope with the rapid change and uncertainty that characterizes globalization. As a result, the two concepts are often seen to overlap. Yemini (2015: 21), for instance, views internationalization as 'a process of encouraging integration of multicultural, multilingual, and global dimensions within the education system, with the aim of instilling in learners a sense of global citizenship'.

Similarly to the literature on internationalization, academic discussions of global citizenship have also raised key questions about both the core meaning of the concept, as well as its implementation in educational practice. The conceptual confusion sometimes found around the term is succinctly presented by Peters *et al.* (2008: 11) who notice that 'one thing is sure ... there can be no one dominant notion of global citizenship ... as notions of "global", [and] "citizenship" ... are all contested and open to further argument and revision'.

Some theorists, for instance, have seen the concept as 'not so much a static identity ... [but] an ability, disposition or commitment' (Rhoads and Szelényi, 2011: 267). This understanding emphasizes attributes such as awareness, responsibility, participation and cross-cultural empathy, achievement and international mobility (Schattle, 2008). In other words, global citizenship is demonstrated in an awareness of self, the world and one's position within it. This in turn triggers a sense of responsibility for the world at large and results in calls for both individual and collective action.

While these theoretical understandings of global citizenship have emerged from academic research, within higher education practice global citizenship has often tended instead to be seen as a route to increase graduate employment. This includes, for instance, initiatives and programmes that aim to provide students with skills that will make them more appealing to international employers (e.g. foreign languages, cultural awareness, intercultural communication).

These two approaches to global citizenship are, of course, based on radically different philosophical, epistemological and ideological perceptions, and interpretations of the world and its processes. The first sees a global citizen as someone who is comfortable enacting their rights and responsibilities anywhere in the world and therefore tends to fall within a liberal-humanistic discourse. The second focuses on equipping graduates with the skills that enable them to be competitive within the global marketplace. This approach situates global citizenship within more neoliberal agendas for economic growth and international competition.

In the following sections, we explore in more depth the ways in which understandings of internationalization and global citizenship are interpreted from both the neoliberal and liberal-humanistic perspectives. In line with emerging academic research and writing, we also suggest a third – critical – interpretation of the two concepts and how they might be meaningfully applied in practice within higher education.

Neoliberal perspectives

The neoliberal economic discourse has a strong influence on definitions, conceptualizations and applications of both internationalization and global citizenship within higher education around the world. In particular, higher education is often conceptualized as a commodity in line with the General Agreement on Trade in Services (Humfrey, 2011: 650) – a trend that is visible in the commercialization of HEIs and the drive for accountability in higher education. From this perspective, the university is viewed as having a mandate to manage knowledge and plays a vital role in securing national competitiveness on a global scale.

This objective is reinforced by curricula and pedagogical approaches that overwhelmingly focus on preparing graduates to secure employment in the international marketplace. Research suggests that there is a shift towards performativity wherein 'what counts is less what individuals know and more what individuals can do (as represented in their demonstrable "skills")' (Barnett, 2000: 255). A focus on disciplinary knowledge and the creation of degree programmes in non-traditional areas (for example, business management) reinforce this rationale for the role HEIs play in promoting graduate employability.

Given the current pressures on universities – including the need to diversify sources of funding as access to public funds becomes more restricted, as well as increasing international competition for both students and resources – it is perhaps no surprise that there is evidence of a movement towards such entrepreneurialism and managerialism within higher education. The management of complex organizations, like universities, with mandates for research and teaching, extensive budgets, human capital, physical and intellectual property requires universities to find a balance between economic imperatives and their perceived responsibilities to society.

Liberal-humanistic perspectives

A key critique of neoliberal perspectives on higher education is that they do not tend to account for the array of challenges that the modern world presents to students and graduates. This is because the reality in which modern universities are operating is in fact supercomplex. As Barnett notes:

> ... the very frameworks by which we orient ourselves to the world
> are themselves contested. Supercomplexity denotes a fragile

world but it is a fragility brought on not merely by social and technological change; it is fragility in the way that we understand the world, in the way in which we understand ourselves and in the ways in which we feel secure about acting in the world. (Barnett, 2000: 257)

According to liberal-humanistic perspectives, this demands that universities' purpose should be to educate individuals who are able to comprehend the complex world around them (epistemology), understand their identity within it (ontology) and have the ability to prosper (praxis). In other words, it is to prepare individuals to participate in a society. Universities are therefore seen as responsible for creating public spaces to foster and lead debate on a range of issues, and for developing in graduates a sense of the wider world. These aims are linked to teaching and learning approaches that encourage critical thinking and active debate, rather than emphasizing mastery of particular areas of knowledge or skills for employment.

Furthermore, in the neoliberally entangled university the characteristics of a graduate are in line with the liberal idea of a citizen who is individualistic, passive and private, de-solidarized (Balarin, 2011), de-politicized and complacent to the status quo, treats political participation as a right to exercise depending on an individual inclination (Caruana, 2010), and is equipped with skills and knowledge necessary to secure employment. From a liberal-humanistic perspective, what is missing in this image of a graduate are the skills and dispositions to nurture civic values (see McCowan, 2012; Balarin, 2011). This means equipping graduates with skills for life, to be able to engage as citizens in society.

Critical perspectives on internationalization and global citizenship

While the two perspectives presented above provide useful lenses for analysis of approaches to both internationalization and global citizenship, we suggest that a third approach provides even greater conceptual clarity. This critical approach actively questions both the neoliberal and liberal interpretations and encourages learners not only to develop greater awareness of global issues, but also to review existing systems and structures critically.

The critical approach is rooted in an understanding that students need to be equipped with knowledge, skills and dispositions to be able to cope with a world that is uncertain and complex. Shultz (2010), for instance, suggests that global citizenship discourse can provide a space for 'dealing' with difficult knowledge and difficult justice, and for managing diversity, all of which are inherent in today's world. The multiplicity and diversity of all humanity, with its languages, visions, knowledges and interpretations of the world, is not only present but also essential for existence (Davis quoted in Shultz, 2010: 11) and can be 'dealt with' through the lens of global citizenship. In this view, diversity is seen as a natural characteristic of the world, rather than a problem or a challenge to be managed (Osler, 2010: 220).

Similarly, Western-centric interpretations of citizenship, values or identities can be questioned and alternative conceptualizations given equal status, such as in Spivak's 'planetary subjectship', where the world is not seen as 'a globe that can be mastered and controlled' but as 'a planet, which we inhabit "on loan"' (de Oliveira Andreotti, 2011: 307). Global citizenship, in this understanding, is therefore not contradictory to national citizenship, but is a framework for managing multiple and diverse citizenships in 'the heterogeneity of today's globalized world' (Tully cited in Balarin, 2011: 357).

This view of global citizenship stands in opposition to the individualized and fragmented vision of citizenship forged by the neoliberal forces influencing education. By fostering the idea of belonging to a global community, it creates a sense of unity above partitions and opens doors for identifications for all people living on our globe. It also moves away from the idea of cosmopolitan citizenship, which has often come to be associated with a transnational capitalist elite with the power to exercise the benefits of citizenship when inclined to do so.

Global citizenship within teaching and learning in health and engineering degree courses

Having set out the three theoretical perspectives above, the chapter now moves to exploring how these are expressed within practice in higher education. In particular, it looks at undergraduate health and engineering programmes in the UK and is based on ongoing research by two of the chapter's authors (see Blum and Bourn, 2013).

Health and engineering are excellent examples to use to explore the relevance and influence of global citizenship within higher education. This is because not only do these professions have a clear global context – in that their key skills and knowledge bases are arguably relevant throughout the world – but professionals in these areas also have a high degree of economic and social mobility. In addition, they are areas of work that are key to global social and economic change.

The tendency in both areas within higher education, however, has been to treat global themes as 'optional' extras or areas of specialization that students can choose to explore alongside developing 'core' skills and knowledge (see Bourn and Neal, 2008; Bateman *et al.*, 2001). For example, within health-related courses in the UK, students are most likely to have opportunities to learn about global issues as part of optional sessions (e.g. one-off lectures or workshops), specialist programmes (e.g. intercalated global health degree programmes are offered in several UK medical schools), extracurricular activities (e.g. through involvement in student societies) or self-organized (usually short-term) overseas voluntary placements (Bourn *et al.*, 2006; Willott *et al.*, 2012). By their very nature, these tend to lead to students with an existing interest in global and development issues being the most likely to pursue these kinds of activities. It has also meant that global issues have largely remained marginalized from mainstream learning for health professionals.

In response to these challenges, a range of initiatives emanated from the Institute of Education[2] between 2007 and 2013. In partnership with other universities and a range of civil society organizations, these projects aimed both to understand better and encourage the promotion of terms like 'the global doctor', 'the global vet', 'the global pharmacist' and the 'global engineer'. The results of these initiatives were a series of reports and papers aimed at policymakers and practitioners.

The Global Engineer (Bourn and Neal, 2008), for example, calls on HEIs to include global themes within engineering degree courses and to show the relevance of themes such as global poverty, sustainable development and climate change to future engineers. Above all it suggests that 'higher education needs to prepare engineers of the future with the skills and knowledge they will need to manage rapid change, uncertainty and complexity' (ibid.: 2).

Similarly, *The Global Doctor* references a proposed list of learning outcomes for medical students that refer both to knowledge of specific themes, such as understanding of global diseases, health systems and the global determinants of health, and the importance of understanding of human rights and cultural diversity (Willott *et al.*, 2012: 24–5). Similar themes can be seen in the publications on Global Pharmacy (Murdan *et al.*, 2014) and Veterinary Medicine (Maud *et al.*, 2012).

These publications have resonated strongly with recent academic debates within the disciplines. For example, there has been a growing understanding that all health professionals require not only an understanding of global health concerns, but also that health research and practice can make a significant contribution to global economic and social change (see Johnson *et al.*, 2012; Frenk *et al.*, 2010). Within engineering over the past decade there has also been an increased recognition of the need to respond to the challenges of globalization and questions of ethical social responsibility (Dodds and Venables, 2005; Jesiek *et al.*, 2014; Passow, 2012; Ragusa, 2014).

These discussions have focused not only on the need for increased knowledge of global issues within the professions, but also on the need to prioritize forms of teaching and learning that can encourage skills such as critical thinking, the ability to recognize different perspectives, to work with diverse groups of people, and to understand the links between local and global events and circumstances. This links clearly to debates around the meaning of global citizenship within higher education: is the core aim to make graduates employable (a *neoliberal* agenda), to prepare them to live and work in an era of complexity and globalization (a *liberal* agenda) or understand, critique and perhaps even work to change the world (a *critical* agenda)?

These diverse approaches to global citizenship within higher education can clearly be seen in the debates and practices around both health and engineering professions. For example, most academic responses to the challenge of globalization within engineering have tended to focus on the competencies required to compete in an international market for engineering know-how. This has included, for instance, knowledge of other languages, developing intercultural skills and working more effectively in teams (Fenner *et al.*, 2005). A more cosmopolitan view can also be seen from research at Northumbria University where there was a call for more practical and real-life experiences within the teaching and learning in engineering. The evidence from dialogue with students suggested that what was needed was for a 'global engineer' to be a multi-literate all-rounder, who may be multilingual, culturally diverse and aware of different applications (Montgomery *et al.*, 2011: 7).

There is also recognition within the health professions of the need for professionals who understand and are prepared to cope with global health concerns. This has been particularly noticeable in the growing popularity of the field of global health, which advocates argue is key to addressing the challenges that globalization poses for health, including through the increasingly rapid movement of both people and disease (see Kickbusch, 2002; Howson *et al.*, 1998).

The need to prepare graduates to deal with the impacts of globalization on health, however, has also fuelled significant debates about the nature of teaching and learning within medical education:

> A key skill that is central to any global health course is the development of critical thinking and analysis. Much traditional medical education revolves around rote learning, though recent initiatives to introduce problem-based curricula have changed this. Global health, by contrast, asks students to become critical thinkers, in their appraisal of problems and their likely solutions, and the logic and evidence base underpinning them. (Willott *et al.*, 2012: 15–16)

This emphasis on critical thinking resonates strongly with the critical approach to global citizenship, which similarly calls for critique of existing power structures.

Tensions have also often emerged about the role and place of values within engineering education, and these are clearly related to the different discourses on global citizenship. For example, there are significant tensions between professional and societal values, as well as diverse value bases around the world. As Mitchell and Baillie (1998: 15) suggest, 'our values are the lenses through which we view the world; they stem from our underlying beliefs and assumptions, which are generally neither articulated nor questioned'. As van der Steen notes:

> For the bulk of the history of engineering, engineering practice has been seen as a neutral endeavour; but the more engineering becomes the major mode of human action to resolve human problems, the less it can get away with this value reference. (van der Steen, 2008: 54)

It is perhaps the recognition of values and criticality that could be key to a distinctive critical global citizenship approach to higher education. This approach is currently evident in the work of a number of NGOs related to both engineering and health, including Engineers Against Poverty and Students for Global Health (formerly called Medsin).

Engineers Against Poverty, for instance, advocates for engineering education that includes a critical understanding of power within the context of development, as well as a commitment to social justice, critical reflection, dialogue and diverse perspectives. Key elements of this include educational approaches that:

- imagine a range of global perspectives
- look critically at how engineers perceive other countries and what has influenced their perceptions
- look at the causes of inequality
- explore power relations, including questions such as who has power, who is voiceless and who benefits? (Bourn, 2014: 16).

There is evidence that aspects of these points are being taken up within the literature on formal engineering education. In looking at sustainable development, for example, Guerra (2012) refers to the need not only to understand how to resolve problems, but also to reflect on how decisions are made and their consequences. Pawley (2012) in her discussions on the role of an engineering academic, mentions the importance of critical self-reflection and questions who determines what engineering problems are and who benefits from their solutions.

The student-led organization Students for Global Health also plays an active role in advocating for the inclusion of global health within medical education. Students for Global Health's vision is of 'a fair and just world in which equity in health is a reality for all'.[3] Its mission is 'to create a network of students empowered to effect tangible social and political change at a local, national and global level through education, advocacy and community action'.[4] The organization was influential in getting global health added to the General Medical Council's guidelines for medical education in 2009 (see GMC, 2009). This addition requires all UK medical schools to provide core teaching in global health for all students for the first time.

One example of this is UCL Medical School which, working in conjunction with the UCL Institute for Global Health (IGH), has embraced recommendations to integrate global health into its curriculum. The UCL MBBS 2012 curriculum aims to instil students with 'an appreciation of the role of the future doctor within the healthcare environment in the UK and globally' (Willott *et al.*, 2012: 25). Global health is also part of a vertical spine on the social determinants of health that runs across all six years of the curriculum.

More generally, the inclusion of global issues within higher education will require the broadening of curricula and the inclusion of new approaches to teaching and learning. This will mean not only incorporating particular themes (e.g. the social determinants of health, sustainable development, global forces and processes, the role of the student as a global citizen) within existing curricula, but also attending carefully to the nature of the learning taking place in order to encourage critical assessment of global concerns and processes. This critical approach may represent a real challenge to dominant notions of learning in some institutions, however, particularly where the pressures of globalization (and accompanying neoliberal agendas) are high.

Conclusion

These examples and the review of the discourses around the practices of global citizenship within education suggest that while the concepts are often contested within both the literature and practice, they resonate with wider debates about the purpose and role of higher education in an era of globalization. The aim here is not to suggest that one of the three approaches cited is more important or relevant than the other, more that they all have a role within understanding the nature of contemporary universities and the challenges they face.

In a world where higher education is significantly affected by the impacts of globalization, the need to educate global citizens is increasingly seen as an important rationale for the contemporary university. However, what it means to be a 'global citizen' and to 'internationalize' a university can have a range of different interpretations and implementations depending on the epistemological, philosophical and ideological perspectives through which both ideas are viewed. We suggest that while neoliberal and liberal-humanistic approaches have historically been central to these discussions, the emerging idea of critical approaches to global citizenship and internationalization provide a useful conceptual lens for analysis of contemporary higher education around the world.

Notes

[1] Addresses for correspondence: monika.kraska13@gmail.com; d.bourn@ucl.ac.uk; n.blum@ucl.ac.uk

[2] Part of the University of London until December 2014, when it merged with UCL.

[3] https://studentsforglobalhealth.org/vision-mission/

[4] https://studentsforglobalhealth.org/vision-mission/

References

Balarin, M. (2011) 'Global citizenship and marginalisation: Contributions towards a political economy of global citizenship'. *Globalisation, Societies and Education*, 9 (3–4), 355–66.

Barnett, R. (2000) 'Supercomplexity and the curriculum'. *Studies in Higher Education*, 25 (3), 255–65.

Bateman, C., Baker, T., Hoornenborg, E. and Ericsson, U. (2001) 'Bringing global issues to medical teaching'. *The Lancet*, 358 (9292): 1539–42.

Blum, N. and Bourn, D. (2013) 'Global perspectives for global professionals in the UK: Engaging students within engineering and health'. *Compare: A Journal of Comparative and International Education*, 43 (1), 37–55.

Bourn, D. (2011) 'From internationalisation to global perspectives'. *Higher Education Research and Development*, 30 (5), 559–71.

Bourn, D. (2014) 'The global dimension to engineering education'. In GDEE (eds) *Making the Case for a Critical Global Engineer*. Barcelona: GDEE. Online. https://tinyurl.com/ybotlpz3 (accessed 13 March 2018).

Bourn, D., McKenzie, A. and Shiel, C. (2006) *The Global University: The role of the curriculum*. London: Development Education Association.

Bourn, D. and Neal, I. (2008) *The Global Engineer: Incorporating global skills within UK higher education of engineers*. London: Engineers Against Poverty.

Caruana, V. (2010) 'Global citizenship for all: Putting the "higher" back into UK higher education?'. In Maringe, F. and Foskett, N. (eds) *Globalization and Internationalization in Higher Education: Theoretical, strategic and management perspectives*. London: Continuum, 51–64.

Cross, M., Mhlanga, E. and Ojo, E. (2009) 'Emerging concept of internationalisation in South African higher education: Conversations on local and global exposure at the University of the Witwatersrand (Wits)'. *Journal of Studies in International Education*, 15 (1): 75–92.

de Oliveira Andreotti, V. (2011) 'The political economy of global citizenship education'. *Globalisation, Societies and Education*, 9 (3–4), 307–10.

Dodds, R. and Venables, R. (2005) *Engineering for Sustainable Development: Guiding principles*. London: Royal Academy of Engineering. Online. www.raeng.org.uk/publications/other/engineering-for-sustainable-development (accessed 6 April 2018).

Fenner, R.A., Ainger, C.M., Cruickshank, H.J. and Guthrie, P.M. (2005) 'Embedding sustainable development at Cambridge University Engineering Department'. *International Journal of Sustainability in Higher Education*, 6 (3), 229–41.

Frenk, J., Chen, L., Bhutta, Z.A., Cohen, J., Crisp, N., Evans, T., Fineberg, H., Garcia, P., Ke, Y., Kelley, P., Kistnasamy, B., Meleis, A., Naylor, D., Pablos-Mendez, A., Reddy, S., Scrimshaw, S., Sepulveda, J., Serwadda, D. and Zurayk, H. (2010) 'Health professionals for a new century: Transforming education to strengthen health systems in an interdependent world.' *The Lancet*, 376 (9756): 1923–58.

GMC (General Medical Council) (2009) *Tomorrow's Doctors: Outcomes and standards for undergraduate medical education*. Manchester: General Medical Council.

Guerra, A. (2012) 'What are the common knowledge and competencies for education for sustainable development and for engineering education for sustainable development?'. Paper presented at the 40th European Society for Engineering Education (SEFI) Annual Conference, Thessaloniki, 23–26 September 2012.

Howson, C.P., Fineberg, H.V. and Bloom, B.R. (1998) 'The pursuit of global health: The relevance of engagement for developed countries'. *The Lancet*, 351 (9102), 586–90.

Humfrey, C. (2011) 'The long and winding road: A review of the policy, practice and development of the internationalisation of higher education in the UK'. *Teachers and Teaching: Theory and Practice*, 17 (6), 649–61.

Huisman, J. and van der Wende, M. (eds) (2005) *On Cooperation and Competition II: Institutional responses to internationalisation, Europeanisation, and globalisation.* Bonn: Lemmens Verlag.

Johnson, O., Bailey, S.L., Willott, C., Crocker-Buque, T., Jessop, V., Birch, M., Ward, H. and Yudkin, J. (2012) 'Global health learning outcomes for medical students in the UK'. *The Lancet* , 379 (9831): 2033–5.

Kickbusch, I. (2002) *Global Health: A definition.* Online. www.ilonakickbusch.com/kickbusch-wAssets/docs/global-health.pdf (accessed 6 April 2018).

Knight, J. (2012) 'Concepts, rationales, and interpretative frameworks in the internationalization of higher education'. In Deardorff, D.K., de Wit, H., Heyl, J.D. and Adams, T. (eds) *The SAGE Handbook of International Higher Education.* Thousand Oaks, CA: SAGE Publications, 27–42.

Jesiek, B.K., Zhu, Q., Woo, S.E., Thompson, J. and Mazzurco, A. (2014) 'Global engineering competency in context: Situations and behaviors'. *Online Journal for Global Engineering Education*, 8 (1), 1–14.

Maud, J., Blum, N., Short, N. and Goode, N. (2012) *Veterinary Students as Global Citizens: Exploring opportunities for embedding the global dimension in the undergraduate veterinary curriculum.* London: Royal Veterinary College and Institute of Education.

McCowan, T. (2012) 'Opening spaces for citizenship in higher education: Three initiatives in English universities'. *Studies in Higher Education*, 37 (1), 51–67.

Mitchell, C. and Baillie, C. (1998) 'On values, role models, and the importance of being me'. Paper presented at the American Society for Engineering Education (ASEE) Annual Conference, Seattle, 28 June–1 July 1998.

Montgomery, C., Penlington, R., Perera, N., Tudor, N.J. and Wilson, A. (2011) *Educating the Global Engineer: Staff and student perspectives on embedding sustainable development practices into the engineering curriculum.* York: Higher Education Academy-Engineering Subject Centre. Online. https://tinyurl.com/y85ob6sh (accessed 16 April 2018).

Murdan, S., Blum, N., Francis, S.-A., Slater, E., Alem, N., Munday, M., Taylor, J. and Smith, F. (2014) *The Global Pharmacist.* London: UCL School of Pharmacy and Institute of Education.

Osler, A. (2010). 'Citizenship and the nation-state: Affinity, identity and belonging'. In Reid, A., Gill, J., Sears, A. (eds) *Globalization, the Nation-State and the Citizen: Dilemmas and directions for civics and citizenship education.* New York: Routledge, 216–22.

Passow, H.J. (2012) 'Which ABET competencies do engineering graduates find most important in their work?' *Journal of Engineering Education*, 101 (1), 95–118.

Pawley, A.L. (2012) 'What counts as "engineering": Toward a redefinition'. In Baillie, C., Pawley, A.L. and Riley, D. (eds) *Engineering and Social Justice: In the university and beyond.* West Lafayette, IN: Purdue University Press, 59–85.

Peters, M.A., Britton, A. and Blee, H. (eds) (2008) *Global Citizenship Education: Philosophy, theory and pedagogy.* Rotterdam: Sense Publishers.

Ragusa, G. (2014) 'Engineering global preparedness: Parallel pedagogies, experientially focused instructional practices.' *International Journal of Engineering Education*, 30 (2), 400–11.

Rhoads, R.A. and Szelényi, K. (2011) *Global Citizenship and the University: Advancing social life and relations in an interdependent world*. Stanford, CA: Stanford University Press.

Robson, S. (2011) 'Internationalization: A transformative agenda for higher education?'. *Teachers and Teaching: Theory and Practice*, 17 (6), 619–30.

Rumbley, L.E., Altbach, P.G. and Reisberg, L. (2012) 'Internationalization within the higher education context'. In Deardorff, D.K., de Wit, H., Heyl, J.D. and Adams, T. (eds) *The SAGE Handbook of International Higher Education*. Thousand Oaks, CA: SAGE Publications, 3–26.

Schattle, H. (2008) *The Practices of Global Citizenship*. Lanham, MD: Rowman and Littlefield.

Shultz, L. (2010) 'What do we ask of global citizenship education? A study of global citizenship education in a Canadian university'. *International Journal of Development Education and Global Learning*, 3 (1), 5–22.

Takagi, H. (2012) 'The Internationalisation of Undergraduate Curricula in England and Japan: The complexity and diversity of meaning'. Unpublished PhD thesis, Institute of Education, University of London.

van der Steen, J.D.J. (2008) 'Humanitarian Engineering in the Engineering Curriculum'. Unpublished PhD thesis, Queen's University, Kingston, Ontario.

Willott, C., Blum, N., Burch, W., Page, B. and Rowson, M. (2012) *The Global Doctor*. London: UCL Institute for Global Health and Development Education Research Centre.

Yemini, M. (2015) 'Internationalisation discourse hits the tipping point: A new definition is needed'. *Perspectives: Policy and Practice in Higher Education*, 19 (1), 19–22.

Chapter 7

Liberating the Curriculum at UCL

Teresa McConlogue[1]

The previous chapter was predominantly focused on how we prepare students for the wider world; but this will be worthless if our educational environment does not reflect that world and enquire into why things are the way they are to make room for how they might be. UCL is a particularly cosmopolitan university in an exceptionally multicultural city; it is also old enough to have its own legacy from colonial times and indeed has prominent alumni who played key roles in shaping a world we are still endeavouring to move away from. For example, the racist work and name of Francis Galton, who coined the term 'eugenics', is deeply problematic. Students, student union staff and UCL staff have recently begun the difficult process of tackling the exclusion of minorities of all kinds in the curriculum, seeking to redress the white, male-centred authorities who dominate the vast majority of what is considered worthwhile knowledge. Here especially, the student voice must come to the fore and be supported in taking the lead, given how under-represented minorities are among teaching-related staff. One initiative within the Connected Curriculum has therefore set itself the task of being part of Liberating the Curriculum. During the finalization of this book, the press seized on such initiatives as evidence that universities were being made to remove Shakespeare from the curriculum (and other such exaggerations), but if universities are not places to be curious about what we have been overlooking, and making efforts to put it right, then they are surely surrendering one of their key claims to be a conscience and the thinking-space for society as a whole. A great deal of work remains to be done but no one, least of all Shakespeare, will lose out if our curricula embrace a wider canon, develop a fuller picture and explore hitherto marginalized areas of science, health, literature, culture, and so on.

> Centres of state bureaucracies, ... imperialistic states and
> dominant ethnic minorities often declare their own epistemic
> position – their knowledge competence, technology and
> interpretations of the world – to be objective, scientific, modern,
> progressive, or forward-looking. Simultaneously they declare
> the epistemic position of their opponents, peripheries, colonies,
> or nondominant ethnic minorities to be traditional, outmoded,
> unscientific, or indigenous. (Meusburger *et al.*, 2016: 3)

Introduction

Across the higher education sector, there is a movement for change towards
more inclusive curricula. This movement for change is seen both in scholarly
work that contests traditional, non-inclusive curricula, and in the many
examples of practice that demonstrate how curricula can become more
inclusive, more representative and more liberated. At UCL, as part of the
Connected Curriculum (CC) initiative a Liberating the Curriculum (LTC)
working group, composed of staff and students, has been set up to find
ways of reviewing curricula and ensuring that thought from marginalized
scholars in race, gender, sexuality and disability is fairly represented. This
chapter describes why the group was formed, how it works, what it has
achieved and how it plans to move forward.

How we got here

The impetus for LTC work came initially from student representatives. In
2013 UCL's student union appointed a full-time Black and Minority Ethnic
(BME) Sabbatical Officer: the first post of its kind in the UK. The elected
post holder, Shanell Johnson, raised the issue of BME student attainment.
She cited work at the Open University (Richardson, 2008) on the attainment
gap between BME students and white students. Richardson analysed data
from the Higher Education Statistics Agency (HESA) on all UK-domiciled
students in 2004/05 and carried out logistic regression analysis to identify
the effect of variables such as age, gender, entry qualifications, mode of
study and subject of study. He concluded there was an attainment gap
and that:

> ... graduates from ethnic minorities are less likely to be
> awarded good degrees by UK institutions of Higher Education
> than are White students. In particular, the odds of an Asian
> student obtaining a good degree are half of those of a White
> student obtaining a good degree, and the odds of a Black Student

obtaining a good degree are only a third of those of a White student obtaining a good degree. (Richardson, 2008: 44)

Work by Woolf *et al.* on BME student attainment in medical schools reached a similar conclusion. In a meta-analysis of 23 reports on the performance of medical students and doctors in the UK, they concluded that 'ethnic differences are widespread ... have persisted for many years and cannot be dismissed as atypical or local problems' (Woolf *et al.*, 2011: abstract).

Drawing on this work, a small research group at UCL carried out an analysis of BME student attainment at UCL and found attainment differences, with the most marked difference for students of African-Caribbean ethnicity. The group presented their work at the UCL Education Committee and made several recommendations including a proposal to review existing and new courses and ensure diversity is represented in curricula.

In 2014/15, the new Students' Union UCL BME Sabbatical Officer, Hajera Begum, was involved in a campaign, led by Dr Nathaniel Coleman, to investigate BME student perspectives of their curriculum. The 'Why is My Curriculum White?' campaign video[2] was extensively viewed and prompted similar videos from other institutions e.g. LSE[3] and Warwick.[4] In the Students' Union video, students reported dissatisfaction with Eurocentric curricula. They called for curricula that recognized the historical development of the disciplines and represented marginalized thinkers fairly.

This call, for a curriculum that fairly recognizes the work of marginalized scholars, is part of a much wider movement, e.g. the 'Rhodes Must Fall' campaign in South Africa (Kamanzi, 2015), which has spread to other universities, including Oxford, and the 'Decolonising the Curriculum' movement, e.g. at Cambridge.[5] Students have been at the forefront of demanding curriculum change and in response the National Union of Students has produced a race equality toolkit.[6] These campaigns and resources have helped shape the work of the LTC group.

Where we are now

As part of an overall review of curricula at UCL and introduction of the Connected Curriculum initiative, a Liberating the Curriculum working group was formed, to explore ways of ensuring marginalized voices are fairly included in syllabuses. We realized that in order to develop fair and inclusive curricula fit for the twenty-first century, we needed to consider not only race but also gender, sexuality and disability. We needed to look at not just what was taught, but how it was taught and by whom. Other strategic work in UCL complemented the LTC group's endeavour. The Race Equality Steering Group, supported by the UCL Equality and Diversity team and chaired by UCL President and Provost Michael Arthur, successfully applied for the Race Equality Charter (REC)[7] and committed UCL to take action to improve numbers of BME academic staff, as well as reviewing the curriculum. Similarly, the successful Athena Swan submission[8] committed UCL to critically review curricula; both the REC and Athena Swan submissions tasked the LTC group with developing a tool for curriculum review as a first step to change.

What we teach, how we teach and who can teach

There are a growing number of research centres and departments, in the UK and worldwide, developing expertise in areas that have been traditionally marginalized. However, insights and knowledge from these centres may not reach mainstream curricula. Critical race, feminist, queer and disability studies theorists have questioned the traditional norms around race, gender, sexuality and disability. This growing body of expertise has challenged ideas that were previously uncontested in some university programmes; for example, Oliver and Barnes (2012) challenged ways of viewing disability, arguing that the medical model of disability assumes that 'able-bodied/mindedness is normal' (2012: 88). In contrast, a social model of disability emphasizes that it is the systems and processes in society that disable people, hence the importance of ensuring that curriculum content, pedagogy and assessment processes do not exclude or hinder any student.

Specialist centres provide research and scholarship to challenge academic practice in research methodology, curriculum content and pedagogy. But there is a danger in establishing these centres that the work of challenging academic practice is seen as separate to developing inclusive practice in mainstream curricula. Sheridan (1986) discussed the challenges of moving women's studies from the margins of the institution into the mainstream, arguing that marginalized scholars need to be given permanent positions and opportunities for promotion to move from the 'ghettos' of marginalized subjects. More importantly, insights from marginalized thinkers need to impact on traditional disciplines, so that within philosophy, history, medicine, psychology and all other disciplines, academic staff and students draw on critical race theory, feminist research, queer studies and disability studies to consider established perspectives critically.

Changing the curriculum is a major endeavour, and one that can be destabilizing for staff and students. Curriculum change in academia is slow, particularly where change impinges on established, canonical knowledge (Berges, 2015). Clegg (2016: 464) argues that it is important to look '... outwards from the academy to knowledge claims and challenges which originate outside the academy and the traditional professions'. Enabling critical debate around the canon is key to developing an inclusive pedagogy. As Luckett argues:

> At a pedagogic level, students should be provided not only with expanded content, but also with the analytical and methodological tools for debating, challenging and deconstructing inherited canons. (Luckett, 2016: 425)

Changing curricula is not just about changing content. Whoever conducts research, decides what to research, how to research and how to interpret that research, holds power. Sandra Harding, a feminist scholar,[9] argues that 'bias that arrives in research at the stage where problems are identified and hypotheses formulated often cannot be identified or eliminated in the testing process' (Harding, 1989: 12). Research methodology might traditionally exclude large sections of the community. For example, in the behavioural sciences Henrich *et al.* (2010: 61) criticize the practice of carrying out research on undergraduate American students, and other privileged communities, and then generalizing the findings across human populations. They claim participants are often 'drawn entirely from Western, Educated, Industrialized, Rich, and Democratic (WEIRD) societies' and that these WEIRD participants are unusual and not representative of human populations. At Stanford, the Gendered Innovations in Science, Health and Medicine, Engineering, and Environment group[10] consider the role of gender in research such as drug trials and automobile engineering. They reported research showing that seat belts which do not properly fit pregnant women cause foetal death: 'Safety devices, such as safety belts, were first developed to fit the 50th percentile man (taken as the norm). Inattention to humans of different sizes and shapes may result in unintended harm. Conventional seatbelts do not properly fit pregnant women, for example, and vehicle crashes are a leading cause of accidental foetal death due to maternal trauma' (Gendered Innovations, 2017).

Just as content and research methodology need to be deconstructed, so too does traditional pedagogy. Pedagogically sound assessment design is inclusive and time-saving. For example, if assessment is inclusive, then the need for later adjustments is eliminated. Work at Plymouth University on inclusive assessment and accessibility[11] is relevant to all students, as students from different educational cultures all benefit from an assessment that is planned around the students and that gives student choice. Strategies for inclusive assessment include preparing students for assessment, providing a variety of assessment methods and practice in each of these methods, and helping students understand assessment criteria, e.g. though activities like guided marking.[12]

However, viewing the curriculum in terms of only race, gender, sexuality and disability ignores the complex, multiple identities of learners. Crenshaw coined the term 'intersectionality' to explain how multiple identities interconnect to oppress, stating that 'the problem with identity politics is not that it fails to transcend difference, as some critics charge, but rather the opposite – that it frequently conflates or ignores intragroup difference' (Crenshaw, 1991: 1242).

The complexity of learners' lives cannot be understood by looking at only one aspect of their identity, e.g. race or sexuality. Crenshaw explains ways in which multiple categories of vulnerabilities interact in the social world to bring about 'patterns of subordination' (ibid.: 1249). In the traditional white, male-dominated curriculum, other thinking is marginalized. There is a need to bring scholars from the margins into the mainstream so that the humanities, social sciences and sciences are taught with reference to the historical development of the discipline and to the now marginalized voices that shaped the early discipline. Current content needs to be assessed for European, North American and Australian dominance of research and research perspectives. Much work is being done on this at UCL and the case studies below illustrate how the curriculum might be reviewed, and how staff and students can work together to develop resources to facilitate change.

How the group works

The LTC group is a cross-institutional group of staff and students at UCL. The group liaises with the equality and diversity team, the student union, the Office of the Vice Provost for Education and Student Affairs, and other interested groups in UCL. The group is organized and supported by staff in the UCL Arena Centre for Research-based Education, and works with the UCL Connected Curriculum (Fung, 2017) and ChangeMakers (see Marie, Chapter 3 in this volume) initiatives. Additional funding has been provided by the Office of the Vice Provost for Education and Student Affairs and this funding has allowed the group to organize and support events and fund small-scale projects. The group is located in the UCL Arena Centre, which runs educational courses for teaching assistants and probationary staff, supports curriculum change through the Connected Curriculum initiative and engages with students to effect change through UCL ChangeMakers. The LTC group is strongly supported by Arena staff and together they find ways of integrating LTC content in Arena courses. The LTC group also runs sessions as part of the well-publicized UCL Arena programme of events.[13]

The LTC working group is composed of a small group of stalwarts who typically meet several times a term to set the agenda and monitor progress; a larger group (around 400 members) network online in the UCL LTC Forum where members can advertise events, share resources and ask for help and advice. This larger pool of staff and students has been invaluable in supporting LTC work. For example, the group recently made a short animation explaining LTC;[14] a request for names of marginalized scholars to include in the animation was posted on the Forum and received prompt and knowledgeable responses.

LTC recognizes that staff and students need support to develop curricula so the group organizes regular events and develops resources to support change. Recently we have organized myth-busting sessions to provide a space where staff and students can critically question the group's work. Before a myth-busting session, participants post their questions on Moodle, which, to encourage questions on sensitive issues, can be done anonymously. These questions are then answered by a panel of expert staff and students in a two-hour event. Myth-busting events have been well attended and well evaluated. To enable curriculum review, the LTC group collaborated with UCL Connected Curriculum colleagues to develop a guide infused with LTC principles.[15] The guide provides academics and students with a tool for reviewing current curricula and identifying areas for change. To complement the guide, LTC supports the creation of resources to give staff and students ideas about ways of developing curricula. This has involved collecting case studies of good practice, designing an animation and funding small-scale curriculum change projects.[16] By way of illustration, a few case studies and funded projects are described below.

Case studies of liberation

Early Modern Marginalities
In Early Modern Marginalities, Dr Charlotte Roberts, with colleagues and students in the English Department, devised a project to support research into marginal voices in early modern literature. This project, funded by LTC, entailed creating a resources hub on Moodle containing bibliographies, articles, and links to external websites. Race, gender, sexuality, disability and working class literatures are represented and there is a discussion space

for researchers to connect, share and support each other's research. The hub is hosted on an internal open-access Moodle, so any member of UCL, staff or students, can enrol and use the resources. The hub has the potential to be used not only for programmes in the English Department, but also for other programmes in the faculty and throughout UCL.

Including patients in curriculum design

Inclusive healthcare is vitally important but often the voices of marginalized groups are not heard or fully represented in medical curricula. Two LTC-funded projects addressed this issue, bringing clinicians face to face with patients. The first, LGBT+ Healthcare in the Medical School, led by Dr Jayne Kavanagh and Jessica Salkind, brought LGBT+ patients and fifth-year medical students together for a compulsory workshop, looking at LGBT+ healthcare issues. Junior doctors helped to facilitate discussions around LGBT+ clinical scenarios and guest Trans speakers answered questions and discussed their experiences of NHS healthcare. In an evaluation after the session, medical students reported greatly increased confidence in taking medical history from a transgender patient.[17] In Ophthalmology, Rosie Gilbert devised a project to involve visually impaired patients in the curriculum. 'Patients' Perspectives of Visual Loss'[18] aimed at bringing patients and trainee ophthalmologists together in a session to discuss patient perspectives of eye disease. Participants described the impact of the session, which brought to life topics they had studied on their programmes, as 'inspiring' and 'emotional'. These projects demonstrate how important it is to ensure that students in medical fields meet with and develop an understanding of patients' experiences, and how including patient perspectives in the curriculum can change conceptions of disability and LGBT+ medical care.

Black Germany

One barrier to including marginal voices in curricula is the lack of a body of relevant academic literature. Jeff Bowersox has addressed this issue in his module Black Germany.[19] Black Germany looks at the history of black people in the German lands since the Middle Ages, using a wide variety of primary sources, for example maps, film, advertisements, sculpture and painting. The module was designed with colleagues in the USA and connects students in UCL with students at the universities of Michigan and Missouri. The module is taught simultaneously in all three institutions and students participate through online discussions. Students are also engaged in research-based learning (Jenkins *et al.*, 2003), developing a research question and appropriate research methods and working in small groups to present their research on a public website. An aim of the module is to focus on perspectives of communities on the margins of society in order to challenge and critique established interpretations of history. Jeff is part of a research network of academics who are looking at ways of diversifying and effectively teaching German studies, drawing on insights from black German history to explore current issues. Their work was recognized with the 2015 H-German Syllabus award[20] and is beginning to have an effect on the teaching of the discipline, illustrating how contesting ways of thinking within a discipline can help develop new perspectives and move thinking on.

Future directions

These case studies describe ongoing work at UCL and work that has been initiated by LTC funding. We have recently awarded funding to projects that build on this work and extend it, enabling staff and students to develop mainstream programmes for large student cohorts, suffused with LTC values. Example projects are:

- Developing a strand across a six-year medical programme (around 2,000 students), which addresses issues around race, gender, sexuality and disability in medicine
- Reviewing the curriculum of the Integrated Engineering Programme and ensuring inclusivity (around 700 students)
- Researching and producing a guide for non-BME staff supporting BME students
- Collecting narratives of Jewish students' campus experiences.

These projects were completed at the end of 2017, and outputs are being prepared for the LTC webpage.

How to liberate your curriculum

Changing curricula is a complex process and needs to be planned over a period of time. The case studies described in this chapter give guidance on ways of reviewing and developing modules and programmes. A starting point for those embarking on this journey is to form a group of interested staff and students. Mutual support and teamwork are key to collecting resources and developing new insights as is providing ways for the group to meet, in person or virtually, and share understandings.

Groups might start by considering the following questions for curriculum review and development, designed to help disciplinary groups think through ways of reviewing their curriculum.

Who teaches your curriculum?

A liberated curriculum needs to be taught by a diverse group of academics who can bring a range of perspectives. In many institutions, there are low levels of diversity among academic staff. A report by Alexander and Arday (2015: 32) for the Runnymede Trust states that: '... 92.39 per cent of professors (15,905) in UK academia are White, and 0.49 per cent (85) are Black, with just 17 of those being women.'

An interim solution, pending the appointment of more diverse staff, is to invite a diverse range of external speakers (see 'Including patients in curriculum design' case studies above for an example of this).

Who is represented in the reading list?

Think about the representation of the development of the discipline – are women, people with disabilities, LGBT+ and non-Europeans excluded from this history? Reading lists that exclude perspectives from marginalized groups can be reviewed and new resources found by both staff and students. The case study above, 'Early Modern Marginalities', illustrates how staff and students can work together to produce a rich bank of resources that can be shared with other programmes across the institution.

How accessible is your curriculum?

Think about recruitment of students and creating programmes that attract a diverse student cohort. Ensure that all documentation and resources are available in accessible formats and organized accessibly. Ensure lectures are recorded; use virtual learning environments (e.g. Moodle) to make lecture notes, presentations, readings and resources available ahead of teaching sessions, and after the sessions for review. Consider accessibility of all aspects of the programme, e.g. field trips, study abroad. Ask for student feedback on any aspects of the programme that are causing accessibility issues. Monitor student retention and completion and attainment to identify any issues that may disadvantage groups of students; think through adjustments and provide alternatives.

Is the curriculum designed so that learners can learn in a way that suits them? Do they have choice over forms of assessment?

Plymouth University's excellent work on inclusive assessment emphasizes the importance of assessment choice. Guidance on assessment options needs to be given so that all students are assessed in a way that best shows what they can do.[21]

Are learners learning in diverse groups that mix race, gender, sexuality and disability?

Creating opportunities for students to collaborate in diverse groups enhances team working skills and prepares students for employment and diverse working practices. The Higher Education Academy offers guidance on preparing students for diverse group work and managing conflicts.[22]

Are there opportunities for students to value and explore the different knowledges they bring to their studies at university?

Students bring a rich range of prior knowledge to their university studies. Programmes can be enhanced by tapping into this store of knowledge. Inclusive programme design affords opportunities for students to share, value, research and critique the knowledge that they bring to your programme.

Finally, share what you are doing, with colleagues, your department, and your institution and beyond, and disseminate this work through publications and websites. We would be interested in hearing about your work.[23]

Conclusions

Curriculum change is slow and multifaceted; it involves challenging staff and student assumptions and institutional processes. At UCL we are at the early stages of this change but we have already learnt that change needs to be a joint effort between students and staff, constructing their syllabuses and developing shared understandings together. Change is slow as it involves ensuring diversity in staff teams, nurturing PhD students and early academics from excluded minorities to help them build an academic career and ensuring that they are supported to effect change. Changing pedagogy involves reviewing institutional processes and more complex planning to ensure accessibility for all in all areas of the curriculum, and greater student choice in assessment. The case studies described above demonstrate how change can be nurtured and how successful projects can serve as archetypes for future development.

This chapter gives an overview of the development of LTC work at UCL; this work is ongoing and by the end of 2017 we had supported over 18 LTC projects in a range of disciplines. To hear more about our current projects and keep up to date with LTC work visit our webpage.[24]

Acknowledgements

I would like to extend a huge thanks to all staff and students at UCL who have been involved with LTC work over the past few years: their commitment and expertise is much valued. Support and guidance from senior management at UCL, especially Professors Anthony Smith and Dilly Fung, have been essential to the continued growth of LTC work. I am profoundly grateful also to my fellow LTC chairs, Dr Victoria Showunmi and Dr Mira Vogel, whose knowledge and expertise have enabled LTC work to flourish and develop in new directions.

Notes

[1] Address for correspondence: t.mcconlogue@ucl.ac.uk
[2] www.dtmh.ucl.ac.uk/videos/curriculum-white/
[3] https://whitecurriculum.wordpress.com/2015/06/07/lse-students-ask-why-is-my-curriculum-white/
[4] www2.warwick.ac.uk/services/library/mrc/eventsandseries/openeducationseries/2015/curriculumwhite/
[5] www.crassh.cam.ac.uk/programmes/decolonising-the-curriculum-in-theory-and-practice
[6] www.universities-scotland.ac.uk/raceequalitytoolkit/curriculum/
[7] www.ecu.ac.uk/equality-charters/race-equality-charter/members-award-holders/
[8] www.ecu.ac.uk/equality-charters/athena-swan/athena-swan-members/
[9] www.iep.utm.edu/fem-stan/
[10] http://genderedinnovations.stanford.edu/what-is-gendered-innovations.html
[11] www.plymouth.ac.uk/your-university/teaching-and-learning/inclusivity/inclusive-assessment
[12] www.ucl.ac.uk/teaching-learning/sites/teaching-learning/files/quickguide-guidedmarking-v2.pdf
[13] www.ucl.ac.uk/teaching-learning/professional-development/arena-open/arena-events
[14] www.ucl.ac.uk/teaching-learning/education-initiatives/connected-curriculum/liberating-curriculum
[15] www.ucl.ac.uk/teaching-learning/sites/teaching-learning/files/connected_curriculum_brochure_oct_2017.pdf
[16] www.ucl.ac.uk/teaching-learning/education-initiatives/connected-curriculum/liberating-curriculum
[17] https://goo.gl/Xitq5C
[18] https://goo.gl/CFzbn8
[19] https://goo.gl/Zfwtuv
[20] https://networks.h-net.org/node/35008/discussions/68644/ann-2015-syllabus-contest-results
[21] www.plymouth.ac.uk/uploads/production/document/path/2/2401/7_Steps_to_Inclusive_Assessment.pdf
[22] www.heacademy.ac.uk/system/files/group_work.pdf
[23] LTC can be contacted at connectedcurriculm@ucl.ac.uk
[24] www.ucl.ac.uk/teaching-learning/education-initiatives/connected-curriculum/liberating-curriculum

References

Alexander, C. and Arday, J. (eds) (2015) *Aiming Higher: Race, inequality and diversity in the academy* (Runnymede Perspectives). London: Runnymede. Online. www.runnymedetrust.org/uploads/Aiming%20Higher.pdf (accessed 19 March 2018).

Berges, S. (2015) 'On the outskirts of the canon: The myth of the lone female philosopher, and what to do about it'. *Metaphilosophy*, 46 (3), 380–97.

Clegg, S. (2016) 'The necessity and possibility of powerful "regional" knowledge: Curriculum change and renewal'. *Teaching in Higher Education*, 21 (4), 457–70.

Crenshaw, K. (1991) 'Mapping the margins: Intersectionality, identity politics, and violence against women of color'. *Stanford Law Review*, 43 (6), 1241–99.

Fung, D. (2017) *A Connected Curriculum for Higher Education*. London: UCL Press.

Gendered Innovations (2017) 'Pregnant crash test dummies: Rethinking standards and reference models'. Online. http://genderedinnovations.stanford.edu/case-studies/crash.html (accessed 27 April 2017).

Harding, S. (1989) 'Taking responsibility for our own gender, race, class: Transforming science and the social studies of science'. *Rethinking Marxism*, 2 (3), 8–19.

Henrich, J., Heine, S.J. and Norenzayan, A. (2010) 'The weirdest people in the world?'. *Behavioral and Brain Sciences*, 33 (2–3), 61–135.

Jenkins, A., Breen, R., Lindsay, R. and Brew, A. (2003) *Reshaping Teaching in Higher Education: Linking teaching with research*. London: Routledge.

Kamanzi, B. (2015) '"Rhodes must fall": Decolonisation symbolism – what is happening at UCT, South Africa?'. *The Postcolonialist*, 29 March. Online. http://postcolonialist.com/civil-discourse/rhodes-must-fall-decolonisation-symbolism-happening-uct-south-africa/ (accessed 27 April 2017).

Luckett, K. (2016) 'Curriculum contestation in a post-colonial context: A view from the South'. *Teaching in Higher Education*, 21 (4), 415–28.

Meusburger, P., Freytag, T. and Suarsana, L. (2016) 'Ethnic and cultural dimensions of knowledge and education: An introduction'. In Meusburger, P., Freytag, T. and Suarsana, L. (eds) *Ethnic and Cultural Dimensions of Knowledge* (Knowledge and Space 8). Cham: Springer, 1–22.

Oliver, M. and Barnes, C. (2012) *The New Politics of Disablement*. Basingstoke: Palgrave Macmillan.

Richardson, J.T.E. (2008) *Degree Attainment, Ethnicity and Gender: A literature review*. York: Higher Education Academy.

Sheridan, S. (1986) 'From margin to mainstream: Situating women's studies'. *Australian Feminist Studies*, 1 (2), 1–13.

Woolf, K., Potts, H.W.W. and McManus, I.C. (2011) 'Ethnicity and academic performance in UK trained doctors and medical students: Systematic review and meta-analysis'. *BMJ*, 342, Article d901, 1–14.

Chapter 8

Setting the interdisciplinary scene

Jason P. Davies[1]

Interdisciplinarity, working *across* specialities, is something that has been shaping higher education increasingly since the 1990s. It is a mode of working that cuts across the usual habits of a single discipline, focusing on solving a particular problem or situation by drawing on a range of expertise. There are times when grand claims are made for interdisciplinary work, and times when it is seen as a buzzword that needs to be put somewhere because it sounds good in grant applications.

Interdisciplinary research is difficult partly because it goes against the grain of specialization, and going into details deeply is inevitable when one is doing research. Interdisciplinary *education* is even harder because there is often less consensus about what understanding we are trying to impart: subject specialists are themselves often not sure how to agree on these and have to collaborate to find their way to an appropriate understanding in each new collaboration. In this overview, Davies argues that one consequence of this is to emphasize the open-endedness of collaborative research, and that students can be a part of it – indeed they make a vital contribution to judgements about what kinds of knowledge and collaborations are of value.

Since appearing in the 1940s and accelerating from then (Lynch, 2006), 'interdisciplinarity' has become a buzzword in higher education internationally. Its supporters have stressed that great things are made possible when disciplines work together, things that are not possible through traditional research: by pooling different areas of expertise, we can tackle issues that are urgent and large-scale in the world outside the university. It has also created some complicated challenges when it comes to teaching. This chapter offers a brief overview of what it means to be interdisciplinary (or not) and sets the scene for some distinct types of interdisciplinary learning and teaching. If it is guilty of oversimplification, it is because of its brevity, but there is more detail and nuance in the references.

What is interdisciplinarity?

In order to think about what interdisciplinarity is, we need to think briefly about what single academic disciplines are.

Subject matter?

Many academic disciplines are named after their subject matter: we are all familiar with 'Physics', 'History', 'Law', and so on. These examples generally appear to most as stable, relatively unchanging subjects, but they are not as fixed as they might appear. Even with its empirical, provable, repeatable findings, Physics has not stood still by any means: even if a time machine was invented to consult the founder of the modern era, Einstein would have a formidable amount of catching up and readjustment to do. That is despite the fact that the actual physics of the universe has not changed: it is our understanding that has moved on. To be more specific, our *methods*, *questions* and *priorities* have altered as understanding, technology and priorities have changed: Physics as a subject was witness to this as the vast majority of departments added 'astronomy' to their names over the twentieth century.

Methods

In other words, we must also note that academic disciplines have distinct methods and approaches *to* their subject material, and different ways of identifying suitable material in the first place. Anthropology, sociology and history all study 'people', for instance, but in very different ways and with different intentions.

Evidence

As a result of these different approaches, what counts as *evidence* changes profoundly from one discipline to another: science, especially medical science, is dismissive of 'anecdotal' evidence (by which they mean evidence that cannot be tested, was not gathered in controlled conditions and might therefore be a red herring, and so on). In contrast, and for example, those studying cultures without writing systems frequently have nothing *but* isolated comments, i.e. *just* 'anecdotal evidence'. They have found other ways of dealing with all the hazards that come with isolated and 'unprovable' pieces of information (for example, see Jenkins, 1995). Anthropological fieldwork, for instance, after over a century of direct experience of unfamiliar cultures, generally warns its practitioners to be deeply cautious of asking people direct questions and accepting their replies at face value. They are sensitive, for instance, to the fact that people tend to be influenced by what they think their audience wants to hear and that statements are rarely to be taken literally and superficially. Perhaps the statements 'really' mean, 'I wish this tiring person would stop asking strange questions'; or they might give jokey or boastful answers that make the findings 'unreliable' (certainly not literal): it is very hard to tell what to believe – see, for instance, Peoples and Bailey (2011: 123) for an example of the authors *thinking* they were being teased.

Anthropologists therefore tend not to carry notebooks around visibly, instead making their fieldnotes at suitable moments in private, and preferring to observe and ask a very limited number of direct questions: they want to see things as 'naturally' as possible. They might not even fully reveal what they are trying to find out, and go 'undercover', which makes patient and quiet observation far more important than a series of questions. One American anthropologist joined her own university as a first-year undergraduate to find out more about her students' world, and spent a year immersed there, for the most part just watching and listening: that way she could notice things that she would never have thought of asking about (Nathan, 2006).

In stark contrast to this, some areas of the social sciences rely almost completely on semi-structured interviews, which may well be recorded and transcribed, arranged in advance and conducted in a semi-formal setting. This provides comparable material that can be aggregated (e.g. '57 per cent of respondents preferred tutorials to lectures') as well as more qualitative findings and considerations. The concerns of anthropological ethnography are less prevalent in this kind of situation (because the interviewers have a common culture and understanding, to a very large extent) and different kinds of judgements are being made. As a rule of thumb, sciences (including many of the social sciences) tend to favour generalizable findings, while the humanities are more interested in the distinct and the particular. Though this is a gross simplification, it illustrates the kind of broad differences and the implications for gathering evidence and choice of methods across academia.

Good questions

An awareness of the limits of evidence and methods means that there is a knack, which has to be acquired, of identifying what a good *question* is: is it meaningful, and answerable, to the satisfaction of other experts in that field? 'Answerable' can depend on all kinds of external factors.

For instance, Thomas Bayes formulated a theorem, which now underpins Bayesian probability, in the mid-eighteenth century. It was not until the mid-twentieth century that computers could actually begin exploring its implications: the calculations were simply too complex to be practical before then.

Being able to identify a meaningful ('good') question in an academic environment is perhaps the most critical skill one can acquire, and it is a skill that requires a thorough acquaintance with the discipline. A question that cuts to the heart of one discipline's priorities may pass another by completely. For example, Dame Mary Douglas spent much of her career as an anthropologist exploring how particular social structures shape knowledge and influence what is considered important. I do not mean to imply she was alone in this, but her *Missing Persons* (Douglas and Ney, 1998) is a good example of the antipathy many of her discipline have for individualized approaches such as psychology and economics, with a running critique that borders on scathing arising from the assumption that people and ideas exist in a vacuum. I once happened to be at the same seminar as her, presented by a historian, about the ideas of a particular group in the first millennium CE (Common Era). She asked if he knew whether they lived alone or in groups and received the slightly wrong-footed reply, 'I have no idea'. The question was polite, and was asked in full awareness that had the speaker spent years learning anthropology, he would not have mastered the range of ancient languages that enabled him to read the texts in the first place; besides that, she would also have been aware that most of the texts were simply found in the desert with very little accompanying evidence of how their authors had lived. But she had to ask, to try to bring her disciplinary understanding to bear. Each of them had focused on different aspects to the extent that some things were almost never considered (for various reasons), while others had become central: but anthropology and textual history had not explored the same paths, and so different questions were of interest.

Disciplinary practices and culture

Writing

There is more to this 'disciplining' than simply identifying relevant evidence and interrogating it in a relevant way, though. Each has its own ways of *writing* that must be learnt: reports must have a particular style if they are to be understood; essays need to be structured in a particular way; a portfolio is another kind of writing that is harder than it looks, as is a legal brief (on which see Wilcox, 2007; or for biomedical research, Budgell, 2009).

Even the decision to write with or without footnotes fundamentally changes the way one communicates; these are all things that must be learnt by application, practice and review. Habitually writing in a particular way has a surprisingly profound effect on how one thinks and behaves. For instance, the question of whether one should write in the active or passive voice runs deep and in alignment with deeper currents: the passive *is* traditionally used heavily in science and emphasizes that the evidence is what legitimizes the argument; attention is drawn to the process and the findings rather than the scientist to emphasize that facts are established irrespective of the person by whom an experiment is undertaken. By contrast, in the humanities and social sciences we use the active to stress that we are taking responsibility for making a judgement; to use the passive is to shirk this duty.

Presentation and communication

Presentation of information in general is equally diverse across the disciplines: an hour-long talk is very different from a three-minute presentation, textbooks are written in very different styles, and so on. Do we present our findings at the outset confidently, or even *over*-confidently?[2] Or do we suggest them cautiously within a culture of modest understatement? These will be understood by those who know as simply being normal ways of saying 'I'm sure that ...'.

Practices that would be embarrassing failures in one field are the norm in another, and for good reasons. It also takes practice to judge how much one can expect an audience to know and how much needs to be explained to get the point across. This can be true even within the same discipline, but becomes exponentially more complicated the more disciplines that are involved.

Risk, resources and environment

Everyday matters, like the use of equipment or resources, also have a subtle but far-reaching effect on creating a particular 'disciplinary way of being': is it, for instance, a risk-averse culture that inculcates habits of careful planning and preparation? This can be considered both in literal terms of the physical environment and in the kind of resources available. Ancient history, for instance, is ever-aware of both the remoteness of the cultures being studied and the sheer weight of *lost* evidence, which leads to a general distrust of speculation and a level of detail in footnotes that other disciplines simply do not feel the need to bother with.[3]

Another 'secondary' aspect that might be relevant is *scale* and impact: chemical engineering (which works in multiples of tonnes) is less forgiving of minor spillages or trivial inaccuracies than chemistry (which tends to work in grams or smaller units) because at that scale, expense, waste and risks are all similarly magnified.

Each field will have their own versions of what factors matter and it will affect the culture in many ways: for instance, when visiting a colleague in a science laboratory, I was challenged nervously but determinedly in the lift by a member of the research staff to explain who I was and what I was doing there. He explained afterwards that the building contained a large number of extremely dangerous materials. A stranger would not normally be challenged in this way once they had got past security and/ or reception, which is standard in many universities now. As well as the 'textbook learning', it is all these behaviours, priorities, things to watch out for, and so on that create a disciplinary culture. To be successful in any academic specialism, one must internalize these values and habits. University education is not just about acquiring (ever more) knowledge. As Oliver and Gourlay outline in Chapter 2, it is about a transformation of one's thinking, so that graduates are able to look at a situation and understand what is possible or desirable in a distinctive way: an architect does not see the same muddy field as an archaeologist; an engineer does not look at a town in the same way as an urban designer; a historian does not look at a group of people in the same way as a geographer. If such differences in perspectives did not result, studying a particular subject would be a waste of time.

Academic tribes

The overall effect, then, is that academics think and operate in distinctive, and very different, ways. 'Knowing how to know' arises from the combination of understanding methods and evidence-handling: not just the answers to questions and knowing what a good question is in the first place, but also judgements about how to respond to unexpected events or discoveries. Is an unexpected crystal formation, produced accidentally in a chemistry lab by an undergraduate, the result of misreading the instructions for the experiment, or a discovery?

A quick glimpse of distinct academic *modi operandi* can be had by considering a joke: a physicist, a biologist and a mathematician are having a coffee opposite a house. Two people go into the house and, a little later, three come out. The physicist says, 'our initial measurement wasn't accurate'; the biologist says, 'they have reproduced' and the mathematician says, 'if exactly one more person goes in, the house will be empty again'.

Sustaining discipline

This disciplinary culture is reinforced and reiterated in a whole range of ways. Depending on the extent to which there are well-trodden paths, staff who 'dabble' in a range of fields may struggle to find employment when interviewed alongside those who have kept their interests strictly focused within the discipline. Some commentators see 'amateurism' and research 'of dubious quality' as characteristic of interdisciplinary work (Jacobs and Frickel, 2009: 51–2; or 'dilettantism' in Frodeman, 2014). They will also find that any research or publications that belong to another field will not generally count in their research quotas: people can be sensitive to the opportunity cost – time spent doing *this* means time not spent doing *that*, and *that* may bring in grant income. Doing *this* therefore translates directly into loss of income for the university. A report commissioned in 2015 by the Higher Education Funding Council for England (HEFCE) and the Medical Research Council (MRC) (Pan and Katrenko, 2015) found that interdisciplinary research had a lower citation impact overall and there are comparable findings from Australia (Woelert and Millar, 2013). Even if someone is successful in keeping up with more than one area (an impressive feat itself), the chances are it will only be limited to specific aspects of those areas.

Research publications by UK academics are assessed by subject specialists within the discipline (after all, who can assess whether something is good maths except another mathematician?) through the Research Excellence Framework, so there is a disincentive to publish unorthodox research because it is 'extremely complex to assess' (Jacobs and Frickel, 2009: 52): you risk a low research rating, and therefore income. Grant applications to obtain funds to undertake research must generally stipulate what they expect to find but, as we shall see, interdisciplinary research can, at times, be an exploratory scouting trip to explore possibilities rather than a predictable process. It may be not so much a case of navigating reasonably well-mapped territory as mapping it in the first place.

One hallmark of good research is originality, but originality is not simply doing something that has never been done before – we might better call it *meaningful* originality, since it cannot be so unusual that no one knows what to make of it. And, while a creative borrowing of methods from other disciplines does appear to promise that, the outcomes are much less certain. Conversely, interesting and valuable work *can* fail to count as original by a particular assessing body: something like the application of a statistical method to historical texts may be highly original in history (if it turns out to work) but bog-standard work for a statistician, who may receive little or no formal recognition for similar work in *statistics* since they may not have contributed much to understanding in that field.

Because so much income depends on these judgements, it is safer to stay close to the heart of the discipline. The more promising and experimental it is, the more one can risk a project being seen as an indulgence that may be no more than a distracting curiosity: such things can lead to breakthroughs, but is more likely to be a dead end and there is always plenty to be done closer to home. This is why interdisciplinary research is generally less likely to receive funding (Bromham *et al.*, 2016), unless tailored and specific funding is made available as a result of social, policy or legal initiatives or efforts. That can change much more rapidly than 'normal' disciplinary research.

Day-to-day operations will heavily and continuously reinforce disciplinary norms: working in teams; publishing (which involves review by and of one's peers, and includes feedback that will tend to bring everyone back to disciplinary norms); teaching (possibly in teams, and within curricula decided to varying extents by the rest of the department and scrutinized by an external examiner); presenting one's research, or perhaps ways of teaching what is already generally agreed and established knowledge within a discipline; attending conferences and hearing about what others have been working on; attending departmental meetings, which again underline what is 'normal' in the discipline and occasionally draw adverse attention to what is not; and the substantial work of keeping up with one's own area of expertise. All these are an unending repetition of the disciplinary norms that are likely to drown out other perspectives, but constitute the key ways by which institutions, including academic disciplines, continuously create and reinforce disciplinary coherence.

There is generally little sense that extra-curricular areas are important, even if they are not far from the core subject area: physicists and chemists, for instance, are not required or even encouraged to know much of the history of their subject but are almost constantly reminded of the need to research and publish about physics or chemistry. They are certainly not paid to find out about literature, epidemiology or teacher education, however interested they might be in those or any other areas. Such interests are precisely that: 'just' interests that lie outside their main fields.

Metaphors for disciplines

The net result of this has been described in a number of ways: 'silos' is commonly used, as is the idea of liberating ourselves by 'knocking down walls' between disciplines – but it is more complicated than that. Getting into the next room doesn't necessarily mean you know how to speak the language or share the concerns of its occupants. More fruitful is the metaphor of 'tribes and territories'; the phrase was coined by Tony Becher in 1989 and the description here draws heavily on his study (Becher, 1989) and subsequent revisions.[4] The articulation of 'communities of practice' (Wenger, 1998) also lent weight to this sense of disciplines as identifiable communities that develop distinct interests and, by default, maintain their own ways of thinking and operating.

Teaching a discipline

Put simply, a university teacher's role is to induct students into their 'tribe'. Their mission is to displace previous assumptions and ideas, with the expectation that students will be in an environment and in peer groups that will reinforce the new ideas and behaviours that must be learnt to become a member of the 'tribe'. The curriculum, resources, environment and teaching colleagues will all immerse students in the department's usual practices and environment. Each will make their own way, more or less successfully, through the process of internalizing all these different facets of learning. When it works well it becomes second nature, and virtually automatic – the more instinctive, the better. Though many will leave with an undergraduate degree, those who stay on will incorporate the culture and knowledge to the point where they embody them and become fully part of them, to the point that they can now begin more systematically to impart them to the next generation of students anew.

When running an activity with an interdisciplinary group of probationary lecturers, I asked them to describe the room we were in from the perspective of their discipline. I noticed that a civil engineer sitting near me immediately started drawing the shape of the large and oddly shaped room *without looking up*. Watching his outline take shape, I first thought it was wrong but when I looked at the corner in question, I realized he had noticed more about the room's perimeter than I had, even though I had looked around, obviously knowing what activity was about to begin. A civil engineer, an architect, a planner and experts from other disciplines who are sensitive to space, layout, and so on would have noticed the layout without deliberate effort; those (like me) who were not cued to notice space had to look, in a way for the first time. While I was noting these varied reactions, the engineer informed me, still without looking up, that the fire extinguisher by the emergency exit was not where it was legally required to be.

That activity was intended to show those probationers just how deeply and automatically they thought in their particular disciplines. When asked what struck them most about the room, biology-related academics talked about the appalling conditions for life to persist (in a subterranean dry space like that, it had no chance), linguistics lecturers talked about an optimum environment for sound (for virtually the same reasons), historians tried to guess how the room had come to exist in its strange form (it had been converted), and so on. Each group described the room from a completely different set of interests. Put differently, this is about *focus*, but the flipside of focusing on one thing is that you must ignore others: as Woelert and Millar (2013: 757) put it, 'certain things and aspects become visible and in this sense "real", while others are rendered invisible.' Disciplinary learning therefore includes a great deal of learning to ignore or discard information that is of little or no use.

... and learning

From the student's perspective, this massive effort to create coherence and consistency may not be visible. In fact, as it is presented to them, it may be deliberately broken down into what appear to be constituent, even unrelated, slices, to make it more manageable. This can, ironically, be too successful as a teaching strategy, and lead to fragmented learning, where students do not realize that what they learnt in one module is relevant to another – a key impetus for the Connected Curriculum strategy. But the more they engage with the curriculum, with the department, the subject and the environment they find themselves in, the more they internalize the material, the methods, the thinking, the practices and the values. Successful graduates do not emerge the same as they went in, whether or not they continue to work in a related field.

Enter the 'real world'

Given this inherent centripetal tendency, it is not surprising that when academics are consulted about 'real-world' issues, sometimes their expertise does not match those problems. A frequent issue is *timescale*: expert knowledge is not always quick, because universities are not satisfied with quick results that might turn out not to be accurate. Or they might simply not match what is wanted – a mechanical engineer once explained the problems of long-term stress-testing of machines to me by saying rhetorically 'if you want a chicken quickly, boil an egg': in other words, if you expose an egg to the same warmth in three minutes that it would receive from the mother hen sitting on it for three weeks, you will not get the same result.

Alternatively, it might give answers that no one wants to hear and whose relevance (but not accuracy) experts are unsure of: Douglas and Ney's

Missing Persons opens by discussing the paradox faced by anthropologists in a world that wishes to address the global issue of poverty, when a significant part of their understanding was that many 'primitive' societies lacking resources and experiencing gruelling work seemed to consider they had a good life, free from want. What were anthropologists to bring to the efforts to reduce hardship in a world that was trying to address 'not just lack but potentially lethal lack'? (Douglas and Ney, 1998: 5). They wrote the book to 'reorganize the terms of the discourse' for the social sciences, to think again about what they were saying, and what they might usefully say.

This kind of conditional answer to pressing issues is what leads to a general perception that disciplines are insular and that walls need knocking down, though we should swiftly note that if any problem *is* solved by a discipline, it will never become visible: if we are graduating medics to become GPs then there is no 'real-world problem' that needs solving (a lack of recruitment or unwillingness to go on to general practice is not the same issue).

But the world keeps coming with its questions: recent decades have seen increasing calls for academia to overcome these limitations as part of a more general push towards greater engagement with the wider world. There is a long tradition of academia embracing social or political issues that cut across distinct fields of study, often forming 'Studies' as its area of interest: roughly chronologically, we might mention 'interdisciplines' such as Marxist Studies (spanning history, economics and much of the social sciences), Women's or Gender Studies (which had a similar reach but more interest in literature and art than Marxist Studies); Environmental Studies as the precursor to climate change-related issues (this is now deeply embedded in, and critical to, many of its relevant areas, such as Oceanography) and, most recently, variously named but related interests in BME (black/minority/ethnic) issues, such as #WhiteCurriculum, outlined by Teresa McConlogue in Chapter 7. But these are academic-heavy movements that intend to have an effect *on* the world on academic terms by their consideration of a single issue or perspective in any and all contexts, rather than situations where the world defines what *it* wants from academia. In that sense, they are at the *opposite* end of the spectrum from interdisciplinarity as being 'about real-world issues'.

Consider, for example, expertise being brought to a high-crime urban area. Criminologists, legal experts, perhaps anthropologists and/or sociologists, a historian of the area, educationalists and others (perhaps even the people who live there ...) will quickly find that their expertise does not mix easily. Each will come with a different focus, different solutions and competing priorities. They will identify different problems as the most urgent and as soon as they begin talking as experts using expert terminology (otherwise known as 'jargon'), the others will not be able to follow them in any detail and the subtleties of their knowledge will be lost.[5] However, none can solve the problem on their own, and all must learn to work together if a useful outcome is going to be produced, whereas interdisciplines that compromise too much are rapidly in danger of dissolving, organized as they are around particular perspectives.

Interdisciplinary modes

It is possible to distinguish different types of interdisciplinary work but, given that there is no single discipline thinking about it to enforce consistent use of terminology, various terms are used, often interchangeably, to refer to different kinds. What is useful is the distinctions of different modes, and for our purposes the three most likely are:

- *multidisciplinarity*, by which I mean a team where each member contributes their expertise separately and within clearly defined limits: think of a team building a house, where the plumber does the plumbing, the electrician the wiring, and so on. They may well become familiar with each other's work, but do not intrude on it.
- *transdisciplinarity*, often defined as the result of collaboration beyond the university or with an entirely unrelated field, or as V.A. Brown puts it, 'academic knowledge extended by other ways of knowing' (Brown, 2015: 210). For instance, a fictional example (as far as I am aware) might be a geographer coming across a way of thinking about infection and the spread of bacteria in an organism, and applying the idea, with suitable modification, to how human populations move and grow.
- (critical) *interdisciplinarity*, when different disciplines work together to explore something and the fundamental workings of their expertise are challenged by doing so. This contrasts with the first two types, which draw heavily on individual disciplines retaining their basic mode of working but encountering unfamiliar ones and drawing on them.

The different focuses and priorities will clash, with no obvious way to make a judgement. Consider our hypothetical high-crime area:

- Are we usually discarding, or focusing on, anecdotal evidence?
- Are we accustomed to 'big data' in the form we have it?
- Do we interview people to find out more, or rely on ethnographic observation?

Then there is the question of what counts as a satisfactory outcome. Is it lower crime in the *short* term? If so, are we even looking at the medium term? What exactly is 'short term' in this context? Or is it improved educational engagement and prospects for likely offenders, or rebuilding a physical environment because the existing one 'encourages' crime? How concerned are we with the social fabric of the area?

When spelled out, these differences are fairly obvious (and I am not claiming the example is fully developed) but it can be surprisingly difficult to make them clear, and harder to find ways to choose between them. Since most experts have, as explained, internalized their process of judgement-making to the point that it is second nature, automatic and 'obvious', they find it difficult to grasp just how different a perspective someone else is bringing. Typically, they expect that simply explaining what they think is the priority will settle the matter, but their colleague from a different discipline will quite possibly do the same thing, underlining the differences: they may find themselves without any way of resolving the difference (Davies, 2011).

The process can be frustrating and disorientating and it frequently requires more time than is initially expected to learn to work together. Perhaps hardest of all can be deciding what gets priority. Often the only way it is likely to work is when an outside agency defines the issue and what would count as a solution. This not only helps choosing between different solutions, but also hopefully provides resources.

In the midst of the difficulty, though, is the possibility of creativity. Expertise tends to perpetuate itself: 'we do it this way' because it works fairly predictably. But being in a situation where the old techniques simply don't apply forces a potentially fruitful rethink as people step back and see how their knowledge and practices work, possibly for the first time in years, ever since they started being second nature. Similarly, learning to explain disciplinary methods and priorities to others can lead to a greater insight into those long-familiar understandings. Others might be able to bring ideas from their fields to the discussion, even bringing solutions to long-standing issues in another discipline. We cannot *guarantee* this happening, but it does happen.

This kind of process is not new, despite frequent claims to that effect: 'traditional' disciplines have always done this. Sider (2005: 48–53), for instance, tells the story of multidisciplinary efforts in the eighteenth century to read severely damaged papyrus rolls found in the Villa del Papiri at Herculaneum, charred – but thereby preserved – when Vesuvius erupted in 79 CE. They tried mercury as a lubricant (it crushed the fragile papyri), rose water, and then a 'vegetable gas' that destroyed the rolls and stank the palace out. Nowadays, X-rays, infrared and ultraviolet light are more effective at reading these texts, which have lasted two millennia. Disciplines have always adapted as knowledge, technology (possibilities) and needs have emerged. Sometimes, but not always, this leads to the foundation of new disciplines: well-known examples include biochemistry and neuroscience (for example, see Jacobs, 2014).

What *is* new is the systematic promotion of interdisciplinarity on a large (and small) scale: perhaps the most material difference in recent years is the sheer scale of recognition and promotion of, and universities' application to, unprecedented, urgent large-scale issues in the world as a whole (Jacobs and Frickel, 2009; Frodeman, 2014). There has also been a change in terms of institutional support: in the 1968 European student uprisings, it was the students who were calling for interdisciplinary work, but it is now just as likely to be the central management, administration and funding bodies (Castronovo, 2000). This goes beyond the deliberate embedding of interdisciplinary research: it has also embraced the question of bringing new and profoundly interdisciplinary students into academia, such as those on UCL's Arts and Sciences degree, the BASc. These share the 'real-world' and applied focus of interdisciplinary research: for instance, at the time of writing, there is a Wellcome Trust-funded four-year PhD interdisciplinary programme available, based at UCL, Birkbeck and the Francis Crick Institute, which speaks of training in 'all aspects … necessary to address important problems in biomedicine'.[6]

Implications for teaching

Interdisciplinary research is tricky but arguably interdisciplinary education, and particularly interdisciplinary *learning*, are much harder (as recognized by many, e.g. Balsiger, 2015). To think this through, I suggest three main categories.

'Incidental'

First, 'incidental' interdisciplinary work, where a course that is predominantly one discipline borrows items, ideas or findings from another. Though this does have an overall structure (the main discipline), we should not underestimate the difficulties that might arise. Imagine a student intending to become a GP being exposed to ethnographic methods by someone who typically has students doing months of immersive fieldwork, in an attempt to improve their ability to understand the broader picture of their patients' lives and underlying health issues. The default medical training will focus on sifting through what they are told by patients for relevant factors (for instance, diet and whether they smoke, and so on). Should they become sensitized to the subtleties of ethnographic research, they might start considering that having a surgery is intimidating to some patients and thereby affecting the stories they tell; they start to suspect they should instead make home visits to get to the salient facts. Anthropological fieldwork (ideally) involves immersion in a culture for extended periods, but making each medical consultation into a year-long study seems a little impractical.

But, more seriously, where *would* you stop? These are judgements that must eventually fit into the working of the 'borrowing' discipline. Would you listen for an extra five minutes without intervening, and allow patients to chatter freely? Ten minutes? Ask for relatives to attend to observe the dynamics and perhaps reduce tendencies to exaggerate or understate symptoms? The new medic is ill-equipped to make these judgements themselves: the 'home' discipline has a duty to guide these judgements, which will probably seem arbitrary and rather unambitious to the anthropologist brought in for a guest lecture. Such a guest lecturer will already be worrying about how much background to expect, and what they can realistically ask students to do.

This example began as an imaginary scenario (because my knowledge is inevitably limited) but my efforts to find examples confirmed the basic logic. In discussing 'narrative-based medicine', Kalitzkus and Matthiessen (2009: 84) say that it:

> takes time and effort because 'significant technical and attitudinal change that is necessary does not come quickly.' … At the beginning, [it] can lead through a phase of destabilization and doubt about one's own approach to medical practice … 'The biggest challenge in taking a narrative approach is knowing when to stop.' (Kalitzkus and Matthiessen, 2009: 84, citing Launer, 2002)

I would argue, then, that this is a vivid example of 'small-scale' interdisciplinary interactions; it is not a special case. This highlights another issue: most university teachers able to teach about a particular topic are experts only in that area – the more interdisciplinary the situation, the less likely it will be that our guest lecturer understands other aspects of what the students are studying. Their ability to guide the students on these kinds of questions will be limited and unpredictable. A single lecture within a series may send ripples throughout the course: the difficulties of interdisciplinary teaching and learning are not always easily judged by the proportion of the curriculum they appear to occupy.

A *new discipline*

My second category pertains mostly to those who have completed one degree and are moving to a different area. Moving from one discipline to one that looks similar may be counterintuitively harder than it looks. Moving from chemistry to chemical engineering, for example, will involve more un-learning than one might expect as, for instance, the scale of operations may become an important factor: a minute error in formulating a chemical reaction will be undetectable when using test-tubes but translate into tonnes when scaled up to the size of an industrial plant. A literature specialist may have to ignore much (but not all) of the subtlety they see in a text if they shift into a more historical area and start interrogating the text for different purposes. But if this changeover is a one-off process, they can at least neglect aspects of their expertise that are no longer relevant, and have a coherent process of changeover, however difficult the transition might be (Land, 2012; Davies, 2016).

Competing and cooperating

Third, we have students learning across a wider set of areas simultaneously. 'Parallel' learning in two or more fields is likely to cause the most turbulence for students. Discerning the undercurrents of a distinctive field typically requires immersion in that field, just as the best way to learn a new language is to move to where it is spoken. This immersion means that there is constant feedback and reiteration of the new ideas and general culture of the discipline, as explained earlier: almost everything reinforces aspects of the discipline.

If students are encountering a range of disciplines, they might well be able to pick up the information they need to master, and start becoming familiar with the underlying methods, ways of handling evidence and methods, and so on, but it will be a challenge to integrate this into anything coherent – before they get a chance, they may well be encountering another one and what they learn will be fragmented beyond their ability to integrate it, or at least to be sure they have integrated it in a way that will be accepted by their peers and assessors.

Students in interdisciplinary scenarios may never get to enjoy settling into the predictable life of one well-established and fairly coherent set of frameworks. As they master their fields, they will need to learn not just to question but when to question, and when to stop, often not because they have reached a 'natural' point of resolution but because they need to integrate answers into an eclectic solution rather than pursue a particular detail.

In many instances this is not critical: they learn what they need to, like medics becoming familiar but not *too* expert in narrative-based medicine. Fragmentation is certainly one possible response to the challenge of integrating one's learning, and in modularized courses even makes it appear easier to prepare for exams, but it is a version of 'surface learning' where one only mimics understanding but has not grasped the underlying principles of the subject (for example, see Cousin, 2006). The ambition of an interdisciplinary degree is not only to grant access to the creativity that comes from being able to take an expert perspective, but also to refuse to see it only that way. They will need to be ever-conscious of the context they are in and adjust their focus and practices. They will be simultaneously adopting multiple sets of practices that may appear to contradict one another and adjusting to the way staff steeped in one discipline may even appear to dismiss the ideas, evidence, priorities and values of another. It is likely that guest teaching staff, brought in as experts on a particular topic, will be at best *unaware* of the extent to which they are treading on the toes of another discipline, a discipline about which the students may have learnt just the previous week. All the issues highlighted in this chapter will probably come to the fore at some point.

This challenge is shared by the teaching staff and the students: it can be no other way. There are issues staff can be mindful of – they must think particularly hard about assessment and feedback. For instance, students who are mainly learning how to write reports should be supported when they are then asked to write an essay. But given the scarcity of genuinely interdisciplinary staff who are also teaching as well as researching, and the inevitable reality that *no* academic staff member can possibly master a wide range of disciplinary modes, the staff and students are inevitably going to be puzzling things out together.

This might surprise some, who are used to thinking of university staff as experts in their fields, but it is, in many ways, a perfect preparation for the wider world. It is a common saying now that most of our graduates will do jobs that do not yet exist: we are preparing them not just to know, but to *not* know. Keeping one's head when faced with apparently insoluble problems, and then finding a way to proceed, is a skill that requires practice (and aligns perfectly with a focus on research-based education). Interdisciplinary teaching and learning is challenging and requires careful preparation by the teachers, and a commitment and resilience on the part of the students, but in changing and complex times, is something that offers the opportunity for a unique kind of creativity.

It will be obvious that many of the case studies that follow in Part Two, as well as the dimensions of UCL's Connected Curriculum and ChangeMakers, fit well with many of the themes that traditionally sit under the heading of 'interdisciplinarity'. University research and teaching have changed beyond recognition in recent decades as they consider their role in wider society, both in terms of what is researched (and why) and how this can become a dynamic process that is reflected in the teaching that is on offer.

Acknowledgements
My thanks are due to Ginny Brunton of UCL IOE for her comments on a draft of this chapter.

Notes
[1] Address for correspondence: j.p.davies@ucl.ac.uk
[2] See Boutron *et al.* (2010) for a study of 'spin' in medical publications.
[3] The 'master' of historical footnotes is probably Jonathan Z. Smith, whose n.24 runs across three pages in Smith, 1990.
[4] There was a second edition with Trowler in 2001, and a rethink in Trowler *et al.*, 2012.
[5] The classic article about this happening is Wynne, 1992.
[6] www.ismb.lon.ac.uk/wt_studentships.html

References
Balsiger, J. (2015) 'Transdisciplinarity in the class room? Simulating the co-production of sustainability knowledge'. *Futures*, 65, 185–94.

Becher, T. (1989) *Academic Tribes and Territories: Intellectual enquiry and the cultures of discipline.* Milton Keynes: Society for Research into Higher Education and the Open University Press.

Becher, T. and Trowler, P.R. (2001) *Academic Tribes and Territories: Intellectual enquiry and the cultures of discipline.* 2nd ed. Buckingham: Society for Research into Higher Education and the Open University Press.

Boutron, I., Dutton, S., Ravaud, P. and Altman, D.G. (2010) 'Reporting and interpretation of randomized controlled trials with statistically nonsignificant results for primary outcomes'. *JAMA: Journal of the American Medical Association*, 303 (20), 2058–64.

Bromham, L., Dinnage, R. and Hua, X. (2016) 'Interdisciplinary research has consistently lower funding success'. *Nature*, 534 (7609), 684–7.

Brown, V.A. (2015) 'Utopian thinking and the collective mind: Beyond transdisciplinarity'. *Futures*, 65, 209–16.

Budgell, B.S. (2009) *Writing a Biomedical Research Paper: A guide to structure and style.* Tokyo: Springer.

Castronovo, R. (2000) 'Within the veil of interdisciplinary knowledge? Jefferson, Du Bois, and the negation of politics'. *New Literary History*, 31 (4), 781–804.

Cousin, G. (2006) 'Threshold concepts, troublesome knowledge and emotional capital: An exploration into learning about others'. In Meyer, J.H.F. and Land, R. (eds) *Overcoming Barriers to Student Understanding: Threshold concepts and troublesome knowledge.* London: Routledge, 134–47.

Davies, J.P. (2011) 'Disciplining the disciplines'. In Dawid, P., Twining, W. and Vasilaki, M. (eds) *Evidence, Inference and Enquiry* (Proceedings of the British Academy 171). Oxford: Oxford University Press, 37–72.

Davies, J. (2016) '"Threshold guardians": Threshold concepts as guardians of the discipline'. In Land, R., Meyer, J.H.F. and Flanagan, M.T. (eds) *Threshold Concepts in Practice*. Rotterdam: Sense Publishers, 121–34.

Douglas, M. and Ney S. (1998) *Missing Persons: A critique of personhood in the social sciences*. Berkeley and Los Angeles: University of California Press.

Frodeman, R. (2014) *Sustainable Knowledge: A theory of interdisciplinarity*. Basingstoke: Palgrave Macmillan.

Jacobs, J.A. (2014) *In Defense of Disciplines: Interdisciplinarity and specialization in the research university*. Chicago: University of Chicago Press.

Jacobs, J.A. and Frickel, S. (2009) 'Interdisciplinarity: A critical assessment'. *Annual Review of Sociology*, 35, 43–65.

Jenkins, K. (1995) *On "What is History?": From Carr and Elton to Rorty and White*. London: Routledge.

Kalitzkus, V. and Matthiessen, P.F. (2009) 'Narrative-based medicine: Potential, pitfalls, and practice'. *The Permanente Journal*, 13 (1), 80–6.

Land, R. (2012) 'Crossing tribal boundaries: Interdisciplinarity as a threshold concept'. In Trowler, P., Saunders, M. and Bamber, V. (eds) *Tribes and Territories in the 21st Century: Rethinking the significance of disciplines in higher education*. Abingdon: Routledge, 175–85.

Launer, J. (2002) *Narrative-based Primary Care: A practical guide*. Oxford: Radcliffe Medical Press.

Lynch, J. (2006) 'It's not easy being interdisciplinary'. *International Journal of Epidemiology*, 35 (5), 1119–22.

Nathan, R. (2006) *My Freshman Year: What a professor learned by becoming a student*. London: Penguin.

Pan, L., Katrenko, S. (2015), *A Review of the UK's Interdisciplinary Research Using a Citation-Based Approach*, Amsterdam: Elsevier.

Peoples, J. and Bailey, G. (2012) *Humanity: An introduction to cultural anthropology*. 9th ed. Belmont, CA: Wadsworth.

Sider, D. (2005) *The Library of the Villa dei Papiri at Herculaneum*. Los Angeles: J. Paul Getty Museum.

Smith, J.Z. (1990) *Drudgery Divine: On the comparison of early Christianities and the religions of Late Antiquity*. Chicago: University of Chicago Press.

Trowler, P., Saunders, M. and Bamber, V. (eds) (2012) *Tribes and Territories in the 21st Century: Rethinking the significance of disciplines in higher education*. Abingdon: Routledge.

Wenger, E. (1998) *Communities of Practice : Learning, meaning, and identity*. Cambridge: Cambridge University Press.

Wilcox, J. (2007) 'Teaching legal drafting effectively and efficiently – by dispensing with the myths'. *Journal of Legal Education*, 57 (3), 448–66.

Woelert, P. and Millar, V. (2013) 'The "paradox of interdisciplinarity" in Australian research governance'. *Higher Education*, 66 (6), 755–67.

Wynne, B. (1992) 'Misunderstood misunderstanding: Social identities and public uptake of science'. *Public Understanding of Science*, 1 (3), 281–304.

Part Two

Case studies

This second part draws eclectically on the themes presented in the position papers of Part One: they are written by staff who do the actual teaching in a range of disciplines. It is impossible to cover the full range here: a university the size of UCL has about 80 different departments, each of which specializes in often quite broad subject areas (such as 'History', an umbrella term for an array of periods and cultures). Instead, we offer these snapshots of academics responding to the various initiatives already outlined and doing the difficult job of anchoring these in the classroom, which, as we will see, is often metaphorical.

Chapter 9

Contextualizing and connecting learning

Kerstin Sailer and Jonathan Kendall[1]

In this case study, two academics from The Bartlett, UCL's global faculty of the built environment, think through how two modules can bring together research and teaching in interdisciplinary education. They use 'real life' as a resource to bring together a whole range of knowledge and activities by having students explore cities and organizational networks. Assessment is particularly tricky in such courses, as is also argued by Jessop and Hughes in Chapter 5; interdisciplinary learning is messy and complicated, as Davies outlines in Chapter 8; and global perspectives must be embedded for such courses to be meaningful, as Kraska, Bourn and Blum highlight in Chapter 6. The authors turn these challenges into a chance for students to learn not just dry, isolated and theoretical ideas, but rather to engage publicly, for instance through blogs. There are many benefits to such education: the students see the city and organizational networks around them in a new light, and tackle realistic skills such as working in groups along the way.

Introduction

Bringing research and teaching closer together means establishing and integrating students into 'academic communities of practice', according to Brew (2012). UCL has conceptualized this closer relationship between research and teaching in the form of the 'Connected Curriculum', a framework for research-based teaching that aims at fostering student learning through research and enquiry (Fung and Cárnell, 2017).

Six different types of connections are highlighted in the framework: 1) students connect with research, 2) students experience a connected sequence of learning activities, 3) students make connections across subjects and out to the world, 4) programmes allow students to connect with wider learning and skills, 5) students connect with external audiences and 6) students connect with each other, across phases and with alumni.

In this chapter we aim to present the teaching practice of two different modules taught at the Bartlett Faculty of the Built Environment, UCL, which particularly address three of the six dimensions of the framework: connections across subjects and out to the world, connections with wider learning, and connections with audiences.

This means the many different ways in which learning can be connected and contextualized will be highlighted and discussed.

Background: Two built environment courses

This chapter draws on the module Making Cities: The Production of the Built Environment, which is offered to first-year undergraduates taking otherwise separate programmes in Architecture, Planning, and Construction and Project Management; and the module Buildings Organisations Networks, which is part of the postgraduate MSc Space Syntax: Architecture and Cities. We will introduce both modules in the following section to give some background on teaching modes, learning outcomes, cohort sizes and assessment.

Making Cities: The Production of the Built Environment

Although recently restructured (by Jonathan Kendall in 2014), Making Cities is one of the most long-standing components of professional built environment education at The Bartlett, UCL. Its origins lie in the leadership of Professor Richard Llewellyn Davies (Bartlett Professor 1960–9) and his desire to facilitate an integrated and cross-disciplinary approach to the training of architects, town planners and other construction professionals. His concern in the 1950s – no less relevant today – was that built environment education has a tendency towards professional specialization, differentiation and introversion, which is at odds with the inevitable and necessary interrelationships through which practice does (or should) operate. The module is unique within the institution: it is the only one taught to all undergraduate students from the schools of Architecture, Planning, and Construction and Project Management – a total of more than 200 students per year. It takes place in the first term of the first year of the degree programmes, a moment in time when those students are nascent professionals in their own discipline, many with only the loosest sense of their own subject, let alone its relationship to others.

It seeks to build an understanding of how each of these disciplines relates to one another and – as importantly – to the idea of the city as a whole. The focus of the module is on the formation of relationships between members of professional teams, how these teams come together to design and deliver projects within the built environment (see also Edwards *et al.*, 2009), and how the accumulation of these projects shapes (and is shaped by) their urban context.

The module exploits London as its primary resource. Students undertake critical and creative research on specific built and emerging projects within the city, which they primarily explore by producing short films, conceived and executed in interdisciplinary groups. A parallel and interlinked programme of lectures and events provides a panorama of perspectives on the process of shaping cities, delivered by a range of speakers from across UCL and those operating in professional practice.

There is a single coursework project to be completed, with two components within it. The project comprises the creation of a four-minute film, and a written and illustrated report regarding the objectives, research, outcomes and process of its creation. The weighting of the marks is 60 per cent film and 40 per cent report. The report is complementary to the film and provides each student an opportunity to submit an individual reflective commentary on the project studied and the lessons learnt in working as part of a group to undertake the research.

Students are organized into ten teaching groups of approximately twenty members, and are supervised in seminars, group discussions and project workshops by a pair of tutors. Student groups, and tutors, are cross-disciplinary in proportion to the numbers of students undertaking the module. Each project is created by a team of approximately four or five students.

Buildings Organisations Networks

The module Buildings Organisations Networks (BON) is led by Kerstin Sailer as part of the MSc Space Syntax: Architecture and Cities (SSAC). The SSAC attracts around 20 postgraduate students, most of whom come from overseas, have a first degree in architecture or planning, and have worked in practice for a few years.

The module focuses on the relationship between architectural morphology, organizations and social networks in complex buildings such as hospitals, schools, offices and laboratories. London-based site visits provide students with an opportunity to reflect on the theoretical arguments presented in the ten-week lecture series and apply them to real-world examples.

Students of the SSAC develop an in-depth theoretical and practical knowledge of the built environment and its functions and acquire a high level of skill in research and analysis. Critical thinking and being able to express this in written form is indeed a crucial skill for all students in evaluating ideas, applying concepts to real-life situations and solving problems. (Marton and Säljö, 1976). For SSAC students this can present an additional challenge since they may not have read intensively in their previous studies and writing is not one of the main skill sets for architects either, yet both are required for a successful completion of this particular course. Students choose the course for a variety of reasons, but a desire to become more reflective and critical architects is frequently mentioned. However, as a deep approach to learning, critical thinking is inherently difficult to teach (ibid.).

In order to address this learning challenge and assist the students in developing their critical expression, an innovative assignment system for the module was devised using short fortnightly writing exercises in a blog format that helps students to test their writing in a trial and error mode, allowing them to learn and progress week by week. The format of the blog also highlights that writing is always meant for an audience. This helps the students to avoid jargon, explain their thoughts in detail, and construct arguments based on evidence (things they've seen, heard or read), since there is an audience that needs convincing.

In detail, the module works as follows:[2] first, in a series of weekly lectures the students are introduced to theories and empirical studies based on original research. Second, in an associated building visit they observe space usage and discuss spatial configuration and behaviours of people in buildings. Third, the students each set up a blog and write an entry (up to 500 words) reflecting on the site visit. Half of the class write in one week and the other half in the following. The students take turns to review the writing of their peers by completing a predesigned form. High-quality blogs from the previous week are praised in class, so that everyone can understand what a successful contribution looks like.[3] As the course progresses, ways for improving are highlighted. Midway through the term the students receive a 15-minute one-to-one tutorial, where they discuss their own writing and address any challenges and possible ways forward. For the final assessment, the students choose their three best contributions, receive comprehensive formative feedback in written form and finally turn their texts into a single 2,000-word 'reflective report', which is marked against the criteria in the assignment.

Contextualizing and connecting learning
Both modules, Making Cities and BON, share the philosophy that learning occurs when students make connections – connections between

academic content and real-life examples, connections between the different stakeholders producing and reproducing the built environment, connections between scholarly thinking and different forms of expression. Thus learning is contextualized and embedded in wider systems in many ways.

In the following section we will show how the contextualization and connection of learning take place in detail by focusing on five different aspects: telling stories, engaging with live projects, using a new medium, team versus individual efforts, and feedback and iterations. We also reflect on student reactions.

Academic discipline: Telling stories and structuring arguments

For Making Cities, the use of film places an opportunity and obligation on students to distil a complex situation (a project in the built environment, its agents and the underlying social, economic and creative forces it encapsulates) and communicate its essence within a time-limited format. In doing this, it is inevitable that decisions need to be made in filtering, getting to the heart of a salient issue and, by implication, eliminating multiple other considerations. Film, as a dynamic visual and acoustic medium, supports the telling of stories: a narrative. Its use within an academic context places a requirement on students to do so not in a whimsical manner but as a device for the communication and structuring of an argument, a considered position that supports a research question.

Likewise, BON requires students to learn how to structure a scholarly argument that is communicated in a way that still remains understandable to wider audiences. The format of a blog does not automatically mean subjective and unprofessional commenting, although some students associate blogs with unsolicited and unserious arguments. Quite the contrary, telling a story of how a building is used and how this relates to its physical layout requires systematic thinking. We therefore train our students in writing in understandable ways, but without losing the scientific foundation of considering literature and taking evidence into account. The shortness of a blog requires students to develop focus and choose a single topic for consideration, filtering the wealth of information available from a building visit.

Telling stories, sifting information and constructing a sound and logical argument is a critically important discipline, both academically and within a future professional context. Both modules address this in slightly different ways.

Engagement with live projects

Making Cities and BON both exploit London as a resource, first in terms of its direct physical manifestation, and second in access to those who live and work within it.

BON chooses a selection of high-profile architecture in London to understand how these buildings afford social life and space usage behaviours, among them the British Library, the British Museum, the offices of the drinks company Innocent, but also leading architectural practices including Rogers Stirk Harbour and Partners, Foster and Partners and Zaha Hadid, Kings Place (a hub for music, art, dialogue and food in London's Kings Cross), the Royal Courts of Justice, the secondary school UCL Academy, University College Hospital, the UCL Cancer Institute and many others. Making Cities also engages with one of the most physically significant projects currently under way in London: the construction of the massive east–west Crossrail infrastructure. The module does not focus on Crossrail as a project itself, though the project's Technical Director has provided lecture input to the students, but uses its route as a conceptual organizing device for the investigations. As a contemporary superimposition on the movement systems of the city, adding another layer to networks that have been incrementally grown since the Victorian age, it will significantly increase both capacity and speed of connectivity within and beyond the boundaries of London. It will lead to potentially dramatic impacts as it strengthens connectivity between diverse areas of the city and helps seed change for the decades ahead. Within the framework of the pan-London project, Crossrail is used to establish a conceptual transect through the city. Each tutor group is focused on a specific area, loosely organized around one of the Crossrail stations currently under construction. The groups receive detailed guidance from their tutors regarding specific locations, projects and additional readings that relate to their area of focus. The projects studied range from individual pieces of architecture and landscape through to large-scale masterplans. The intention is to have a diverse cross-section of projects across the cohort that can stand in some way as a representative distillation of the city as a whole. Most of the projects are contemporary (currently or recently under construction) but others are older and subject to ongoing adaptation, or are planned but have not yet been implemented.

Using a new medium

The pedagogical argument for Making Cities is that in many ways the act of film-making is analogous to the formation of projects within the built environment. It requires a clearly defined set of objectives, multiple participants to undertake specific roles and collaborate with one another in conceiving and undertaking the production, and it requires organizational skills to synthesize complex overlapping requirements.

One of the reasons for choosing the production of a film as the primary output of the module is the increasing prevalence of low-cost and high-quality video recording and editing equipment in mobile phones or lightweight digital cameras. It is assumed that most students taking the module will already be carrying film equipment with them all day every day – a situation inconceivable only a few years ago. Most desktop computers also include basic video editing software for free.

The emphasis of the module is, emphatically, not on the technical craft of film production. The interest and emphasis are on the creative use of the medium to advance a line of academic enquiry. For any students who do not possess their own equipment, or who want more advanced equipment (cameras, audio recording, additional grips, etc.), these can be accessed within The Bartlett. Software and computers for editing digital footage are available in computer clusters and additional technical tutorials are offered for those who want assistance.

Similarly, BON exploits the fact that blogging, i.e. the creation of web content, has become extremely easy. Within less than an hour, a student can set up their own web presence and start producing content. What is part of the learning here is to make connections to the outside world and train students in responsible and professional use of social media platforms, which will become increasingly important in today's social media and technology-driven world. Within the safety of a learning environment, we discuss what it means to post and go public, but also how blogs can be used as part of an online portfolio and web presence after the end of the course to allow students to shape what is available about them online. Privacy concerns are addressed by allowing students to use pseudonyms if they want to. Still here, as well as in Making Cities, advancing a line of academic enquiry is the focus of the module while the use of a new medium adds to the experience and transferable skill sets.

Team versus individual efforts

The act of group working is integral to the Making Cities module. As in professional practice, teams are often brought together by third parties (e.g. a client) and it is the responsibility of the team members to work together to achieve the aims of the project successfully. It is conceptually the most important aspect of the module – more so, perhaps, than the specific professional roles and relationships – and is simultaneously the most challenging. Many of the challenges are pragmatic and logistical, and derive from the difficulties of alignment of the teaching calendar for three different schools; the afternoon in which the main teaching activity takes place is literally the only moment in the week when all three sets of students are unencumbered by other obligations. The module therefore places challenges on the students to manage their time, allocate tasks and share information.

Working as a group also raises issues of leadership and decision-making that can lead to inevitable tensions. Students often struggle to manage interpersonal relationships that relate to leadership, strategy and implementation. This is exacerbated by the formal assessment of group work, where students can be concerned that their efforts in dragging a reluctant group forward are not fairly credited and recognized, or indeed that those who have contributed less share the same outcome as others. Two important interventions are designed to manage these challenges within an academic context. Students are asked to submit a 'group working declaration' alongside their coursework, in which they can agree to share credit equally or draw assessors' attention to their specific individual contributions. The individual reflective commentary submitted alongside the group written report (20 per cent of the final mark) also provides students with an opportunity to discuss their own role within the group and reflect on their experience. It serves as a useful mechanism to allow tutors to differentiate between students in the assessment process, while recognizing that the predominant output should indeed be regarded as a collective product.

By contrast, BON focuses on individual efforts, but by providing an open forum for exchange and asking students to comment on each other's work, the module highlights the fact that all our endeavours are embedded in a wider context of relationships with others.

Feedback and iterations

Within the compressed period of a single term, it is a challenge to undertake wholesale iteration of the coursework produced on Making Cities. Instead, the tutorial process is structured to allow continuous support for the students throughout the module on a weekly basis, guiding the work as it develops, providing strategic feedback at key stages and supporting the evolution of the work through to the final submission early in the second term. The terminology of film-making is exploited in the structuring of the module, and students are expected, by key dates, to produce a 'pitch', discuss a 'storyboard', submit a 'script' and present a 'rough cut' for review. Each of these terms has direct relevance for the development of a research proposal in any other academic context; these requirements could be recast as the synopsis, abstract, outline and drafts of a thesis.

In contrast to Making Cities, the set-up of BON is geared towards an iterative process with a carefully orchestrated system of feedback, both from peers and from the module leader. Keeping the task for each week deliberately small and relatively easy (500 words, with at least one image and at least one reference), the blog aims to take the fear out of writing. The message to the students is that it does not matter if their first attempt is not perfect, since there will be many more opportunities for trying again and excelling the next time. Indeed, seeing students improve their writing week by week is a rewarding teaching and learning experience, both for students and tutors. Peer review is part of the feedback system. It contributes to the continuous learning experience by encouraging students to analyse in detail what their peers have written. Thus they collect ideas for their own writing, understand how others construct arguments and begin to grasp what a good academically grounded text looks like. Despite well-known drawbacks such as reliability of peer assessors and the negativity around receiving peer feedback (Lundstrom and Baker, 2009; McConlogue, 2015), peer review seemed to work well in the context of the small cohort of BON (see similar results in Carnell, 2016). A short survey with BON students in 2015 confirmed the overall usefulness of the method (rated as 5.78 on a seven-point scale). The highest agreement was obtained for the statements 'I felt encouraged to do better next time' (6.04) and 'I believe this process helps me in achieving a better mark' (6.17), while the most critical issues were considered consistency of feedback across reviewers (4.74) and feeling comfortable writing reviews for peers (4.83). Asked what they liked best about the peer review, students commented that it 'challenges your reading skills and makes you reflect a lot on the writing. It is also a joint learning process'; it was highlighted that 'noticing others' mistakes and not to repeat it in your own writing' is positive. Among the negative aspects were 'it feels bad to judge', 'some of the reviews from fellow students do not make sense' and 'can't debate with them'.

Student reactions

Drilling further into student reactions, it can be concluded that views vary for Making Cities. The cohort is large in number and varied by many characteristics, most particularly their disciplines, nationalities and educational backgrounds. They are new to their subjects, and are taking the module at a moment when they may be living in a new city or country or communicating primarily in English for the first time in their lives. Many are coping with a pedagogical context utterly different to their previous experience, and Making Cities – inevitably, and somewhat unapologetically – confronts them with a challenging combination of issues to address, both academically and socially. Some find it hard and struggle to understand what they are doing or why it is relevant; others relish the module.

On the whole, student reactions to BON are overwhelmingly positive. The students enjoy visiting buildings and exploring London, rather than being stuck in a classroom. Many comment that this has formed the most impressive part of their whole programme. A structured survey in 2013 on the usefulness of different teaching elements revealed that students most valued oral feedback in a one-to-one situation (rated as 4.55 on a 1–5 scale), but also written feedback (4.55). Seeing examples of phenomena on site visits and discussions on site visits were seen as very useful too (4.45 each). However, the students also valued 'writing blogs' highly (4.27). Asked about the single best thing about the module, students commented: 'The weekly blogging exercise. It forces you to quickly assimilate the knowledge and apply it'; 'The site visits and ... especially listening to what the other students thought of the sites, and how they could connect it both to past practice as architects or planners, but also their way of seeing the connection between theory and the site we visited'; 'The personal tutorial on my blog writing ... especially the written feedback on my selected three blog posts'; and 'Learning to write blogs and to talk about buildings'.

Conclusions

We have presented insights from the teaching practice of two case studies, both taught at UCL's Bartlett. We have focused on the many different ways in which learning is contextualized and connected. In particular, both modules – Making Cities as well as Building Organisations Networks – realize a high degree of embedding learning into the built environment of London, taking teaching and learning outside the context of the classroom and treating the rich architecture of London as a laboratory. Despite their differences, one being offered to a large and interdisciplinary group of undergraduate students, the other a specialized offer for a small cohort of MSc students, the modules share a common understanding of encouraging students to use new media to connect to audiences, to explore issues themselves and to build relationships among each other through group work or peer assessment.

Future work on pushing the boundaries of research-based teaching and making connections might investigate further whether and how the multiple levels of connections students make always have a positive impact on the learning experience, how having gone through the process of learning something differently in one module has an impact on their future careers as learners, and how the insights and lessons learnt here can be shared among other practitioners also outside the built environment context.

Notes

[1] Addresses for correspondence: k.sailer@ucl.ac.uk; j.kendall@ucl.ac.uk

[2] The described set-up was used in the academic year 2016/17. As an experimental approach, small changes are introduced every year to improve the learning experience.

[3] Success is measured against the criteria in the assignment, which are: 1) Choice of topic (original, relevant, clear); 2) Logic and coherence of the argument; 3) Evidence (supporting arguments); 4) Quality of writing (thoughtful, balanced, detailed, key concepts understood); 5) Presentation and language (graphics, written English, expression). An example of a blog from a previous student (which is also shared with incoming students) can be seen at https://buildingsthesocialnetwork.wordpress.com (accessed 19 March 2018).

References

Brew, A. (2012) 'Teaching and research: New relationships and their implications for inquiry-based teaching and learning in higher education'. *Higher Education Research and Development*, 31 (1), 101–14.

Carnell, B. (2016) 'Aiming for autonomy: Formative peer assessment in a final-year undergraduate course'. *Assessment and Evaluation in Higher Education*, 41 (8), 1269–83.

Edwards, M., Campkin, B. and Arbaci, S. (2009) 'Exploring roles and relationships in the production of the built environment'. *CEBE Transactions*, 6 (1), 38–61.

Fung, D. and Carnell, B. (2017) *UCL Connected Curriculum: Enhancing programmes of study*. 2nd ed. Online. www.ucl.ac.uk/teaching-learning/sites/teaching-learning/files/connected_curriculum_brochure_oct_2017.pdf (accessed 1 April 2018).

Lundstrom, K. and Baker, W. (2009) 'To give is better than to receive: The benefits of peer review to the reviewer's own writing'. *Journal of Second Language Writing*, 18 (1), 30–43.

Marton, F. and Säljö, R. (1976) 'On qualitative differences in learning: I – Outcome and process'. *British Journal of Educational Psychology*, 46 (1), 4–11.

McConlogue, T. (2015) 'Making judgements: Investigating the process of composing and receiving peer feedback'. *Studies in Higher Education*, 40 (9), 1495–506.

Chapter 10

Scenario-based learning

Matthew Seren Smith, Sarah Warnes and Anne Vanhoestenberghe[1]

Continuing the theme of using the real world as a teaching resource, Smith, Warnes and van Hoestenberghe describe learning scenarios where students find their own way and make their own choices in exploring an authentic situation. The intended learning outcomes are explained to the students to guide them to what is relevant, but these are thoroughly embedded in the tasks set: they do not have to make a special effort to work out what is being assessed. Again, assessment requires careful thought, which makes having student input to the design all the more relevant; this allows the teaching staff to actively guide students through their learning rather than merely acting as dispensers of knowledge: just as the Connected Curriculum strategy invites, students find things out for themselves.

What is scenario-based learning?

Scenario-based learning (SBL) is the use of scenarios as a vehicle for the teaching and learning process, providing students with the opportunity to learn from and apply their learning to realistic experiences. Such scenarios may be a particular set of circumstances, a critical incident, or a narrative (Errington, 2005). Errington (2005) further suggests that they often feature common elements, including role-play, problem-solving, a demonstration of taught skills, the exploration of an issue(s), and the contemplation of outcomes. Scenarios can therefore range from simple sets of circumstances and conditions, to detailed sequences of events that take into account plots, roles and team relationships, which students may navigate via multiple pathways and which therefore have a multitude of possible outcomes.

Scenarios, as Errington (2005: 10) succinctly notes, 'provide an ideal platform for students to experience deep level learning tasks, and attain higher order cognitive skills (decision-making and critical analysis)'. This we fully agree with and have found to be the case in the two scenarios outlined in this paper.

Elements of scenarios

Through our experience of working with scenarios on two different undergraduate modules, Understanding Management and Bone Modelling, we have identified the following five key aspects that we consider are characteristic of scenario-based learning: challenge, narrative, choice, roles and role-play, and authenticity. These will now be discussed in turn.

Challenge

Challenge is inherent in all learning scenarios, be it medical students diagnosing a patient's symptoms, marketing students launching a new product, or archaeology students curating an exhibition.

In Understanding Management, the challenge was presented to students via a written statement on the virtual learning environment (VLE). This described the proposed merger of Burger King and the Canadian-based doughnut chain Tim Hortons and was coupled with an authentic video news clip to add intrigue and engage the students in the scenario. The challenge was simple: through group presentations and individual business reports, the students would present recommendations to company board members as to how the merger should go ahead.

A similar approach was taken on Bone Modelling, where a statement was again displayed on the course page of the VLE, and also emailed direct to students. The statement informed students that they would be modelling bones to estimate their mechanical properties. Additional information was provided in the form of recommended readings, setting the context and demonstrating the potential of the methods. This acted as a way of engaging the students early on in the task.

As can be seen from both of these examples, there is a clear purpose presented to the student in a way that intends to inspire interest and encourage a solution-focused approach. As such, we consider that challenges have the greatest impact when they are communicated clearly to students at the beginning of the scenario, with the most effective challenges simultaneously introducing the learning and setting overall objectives, as well as hooking the student in – igniting their imagination and desire to complete it. The aim is that students will be intrinsically motivated to engage with the scenario and therefore the learning, that they will find the activity rewarding in and of itself rather than being motivated by extrinsic rewards such as receiving a high grade, or obtaining course credits (Nakamura and Csikszentmihalyi, 2002).

Narrative

Another method of hooking students into a scenario is the use of a narrative. In the Bone Modelling scenario, its realistic nature comes from the laboratory environment, and a constructed narrative is not necessary. The short and uninterrupted nature of the scenario means that less intervention is needed to maintain motivation.

By contrast, on Understanding Management the narrative provides an important thread, presenting students with a timeline of the events, such as the merger of the companies and the presentation to the board. As the scenario evolves, there are opportunities to develop the plot in response to levels of student engagement, adding unexpected issues to change its course. The narrative provides a way of introducing conflict to our students, while maintaining a measure of intrigue and surprise. This naturally requires students to think effectively on their feet, thus replicating the pressures found in the workplace (Errington, 2008).

Choice

Choice is fundamental to the learning experience of scenarios. It encourages learner autonomy and critical thinking, allowing students to reach a deeper level of learning as they evaluate the options and analyse the implications of their decisions.

A learner-centred approach allows students to align their personal goals, values and interests with the learning (Ryan, 1993; Ryan and Deci, 2000) and is a key aspect of both modules. On Bone Modelling, students are required on the first day to define a strategy to demonstrate at the end of the week that they have understood the core concepts and met the intended learning objectives. The activity is presented to students as their taking ownership of their education and offering an opportunity to reflect on their strengths and weaknesses in the acquisition of engineering knowledge. A similar activity is applied on Understanding Management, where students are required to identify their expectations for the course and motivations for completing it in the first lecture. The aim of this is to create 'buy in', setting a clear precedent that students are free to approach and engage with the scenario in a way that is valuable to them.

On a more granular level, choice activities are formally built into the timeline of our two scenarios. This is where students are presented with a limited set of predefined options, typical of compromises required in a real situation. First, on Bone Modelling, students are given four academic papers to read two weeks before the scenario begins. From these they must choose one on which their individual assessment will be based. This funnelling approach allows students to narrow their focus to an area in which they are interested while ensuring a concrete grounding for the learning. There is a similarly important decision for students to make on Understanding Management. In Week 2, students are required to select their team management role, which they will adopt for the length of the scenario. Before doing so, however, they are instructed to read overviews of each management role and watch interviews with role professionals. Again, this provides them with a base knowledge of each area before allowing them to specialize. We will explore the undertaking of these roles in the following section.

Roles and role-play

Through our experiences of developing scenarios, we identified two types of roles that students undertake in scenario-based learning. The first are function-based roles in which a student 'plays' a fictional role, e.g. health officer, forensic scientist. The second are intrinsic roles (or natural roles), which people take within a group, for example a leader or a scribe. These are akin to the functional roles and team roles, respectively, proposed by Belbin (Belbin, 2010). Both types will now be explored.

As was mentioned in the 'Choice' section, students of Understanding Management are required early on in the scenario to select function-based management roles that they will adopt for the duration of the merger. These roles reflect the types of roles that exist within the organizational structures of companies, for example marketing manager. This enriches and extends the learning experience in three key ways. First, it places students within the narrative, encouraging them to immerse themselves in the detail of the scenario further and in turn achieve a deeper connection with the learning. Second, it provides an anchor for students, or vantage point, from which they can explore the issues at hand. It is hoped students begin to specialize and form a professional identity, taking on responsibility and considering the specificities of their role when interacting within their team. This encourages them to value a collaborative approach, where the team is greater than the sum of its parts. Working in this way requires them to view issues from varying perspectives, developing skills such as negotiation, communication and consensus building. Third and finally, to a greater or lesser extent role-play imparts to the student what it may be like to work within the profession, introducing the culture, attitudes and language of the sector.

By contrast, in the Bone Modelling scenario students are not explicitly assigned function-based roles and instead the focus is on the intrinsic roles that they adopt. At three points during the scenario (once before, during and after the task) the students reflect and discuss their strengths and weaknesses with their team. They reflect on the role they expected to undertake within the team, how this was influenced by the rest of the team, and so become aware of the team interplay as typical of a real situation. As teamwork is part of the formal teaching material, this experience shows students the value of their learning, and how it is relevant to their future profession from the first year of their study.

Authenticity

One of our key aims in designing the scenarios was to ensure that both the scenarios and the work undertaken were authentic. We consider that for the experience of learning from, and for, real situations to be positive, a certain level of authenticity must be achieved. According to Errington (2011: 87), 'scenarios must not only be authentic in replicating aspects of the professional setting, but also be robust and relevant'; if not, there is a greater risk that students will become bored and disengaged.

Stewart (2003) considers that scenarios are 'essential slices of reality' and therefore demand authenticity. This is observed on the Understanding Management scenario, where the students' interest increased as the scenario became more authentic. This increased authenticity was achieved by simple additions, such as offering students their own business cards and branded lanyards, as well as integrating news clips and articles. In the Bone Modelling scenario, the authenticity is provided by the environment (a biomedical lab) and the real-world methods, tools and technologies used by the students. This was crucial in this scenario, which aimed to develop the students' professional skills.

Context

This chapter is built on our experience of teaching for, and from, real situations. Here we introduce the two courses in which we implemented scenario-based learning, and our reasons for adopting this teaching method.

Course 1: Understanding Management

Understanding Management, run by UCL's School of Management, is an undergraduate elective module with classes scheduled over a ten-week term. Student numbers during the academic session 2014/15 were roughly 80 in Term 1 and 150 in Term 2. A scenario-based approach was introduced as an effective way of linking the class activities (3 hours of lectures and e-seminars each week) with those taking place out of class (expected to be 15 hours each week). It also gave students the opportunity to apply the management theories covered in an authentic context, which we hoped would lead to higher levels of student engagement and sustained motivation over the ten weeks. The assessment was divided between a group presentation (30 per cent) and an individual business report (70 per cent).

UNDERSTANDING MANAGEMENT SCENARIO

This module introduces you to the practice of management, providing you with a real insight into the role of the manager in today's dynamic and exciting business environment. As such, a range of management tools and roles are explored from both a practical and theoretical perspective, including strategic thinking, analysing the business environment, marketing, and motivating the self and others.

The primary learning objectives are as follows:

- Critically approach problems and issues that surround management practice
- Explain and evaluate the main environmental, strategic and operating concerns facing organizations and managers
- Produce, justify, and support arguments in favour of, or against management approaches
- Apply a range of methods and analytical approaches to specific cases

Course 2: Biomedical Engineering

A new programme in Biomedical Engineering started in the academic year 2014/15, as part of the Integrated Engineering Programme run by UCL's Faculty of Engineering. The programme includes six scenarios, each a week long, during which all taught courses are interrupted, so the students can dedicate all of their time, or about 7.5 hours a day, to the scenario. In this chapter we present the scenario that took place at the end of the second term of academic year 2014/15, with 12 first-year Biomedical Engineering students. The aim of integrating a scenario was to demonstrate to students that, after less than one year, they had already acquired knowledge and skills relevant to real situations. By applying these in an authentic environment (the bulk of the work took place in a lab, using real engineering equipment), they would consolidate the knowledge learnt from technical modules while developing transferable soft skills such as teamwork and communication. The students were asked to produce a virtual and a physical model of a section of a bone, and test its mechanical properties, hence this scenario was called the 'Bone Modelling' scenario. They were assessed on theoretical and practical knowledge as well as on collaboration and communications skills. This was done through a group presentation, a personal five-minute pitch with questions and answers, and a brief reflective piece.

> BONE MODELLING SCENARIO
> Successful engineers need to be able to identify and analyse problems, conceive and design potential solutions, liaise with and present to clients, and work with and direct colleagues. They need to do these things efficiently, ethically, professionally, and competently. Our goal is to give you the tools you need to be effective from the start of your career. This will not only help you to work as a competent professional when you graduate, but also help you to achieve more while you are doing your degree.
>
> The primary learning objectives are as follows:
>
> - Demonstrate a general understanding of biomechanics and physiology
> - Understand and apply technical skills such as mechanical concepts, technical drawing and finite element modelling
> - Demonstrate critical thinking, hypothesis testing, iterative evaluation and assessment
> - Develop professional skills such as collaboration, delegation, communication of ideas, planning (and contingency planning), evaluation and decision making, creativity

Although the motivation for employing a scenario on the two courses was distinctly different, we will explore the similarities and differences in the techniques used and their effect.

Practical aspects of developing and delivering a scenario

Learning design
Although there are many similarities in the design and delivery of the two courses, the motivation for employing a scenario and the effect this has on student learning differs.

On Bone Modelling, the primary learning objective is for students to develop professional workplace skills. As this is the focus, the course content (bone modelling) is familiar and should not require much effort to understand. This frees up the student's working memory, allowing them to engage fully with the scenario. Here the content is a vehicle for the scenario. In contrast, on Understanding Management, the primary learning objective is for students to gain a strong foundation in core management theories. Here the scenario quickly becomes familiar, acting as a lens through which students can understand and manipulate the content. The scenario in this case is a vehicle for the content.

In addition, we observed secondary effects on each course. In the bone modelling scenario, although the content is familiar, there is a consolidation of core knowledge. In the management scenario, the secondary effect is the development of professional skills and good practice.

On both courses, we considered the design and progression of the learning, with emphasis on the journey undertaken by students. As the courses progressed we ensured that students were exposed to increasingly demanding activities, requiring them to achieve a deeper level of understanding. The figures below, created with Learning Designer,[2] give a snapshot of Understanding Management at the beginning and towards the end. As can be seen, the time dedicated to higher-order learning activities such as Practice and Produce is greater in the latter stages of the course.

Finally, we found that student input was, and is, vital to the design process. For both scenarios, a student was consulted to evaluate the design, test the scenario and propose changes. Moreover, we collected students' feedback via a scenario-specific questionnaire and ensured that we were available for live and continual feedback throughout the course. On Bone Modelling this was semi-formalized, with students encouraged to meet with the scenario lead to discuss any issues encountered.

Figure 10.1: Understanding Management Week 1: breakdown of learning activities

Figure 10.2: Understanding Management Week 7: breakdown of learning activities

Delivery

As noted at the opening of this chapter, the delivery and duration differed between the two scenarios. The Bone Modelling scenario took place over one week, during which all other teaching activities were suspended. As the work is practical, and relies on previously acquired knowledge, aside from the occasional instruction, none of the course material is delivered online. For Understanding Management, the scenario provided the thread that linked together each week of the ten-week module, with almost all of the non-assessed portions of the scenario taking place online and outside scheduled class time.

Despite these differences, one characteristic common to both courses is the nature of the lecturer's involvement. In both cases, students are encouraged to work independently within the scenario, largely without an academic present. This allows students to practise application freely, learning experientially and constructing their own solutions.

A further similarity is the timing of taught material and student application. On Understanding Management, the content covered is aligned with the development of the scenario and there is a short time between concepts being learnt and their application by students. For example, in Week 6, when the lecture focuses on leadership, teamwork and motivation, students are put into cross-company teams and are required to apply the theories they have just encountered. Equally on Bone Modelling, although the content is not new to students, the theoretical knowledge surrounding the design process and technical practices relating to its analysis are new, and again taught in conjunction with their application.

Assessment and group work

When designing a course around a scenario it is essential that assessment is planned within the context of the scenario, that it is authentic and reflective of the practices found in the professional setting that it intends to imitate (Errington, 2011).

We consider that both courses achieve this in comparable ways. Students of Bone Modelling are required to present the result of their tests to a panel of experts. Presenting research to a panel in this way is reflective of professional practice within the field and therefore authentic. In addition to this, students must present individually, discussing a paper of their choice in the light of what they have learnt during the scenario, as well as completing a written portfolio in which they must reflect on the learning process, demonstrating acquisition of the stated learning objectives. Again, these types of assessment are authentic and akin to the types of appraisals found in industry.

On Understanding Management, students are similarly required to present their findings and recommendations in a way reflective of the industry – to their fellow students, the 'shareholders'; and their tutors, the 'board'. In order to further the authentic nature of the presentation, the students/ shareholders then vote on whether they approve the recommendations, with those groups achieving over 50 per cent of the vote being given the 'backing of the board'. Finally, students must complete an individual business report outlining their recommendations for the merger, using the concepts they have been taught in class and in the light of what they have learnt during the scenario. Again, this aims to mimic the type of reports written by managers in the corporate world.

Student feedback

Students on both courses were positive about the scenario-based approach. Compared with the 2013/14 delivery of Understanding Management, the introduction of SBL contributed to a measured increase in attendance, grades and student satisfaction, as can be seen in Table 10.1 which compares the Term 2 deliveries of the module in each year.

Table 10.1: Student feedback on Term 2 deliveries of Understanding Management

	2013/14 Term 2 (%) Response rate: 66.67%	2014/15 Term 2 (%) Response rate: 88.59%
Average attendance	73.58 (±6.35)	80.00 (±7.58)
Average grades	61.24 (±7.38)	66.28 (±8.26)
Student satisfaction		
Course overall	75.93 (±16.58)	80.90 (±15.21)
Lecturer overall	84.44 (±16.25)	88.12 (±13.97)

On Understanding Management, students appreciated the real and timely nature of the narrative: 'Structuring the course around a real and relevant case study was the best part of this course'; 'Focusing on this real merger made the course current and relevant'. Equally, students of Bone Modelling appreciated the contextual application: 'I often find that I don't fully understand or appreciate the significance of a subject until I have fully practised it myself outside the classroom'; 'There is no way you can fully understand a scientific subject until you have fully engaged with it by predicting and hypothesizing, changing parameters, testing and adapting, and learning from doing.'

On both courses, they were positive about group work. On Understanding Management, 'The best part for me is the group work. We finally got a chance to apply what we learn to a real case and I love the cooperating process!' and on Bone Modelling, 'I enjoyed the teamwork aspect of this week. It is important to divide up tasks between a team, trust each other's work, and then collate all the information usefully at the end of the process.'

Presentations as an assessment method were equally well received. On Understanding Management, students commented that they 'simulated a real professional experience', and 'allowed a communal platform to share ideas'. On Bone Modelling, 'teaching others let me understand someone else's perspective and also showed me that there are sometimes gaps in my path of thinking', and 'presenting my work to others also made me more conscious of what I tried to achieve and let me go back again to what I had done previously and therefore made me understand my own work better'.

Reflections

Despite the differences between the two scenarios, several of the issues encountered were similar. Although the collaborative aspects were received positively by students, this also led to confusion, with students unsure of how to function as a team. To address this, changes have been made on both courses. On Understanding Management, students are provided with a more clearly defined timeline of events to focus their efforts, and details on the formation and merging of groups. For example, students are given in Week 1 of the course a timeline of key dates, stating when initial company teams will form and when management role selection will take place. They are informed that in Week 4 of the course the 'merger' will take place and this will be accompanied by an important 'negotiation meeting'. In this meeting larger student teams are formed, comprising one team from each of the two companies (Burger King and Tim Hortons). On Bone Modelling, more obvious links will be drawn to other modules undertaken by the students in communication and project management, as well as more specific guidance on group work.

Another common issue is that students viewed the presentations more as assessments rather than learning experiences *per se*. This led to a lack of interest from the other teams on Understanding Management. Hence, presentation evaluation sheets have been introduced for students to fill out when not presenting and teams have been paired up, with one acting as the 'board' for the other and being required to ask questions. On Bone Modelling, the assessment has been revised. The group presentations will be formative, and with the introduction of peer assessment, provide an occasion for reflective learning. The personal pitch will be summative, after the students have received feedback from the group presentations.

Additionally, other improvements will be made based on observations by the teachers and student feedback. On Bone Modelling, the work of Cowan (2006), Kolb (2014) and others on reflective learning will be further explored to help students learn more from the presentations and reflective portfolio. For Understanding Management, the use of technology, especially 'flipped classroom' pedagogies, will be incorporated in the module.

Conclusion

Students increasingly want to know that the theories and concepts they are being taught have real-world applications, especially in fields such as management and engineering, where career aspirations are often in direct alignment with the course of study. Scenarios are an effective way of doing this. By creating an environment centred around practice and application, they give purpose to the learning, bridge the gap between theory and application, and improve professional skills.

In our experience, scenarios are effective when teaching professional skills as well as knowledge. They can be successfully augmented using technology, though this is not essential, and they are expedient when run as a single session or a continuous element interspersed with core learning.

Notes
[1] Addresses for correspondence: m.s.smith@ucl.ac.uk; s.warnes@ucl.ac.uk; a.vanhoest@ucl.ac.uk
[2] Learning Designer is a tool developed by the UCL Knowledge Lab to map the breakdown of learning activities by the time spent on them.

References

Belbin, R.M. (2010) *Team Roles at Work*. 2nd ed. Oxford: Butterworth-Heinemann.

Cowan, John (2006) *On Becoming an Innovative University Teacher: Reflection in action*. 2nd ed. Maidenhead: Open University Press and McGraw-Hill Education.

Errington, E. (2005) *Creating Learning Scenarios: A planning guide for adult educators*. Palmerston North, NZ: CoolBooks.

Errington, E.P. (2008) 'Exploring real-world scenarios as vehicles for authentic learning'. *International Journal of Interdisciplinary Social Sciences*, 3, 1–5.

Errington, E.P. (2011) 'Mission possible: Using near-world scenarios to prepare graduates for the professions'. *International Journal of Teaching and Learning in Higher Education*, 23 (1), 84–91.

Kolb, D.A. (2014) *Experiential Learning: Experience as the source of learning and development*. 2nd ed. Upper Saddle River, NJ: Pearson Education.

Nakamura, J. and Csikszentmihalyi, M. (2002) 'The concept of flow'. In Snyder, C.R. and Lopez, S.J. (eds) *Handbook of Positive Psychology*. New York: Oxford University Press, 89–105.

Ryan, R.M. (1993) 'Agency and organization: Intrinsic motivation, autonomy, and the self in psychological development'. In Jacobs, J.E. (ed.) *Developmental Perspectives on Motivation: Nebraska Symposium on Motivation 1992*. Lincoln: University of Nebraska Press, 1–56.

Ryan, R.M. and Deci, E.L. (2000) 'Self-determination theory and the facilitation of intrinsic motivation, social development, and well-being'. *American Psychologist*, 55 (1), 68–78.

Stewart, T.M. (2003) 'Essential slices of reality: Constructing problem-based scenarios that work'. In Errington, E.P. (ed.) *Developing Scenario-Based Learning: Practical insights for tertiary educators*. Palmerston North, NZ: Dunmore Press, 83–91.

Chapter 11

Object-based learning and research-based education: Case studies from the UCL curricula

Thomas Kador, Leonie Hannan, Julianne Nyhan, Melissa Terras, Helen J. Chatterjee and Mark Carnall[1]

The general broadening in recent years of what counts as legitimate learning has included an interest in objects, including those from curated collections such as artefacts, natural history specimens and archival items, which may have complex cultural or scientific meaning in their own right. A more sophisticated interaction with objects has been a particular focus for some time and meshes well with newer initiatives and strategies. Indeed, it was a forerunner of bringing research-based education into university curricula. These case studies describe how students could be part of genuine research projects while drawing on traditionally neglected aspects of learning such as touch and direct experience. It is no artificial exercise: Kador and his colleagues record that students have at times corrected mistakes in cataloguing, as well as reconsidering the ethics of objects often taken without permission as colonial curiosities. Francis Galton and his colleague Flinders Petrie must be reckoned with again, given the provenance of many of the objects available to UCL students on site. They are also concerned with the opposite direction: creating virtual versions of objects gives students the chance not just to learn, but to 'produce', by creating exhibitions.

Overview

This chapter explores the strong relationship that exists between object-based learning and research-based education. Object-based learning as applied here prioritizes interaction with museum objects to enhance critical thinking and key skills in university learners. Research-based education is focused on the students themselves engaging in the process and practice of primary research, rather than teachers imparting their research through their teaching. Our four case studies taken from current teaching at UCL demonstrate how object-based learning using museum objects can be used effectively within research-based curricula. In this context this chapter responds to UCL's Connected Curriculum initiative, which will see a gear-change in teaching and learning at the university – one that prioritizes holistic degree programmes with research practice and teacher–student collaboration at their core.

Introduction

How can cultural resources be utilized to design a research-based education? To answer this question our chapter presents a number of case studies that illustrate the use of museum objects in engendering student research through the practice of object-based learning. As an educational institution, UCL is very fortunate to have ready access to a substantial number of specimens and artefacts from 18 large teaching collections. This includes four public museums: the UCL Art Museum, the Petrie Museum of Egyptian Archaeology, the Pathology Museum and the Grant Museum of Zoology, as well as a further 14 departmental and subject-specific collections of objects, ranging from anatomy to space exploration and totalling approximately 800,000 objects. Students and teachers at UCL are particularly privileged to have access to such a diverse collection. However, most other universities – even if they do not have a university museum of their own – are usually located in proximity to museums or galleries with which they could forge collaborative partnerships. Such partnerships would provide their students with access to collections for object-based educational programmes similar to those discussed here.

Before presenting the case studies we will briefly outline what object-based approaches to learning entail and what the pedagogical benefits of using cultural resources for a research-based education are. Put simply, object-based learning is a pedagogy that prioritizes facilitated interaction with 'material culture' to enhance critical thinking and key skills. Material culture is a very broad term that includes everyday objects, documents, works of art, biological specimens and artefacts, to name but a few (Buchli, 2002). However, in the context of this discussion we are particularly interested in exploring the merits of utilizing objects and specimens from museums' collections in university teaching.

What do collections of museum objects bring to research-based teaching in higher education?

There is a long-standing historical relationship between (higher) education and object handling. Collecting, touching and engaging with physical objects – from artworks and historical artefacts to natural history reference collections – used to be the mainstay of many academic disciplines. This has led to the creation of teaching collections and as they became larger, many of them gave rise to university museums. For example, the oldest university museum in Britain, and probably one of the oldest in the world, is the Ashmolean Museum in Oxford, which dates back to the gift in 1683 of Elias Ashmole's collection, which in turn largely comprised John Tradescant's collection of curiosities and rarities (MacGregor, 2001). There are even some examples of universities that began as museums, such as the University of Bergen in Norway (Lourenço, 2005: 375; Roselaar, 2003: 257). The museums at UCL were established with the founding of the university in 1826, and incorporated Robert Edmond Grant's teaching collection of zoological specimens, growing in 1847 with the donation of a large collection of John Flaxman's sculptures (Chambers, 2008). Similarly, universities in numerous other European cities established museums between the seventeenth and nineteenth centuries, and many such university museums still remain across Europe. However, the use of their collections in day-to-day teaching and their custodial care appears to have declined steadily throughout the (second half of the) twentieth century. A concern with this decline lead to the formation of the University Museums Group in the UK in 1987 (Arnold-Forster, 2000). In the light of mounting evidence for the benefits of object-based learning, this neglect is beginning to reverse, and we can observe a resurgence in the integration of university museums and their collections into mainstream teaching (e.g. Alvord and Friedlaender, 2012; Bartlett *et al.*, 2014; Chatterjee, 2008; Chatterjee *et al.*, 2015). For instance, in 2013, more than 700 university courses were taught in the United Kingdom using university museum collections (Hide *et al.*, 2013).

The value of objects in learning

Objects can be viewed from many different perspectives to reveal multiple, and sometimes contested, meanings. Engagement may start with object-focused questions such as 'What is it? What is it made of? How was it made? Where is it from? When was it made? How was it used?' Answers to these questions open up further research areas about how objects connect people and places, hold multiple meanings, express knowledge and cultural values. In this way objects and collections lend themselves extremely well to active learning (Bonwell and Eison, 1991), as object-focused tasks allow learners to engage with the history, contexts, relationships and even the social life of the object, on an ever more complex level. Students can discover these new avenues of investigation for themselves: as they respond to the prompts the object raises for them personally, they can begin to make their own meaning and are thus much more likely to recall their discoveries subsequently (Kolb, 1984).

In contrast to traditional teaching styles that tend to foreground the verbal and visual, object handling provides opportunities to engage through touch (Chatterjee, 2008). The case studies presented in this chapter, taken from the UCL curricula, provide some good illustrations of this process in action. For example, in both Object Lessons and the Mystery Specimen exercise (discussed below), students are tasked to engage closely with one specific museum object for the duration of an entire term. This offers the students the opportunity to approach the object and make sense of it for themselves from multiple perspectives and choose to apply the approach that works best both for them personally and for the particular object they are working with.

Object-based learning also lends itself extremely well to social learning, as discussed by Vygotsky (1978), and is therefore well suited for students with particular strengths in interpersonal intelligence. Staying with Object Lessons, the second part of this module focuses on a team exercise in which the students, in small groups, have to bring together their individual objects in order to find a common denominator that will provide the theme for a virtual exhibition that they are tasked to design. To do this they must sharpen not only their observational and investigative skills for engaging with the objects, but also their interpersonal, communication, decision-making, delegation and team working abilities.

Directly engaging with objects is a very practical and physical experience. This allows students to relate theoretical concepts to something applied and tangible. For example, looking closely at a number of zoological specimens can make plain seemingly complex taxonomical relationships between different species. Objects demand that learners master these 'threshold concepts' before they can move on and engage with a topic on a higher level (Meyer and Land, 2003, 2005). However, as students are so focused on the object(s) and the task in hand, mastery of difficult concepts can frequently take place almost unnoticed, as part of the broader investigative process. So while students work on achieving an understanding of an object, the learning of the concepts associated with this task does not seem arduous, which is, as we argue here, an attractive model for learning.

In addition to the ever-growing body of literature highlighting the educational benefits of learning through objects (see, for example, contributions in Chatterjee and Hannan, 2015), at a wider and more holistic level there is also an increasing amount of evidence for the broader health and well-being benefits of engaging with objects, especially through touch (Chatterjee and Noble, 2013). Therefore, learning with objects will not only help students in grasping difficult concepts, but could also bring further positive outcomes by providing a more enjoyable learning experience.

The first step in designing object-based learning activities is to identify the right objects for the task and this generally means collaborating with a museum or the curator of a teaching collection. As already discussed, students and teachers at UCL are in an extremely fortunate position in this regard and it is very straightforward for UCL academics interested in utilizing object-based learning in their teaching to get started. What is more, the department responsible for the museums and collections at the university, UCL Culture, has a team of curatorial, conservation, education and public engagement specialists specifically employed to enhance the learning opportunities that these collections present. Therefore, the key mission at UCL Culture is not only to use the collections to drive our own teaching and research programmes, but also to facilitate our colleagues from across UCL (and beyond) to work with these collections in developing innovative teaching and learning programmes appropriate to their own students and academic disciplines. This is well illustrated by the case studies presented here from the Digital Humanities, the BASc Arts and Sciences degree programme and the Biological Sciences. They demonstrate how museum objects can be used to facilitate both disciplinary and interdisciplinary learning and, crucially, most of this learning takes place through student-led investigation in response to the objects. This is precisely the learning achievement associated with our first case study.

Case study 1: Mystery specimens for bioscience students

UCL's Grant Museum of Zoology is an example of a museum collection that was necessarily repurposed to address a number of emerging needs. To begin with, traditional specimen-based teaching has been replaced by broader theoretical learning. There has also been a drive to train students with transferable skills, while the explosion of biological science disciplines (genetics, ecology and modelling) has put pressure on traditional bioscience course content. Across universities, zoology departments became subsumed into biology departments, at first still offering zoology degree programmes but later only zoology modules within biology or biological science programmes. This led some to question whether biology graduates could define the difference between snakes and earthworms (Bowler, 2007). The Mystery Specimen project, developed with staff from the Grant Museum of Zoology and teaching staff from the Department of Genetics, Evolution and Environment, was designed to take advantage of object-based learning to encourage students to put biological theory into practice.

The project is a term-long practical that forms 50 per cent of the final mark of Vertebrate Life and Evolution, a module available to third- and fourth-year undergraduates. Teaching takes place at the Grant Museum where students are each given a vertebrate (an animal with a backbone) specimen that has been 'de-taxonomized'; this means that all of its associated labels and identifying description have been removed. The specimen could be anything from a bone to a piece of skin. The students' first task is to identify which part of the animal it came from, which involves quite detailed anatomical observation and perhaps some drawings or photographs, making use of the wider collections at the Grant Museum. Thinking about where the specimen fits in with the rest of the animal kingdom is the beginning of the process that helps to lead the students to an identification of what type of animal it might be.

There is a wide range of students on the course – most study biological sciences but students also come from Geography, Anthropology or Human Sciences. However, most of them will not previously have been faced with an unidentified specimen as part of their taught curriculum. Over the course of a term, students have several sessions to access their specimen. The first session involves learning how to look at specimens and think about a detailed description (anatomy), starting from the general and moving towards the detail. Does the specimen have a beginning or end, top or bottom? Is it complete or partial? What material does the specimen comprise? Students then have several sessions in the Grant Museum and are given the opportunity to ask museum staff for comparative material to try to match or narrow down the identification (comparative anatomy). Throughout this process they are encouraged to explore other museum collections and the published literature, modelling the same process as genuine specimen-based research in Biology and Palaeontology.

The students have to identify their specimen as far as they can from an unknown part of an unknown animal to the correct class, order, family, genus or species. The written assessment for this practical is to write up their diagnosis in the style of a scientific journal article – modelled on *Trends in Ecology and Evolution* – giving students experience of how to translate observations, description and analysis into the formal language and format of descriptive taxonomy. When presented with their mystery specimens, students are often puzzled as to where to start and it is very difficult to get the answer by using popular internet search engines without being able to describe or define what the specimen is. The Grant Museum staff who select the specimens ensure that students are given diagnostic material and not specimens that are impossible to identify or only possible to identify at a basic level. Most students are able to narrow down their identification to a basic group of vertebrate – whether it is a bird, fish, reptile, amphibian or mammal. Refining the identification further can be more challenging and it is here that students have to start thinking critically about variations in biological specimens. Is their specimen from a male or a female, or from an adult or juvenile? Has their specimen been affected by pathology or altered during preparation? At this stage they need to consult the literature as widely as possible, focusing on detailed searches of relevant journal articles using the online citation indexing service Web of Science,[2] contemporary texts or older material where original descriptions were published.

The students' journal articles are assessed, not on whether the identification was correct according to the museum identifications, but on the quality of the detective work, research and quantification in reaching the identification. Students also need to propose what further work they would ideally undertake to narrow down or confirm the identification and this is where they can reflect on the range of scientific techniques that they have encountered in the course of their degree programme to date. Would isotope analysis, DNA sampling, X-ray or micro-CT scanning aid in a better identification? An added benefit of this practical is that the museum receives copies of the coursework to compare with the identifications in the museum catalogue, as in some cases, students have been able to identify or re-determine previously misidentified specimens through their coursework. In January 2016 the Grant Museum installed an exhibition case with such student discoveries of previously misidentified specimens.

The Mystery Specimen model has been very successful at UCL and has been adapted for use in a range of modules including for Bioscience undergraduate and Museum Studies Master's students. One particularly successful element has been the focus on systematic research-based learning starting from a museum specimen. What is more these practicals also give students a realistic experience of working life, such as what it would be like to work in a museum environment with specimens and in collaboration with museum professionals, thus creating a direct link between academic learning and the workplace.

Moving from the first case study with a primary focus on supporting teaching specific disciplinary skills, the second case study, also based within one particular UCL collection – namely that associated with Sir Francis Galton – demonstrates how museum objects can be employed both to teach practical skills for the workplace and stimulate reflection on key ethical questions.

Case study 2: Object-based learning with the Galton collection

Digital Resources in the Humanities (hereafter DRH) is a core module of UCL's MA/MSc in Digital Humanities programme. This programme was launched in 2010 within UCL's Department of Information Studies (UCL Centre for Digital Humanities, 2015). It is an interdisciplinary programme that investigates the past, present and future roles of digital technologies in the research and teaching of the humanities and cultural heritage. The module provides students with a wide-ranging introduction to established and emerging areas of Digital Humanities, especially the use of computational technologies to explore, interpret and reimagine the 'cultural complex' of the humanities (ESF, 2007).

Elsewhere some of us (Nyhan *et al.*, 2015) have discussed how and why object-based learning has become a pedagogical pillar of this course. At the broadest level, it is useful because it can help students to learn in an 'integrative' way. Integrative learning seeks to help students to notice the connections between the otherwise seemingly disparate subjects, concepts and debates that they study in their various modules (Huber and Hutchings, 2005). The outcome of such learning should be the ability to apply their knowledge independently and creatively to the novel situations (such as research-based teaching exercises) that they encounter within and outside the classroom, now or in the future. Indeed, such learning is *sine qua non* in Digital Humanities because the subject is not only interdisciplinary but also 'extramural' in the sense that successful students can expect to find subsequent employment in a wide range of contexts and industries. We will now briefly introduce the history of UCL's Galton collection and describe how it is integrated into DRH as an object-based learning exercise.

As mentioned above, in addition to its four public museums, UCL is home to a number of other collections that are accessible upon request but not on permanent display. The Galton collection falls into this category. Sir Francis Galton (1822–1911) was born in Birmingham and went on to read mathematics at Cambridge. From today's vantage point Galton is a perplexing and discomfiting character (Bulmer, 2003; Gillham, 2001). He was an important and productive scientist who made many significant contributions such as the science of fingerprinting, weather maps and advancements to statistical analysis. However, he was also a key proponent of so-called 'scientific racism' and coined the term *eugenics* 'to describe the science and idea of breeding human "stock" to "give the more suitable races or strains of blood a better chance of prevailing speedily over the less suitable"' (Challis 2013: 80, citing Galton 1907: 70).

Though he was not directly employed by UCL, he worked closely with some of its professors, such as Karl Pearson and Flinders Petrie. In 1904 UCL also provided Galton with rooms at 50 Gower Street for the 'Eugenics Records Office'. Upon his death, in 1911, he bequeathed £45,000 to UCL for the establishment of a Chair of Eugenics along with a number of objects that form the basis of what is now known as the Galton collection. It comprised his personal effects, objects that he brought back from his travels, and various artefacts relating to the research he did on areas such as Criminology. To many of us, the most challenging and unsettling objects in the collection are those relating to Galton's 'anthropometrics' research, the measurement of human features, which he considered indicators of human ability and behaviour (Galton, 1884: 4–5). For example, the 'Haarfarbentafel' is a collection of 30 samples of dyed hair, numbered from 1–30. Carole Reeves has written of it:

> The hair scale is scientific. It is a 'standard' scale which means that all race scientists invest in its truth. The dark-haired races cannot escape the truth. At Auschwitz-Birkenau, Bergen-Belsen, Dachau, Treblinka, Hadamar, hair shaved from those who perish rarely matches samples 12 to 24. Most are piles of clipped raven's wings. (Reeves, 2013: 61)

The Galton collection catalogue is online and freely accessible; however, it is very difficult to use without prior knowledge of the scope of the collection. Each year students of DRH are asked to explore the catalogue in advance of the object-based learning session, which is usually led by the collection's curator. The class discussion (and inevitable debate) that follows the viewing of the collection offers students a unique opportunity to apply the knowledge they have already gained on the course to a completely new set of objects and, most importantly, to problematize that knowledge.

Once they have viewed the collection, the students are asked to describe the kind of digital collection they would produce if money and resources were no object. We discuss the various approaches and techniques that would allow the collection to be published online and searched with more ease: for example, 3D digitization and faceted browsing. However, the wider social and cultural complexities of digitally recording and publishing such a collection invariably emerge during this discussion. In earlier sessions of the module students will have discussed digitization as an unqualified good and a force for the democratization of access to knowledge and objects. The objects in the Galton collection may not negate this statement but they certainly cast it in a new light. Up to this point the various themes of the module will have been taught on a weekly, and somewhat disjointed, basis. However, using the Galton collection in teaching emphasizes that a rich understanding of Digital Humanities approaches to cultural heritage requires not only knowledge of technological issues but also, among other things, the necessity of sensitive and ethical approaches to making digital collections – in this case, of objects devised for racist purposes – universally available. So too, the object-based learning session affords opportunities to reflect on more far-reaching issues, such as the ubiquity of narratives of techno-triumphalism (McNeil, 2000) and the role of Digital Humanities in disrupting them. In this way the session on the Galton collection prompts students not only to integrate and apply the wide range of knowledge and skills that they will have acquired during the module (and the programme as a whole) to a novel situation but also to consider the future of Digital Humanities and the contribution that they can each make to it.

The third case study – also drawn from the Digital Humanities – will continue with this possibility of students, through their research and enquiries, making an actual and valuable contribution to the wider teaching and research community of UCL and beyond. In fact, making a tangible contribution, beyond the remit of their module of study, has been a feature of both of the previous case studies.

Case study 3: Teaching digitization with the Slade Archive Project

The Slade School of Fine Art, an internationally leading art school based at UCL, which since 1871 has trained generations of world-renowned artists,[3] has an intriguing but underused archive relating to students and staff, and their teaching, artworks and experiences. This extensive archive provides rich evidence of the college culture and includes papers, photographs, class lists, student records, audio recordings, films, prospectuses, death masks and other artefacts. However, this archive is difficult to access, its cataloguing is incomplete, many documentation systems are not interoperable and no attempt has ever been made to present it to a wider audience (Bruchet *et al.*, 2014; Terras *et al.*, 2015).

The Slade Archive Project (n.d.), jointly undertaken by the Slade and UCL Centre for Digital Humanities since 2012, is a highly iterative, exploratory collaboration, investigating how digital tools and techniques can increase engagement with the archive. The project informs and enhances the use and understanding of digital methods available to art historians – a field that has not, to date, made much use of computational research methods (Rodríguez *et al.*, 2012; Rodríguez, 2013; Long and Schonfeld, 2014; Dobrzynski, 2014) – and encourages and supports new archival approaches (Bruchet *et al.*, 2014; Terras *et al.*, 2015). Additionally, using the Slade Archive as part of the teaching on the Digital Humanities programme (set within a Library and Information Studies School) allows students the opportunity to engage with current debates on best practice in archival digitization, contributing both to the digital element of the Slade Archive Project, and to developing students' practical and professional skills.

The project was conceived as a flexible and collaborative framework under which various sub-projects could be developed, driven by the specific interests of those working at the Slade, and governed by available resources. Framing it as a Digital Humanities project enabled access to resources maintained by UCL's Centre for Digital Humanities, such as the multi-modal digitization suite, and allowed embedding activities in teaching delivered as part of the MA/MSc in Digital Humanities module Introduction to Digitisation. Students have to work in groups, with a small, defined set of material from the Slade Archive, to undertake a complete digitization project from 'nail to nail'.[4] This includes taking historical photographic material from the archive, digitizing and creating digital image surrogates, providing full metadata, and delivering the resulting files in such a way that they can be incorporated into UCL's digital library catalogue and Slade Archive site, so others can access the material. The digital materials thus created are then delivered back to the Slade. The teams of students have to establish hierarchies and workflows in this time-limited task, which gives them an understanding of commercial digitization practices within the cultural and heritage sector that would only be possible through undertaking such a practical task. As a second part to the assignment, students are required to produce a self-reflective essay documenting what they have learnt about digitization, and themselves, by undertaking this activity.

In conducting the student projects in this way, we are, as curator Matthew Teitelbaum wrote, 'learning in public' (1996: 40). The range of activities have expanded beyond the familiar art historical activities of researching in, and extracting from, the archive, to encompass the collaborative, digitally iterative and publicly situated work of 'enabling, making public, educating, analysing, criticizing, theorizing, editing, and staging' (von Bismarck *et al.*, 2012: 8). Embedding the archive in teaching provides the means to approach, refine and choose ways in which to interrogate and understand the nature of the archive, while challenging conventional epistemological and disciplinary frames, as it brings methods, practices and theories together in new configurations (Cook, 1997). The teaching element of the Slade Archive Project allows those involved to rethink the remit and scope of such archival projects conceptually, and the role that Digital Humanities programmes have in fostering and exploring new teaching techniques utilizing archival materials. New convergences of collections, teaching, and the digitized spaces between, continue to form new opportunities in pedagogy.

Over the course of the previous three case studies we have seen a move from practical, disciplinary skill to more broadly reflective and interdisciplinary approaches using objects and collections from across the university. The fourth and final case study reports on an innovative module that aims to draw on the entire spectrum of available cultural resources at UCL in a truly interdisciplinary approach to research-based education through object-based learning.

Case study 4: Designing and teaching an interdisciplinary object-centred module

Object Lessons: Communicating Knowledge through Collections is a module on UCL's BASc Arts and Sciences undergraduate degree programme. This programme was launched in 2012 and offers students in UK higher education a new experience – the opportunity to study both arts and sciences within one undergraduate degree programme. While the degree is naturally very broad-based, students are able to tailor their studies by choosing a major pathway: Cultures; Health and Environment; Sciences and Engineering; or Societies. These pathways allow learners to navigate the fantastically broad range of modules available to them (anything from Anthropology to Civil Engineering or Zoology). A series of degree-specific core modules also run through the programme and have been designed to develop students' knowledge and skills in an explicitly interdisciplinary way. Object Lessons is one of these core modules and is taken in the second term of the second year of the BASc programme. Here, we will discuss the way the module was designed with research-based education in mind and will reflect on how teaching the module has shed light on the opportunities and challenges of making our curriculum 'connected'.

Object Lessons is structured around weekly lectures and seminars. The lectures, which form the backbone of the module, are given by a range of speakers and introduce the students to different disciplinary perspectives on studying material things. For example, a lecture on 'Materials and Materiality' by Professor of Archaeological Sciences Marcos Martinón-Torres is followed by one on 'The Social Life of Things' by design anthropologist Dr Adam Drazin. In this way, the lectures move through key conceptual, theoretical and research practice issues as they are encountered in materials science, archaeology, anthropology and historical material culture studies. In the second half of the module, lectures are delivered by curators and museum professionals in order to help students think about objects not only as embodiments of ideas but also as tools for communicating those ideas. The content of the lecture series was chosen to provide students, week by week, with the tools they need to complete their assessed work. The first series of disciplinary approaches to the study of material culture accompanies the students through their own object-based research and report writing, while the second half of the lecture series underpins their group work on an exhibition project. Weekly seminars provide a space to discuss the content of the lectures further and to test things out in practice. The seminars are active, enquiry-based learning sessions conducted in small groups (with a facilitator per group of six students). These classes use museum objects to help students improve their analytical skills and to prepare for their assessments.

The module has two main pieces of assessed work: an object report (conducted individually) and a virtual exhibition group project. At the start of the module, each student is allocated a different object, item or specimen[5] to research from a UCL museum, collection or library. This could be a zoological specimen, an ethnographic or archaeological artefact, an object relating to the history of science, a rare book, manuscript or an artwork. Objects are allocated in such a way as to generate interdisciplinary encounters, for example a student focused mainly on humanities disciplines (in their wider programme pathway) might be given a scientific instrument to research, whereas a student studying sciences might be assigned a work of art. The students are asked to conduct independent research into their object and to make use of more than one disciplinary framework for the study of material culture in this process. They arrange visits to the museum collection and are able to delve into existing museum records as primary research material. The students might also draw on the knowledge of the given curator and are expected to conduct wider secondary reading to contextualize their object and develop an argument for the resulting report. The object report is 2,000 words in length and carries 40 per cent of the total mark for the module. The intention with this assessment is to offer students a genuine, individual research project – in some cases a real mystery as many museum objects have had very little research conducted on them to date and are in need of better documentation, as was seen in case study 1. As each student is given a different object, they must consider how to respond to the particularities of 'their' object and make decisions about how they can use evidence to make an argument in their reports. In this way, students are asked to make decisions about how to use evidence, methods of analysis, methodology and argumentation to the best effect. This is a challenging exercise, but the module provides ample opportunities for one-to-one support as students develop the shape of their research and plan their report writing. There is also an emphasis on students bringing their own cross-disciplinary knowledge to this project, alongside the perspectives offered in lectures, in order to achieve an interdisciplinary response to the object. Student feedback in module evaluation has reflected this ethos:

> There was a lot of flexibility in terms of how to 'interpret' the object report, which at first seemed very daunting. In the end, it ended up being a good learning process, having to figure out yourself how to best structure the assignment according to your object. (Object Lessons student, spring 2015)

In the second half of term, the students work in groups of six to devise a virtual exhibition featuring the six objects that formed the basis of their individual object reports. The first step is to develop a theme that connects the objects and discuss how to communicate this theme through the exhibition. The groups decide on a target audience for the exhibition and tailor the content to this audience. While they draw on the content of their object reports in constructing the exhibition, it is important that they make sure the exhibition achieves an appropriate tone and consistent mode of presentation throughout. The lectures during this second half of the module are very much focused on issues of communication, audience, design, ethics and digital interactivity. The group project itself is worth 40 per cent of the total module mark and the students give an oral presentation on the process of putting together the exhibition, for which they are awarded the remaining 20 per cent of their mark. Through this process of interrogation, research, documentation and presentation, students develop a range of research and practical skills. They acquire an awareness of the strengths and weaknesses of different sources of information, for example the textual, visual and auditory material, and learn how to combine these sources in the analysis of a particular theme or research focus. As one student commented:

> It was enlightening to learn about objects through actually interacting with them. It really helps to get knee-deep into the subject matter and not make it just one more example in the textbook. (Object Lessons student, spring 2015)

From the outset, Object Lessons draws students into the practice of primary research by asking them to conduct an entirely novel research project and providing them with the support they need to access relevant resources and expertise. Students are initially given access to the object they are to research but must, thereafter, make arrangements with curators or librarians to conduct follow-up research visits, thus developing independent research skills. As one student described:

> I enjoyed it. It felt far more independent and investigative than other forms of research. (Object Lessons student, spring 2015)

As with the Mystery Specimen project (case study 1), student research of a good quality is added to existing documentation within the relevant museum or collection archive and forms a part of the research resources made available for future researchers using these collections. In this way, the students actively participate in research culture and contribute their own research findings to institutional holdings. Throughout the module, students are explicitly asked to make connections across subjects, and this is an important assessment criterion for their object report. As a student commented in 2015:

> [Object Lessons is] mind-opening; it is a good introduction to museum curation and it brings us new perspectives to view things around us. I like this very much as we can really touch and learn a real thing and connect them with the culture context. (Object Lessons student, spring 2015)

The virtual exhibition project requires students to develop content aimed at a specified public audience and – in collaboration with colleagues in UCL Digital Education (formerly e-Learning Environments) – the Object

Lessons teaching team have put in place a system whereby students can choose to publish or open their virtual exhibition and have continued access to it for future use. This has converted an assessment that was not publicly accessible into a piece of work that can become part of each student's personal portfolio and a product that can be publicly accessible and invite dialogue with audiences outside UCL. There is more work to be done on streamlining the logistics of making a piece of formal assessment into a usable, public-facing product of ongoing use to the students and the wider (academic) community. It is hoped that by exploring this subject in terms of this module, lessons can be learnt that will be of use to other programmes across the university and beyond.

Object Lessons also aims to connect learners with world-leading research via the lecture series, which introduces them to a range of UCL academics working at the cutting edge of their field. As outlined above, these lectures offer students different theoretical and disciplinary frameworks for thinking about material culture. Through conducting research on collections and working directly with specialists – in the form of curators and librarians – on the project work, they are introduced to the detail of professional life in museums and libraries. Students are asked to consider the opportunities and constraints offered by the museum or library as a custodian of collections when they build their own exhibitions in a virtual environment. In this way, Object Lessons connects them not only with academic research, but also with workplace learning in the museum, library and wider cultural sectors.

Lastly, Object Lessons ensures that students connect with each other during their course of study. Every weekly seminar involves small group work and is based around active, object-based or enquiry-led learning activities. The group project also encourages students to engage with each other's strengths and academic perspectives in order to create the best possible virtual exhibition and thus also bestows upon them essential transferable team working skills.

Conclusions

In a connected curriculum the threshold between expert researchers and novice students is lowered significantly. Learners – in this case university students – are directly and collaboratively integrated into the research process and become thus empowered to construct their own meanings. There are many ways to move current teaching practice in higher education in this direction. We hope that our chapter has highlighted how object-based approaches to learning – primarily using collections of museum (and library) objects – provide excellent opportunities for students to become researchers whether by engaging closely with only one object or dealing with an entire collection. Heritage is always a field of controversy and even conflict (Tunbridge and Ashworth, 1996) and therefore there are never simple, singular ways to understand or engage with material culture. Being given the opportunity to work with real objects and to appreciate their often troublesome and conflicted meanings – as, for example, those from the Galton collection – students will acquire not only subject-specific skills but will also analyse and question the epistemological frameworks within which knowledge is and has been constructed. Finally, with assessments specifically geared to real-world problems, students are also able to contribute to the creation of understandings and the production of resources that will be useful beyond the context of their own course of study. This is the case in relation to all four case studies presented here, where the best and most successful assessments have been adopted by the curators of the relevant collection as future aids for teaching and research.

Notes

[1] Addresses for correspondence: t.kador@ucl.ac.uk; l.hannan@qub.ac.uk; j.nyhan@ucl.ac.uk; m.terras@ed.ac.uk; h.chatterjee@ucl.ac.uk; mark.carnall@oum.ox.ac.uk

[2] http://wok.mimas.ac.uk; www.webofknowledge.com

[3] Famous alumni include Gwen and Augustus John, Stanley Spencer and Ben Nicholson around the turn of the twentieth century, Richard Hamilton and Eduardo Paolozzi in the 1940s, and Derek Jarman, Paula Rego, Euan Uglow and Craigie Aitchison in the 1950s and 1960s. More recent Turner Prize-winning alumni include Martin Creed, Rachel Whiteread, Antony Gormley and Douglas Gordon.

[4] A commonly used term in the Gallery, Library, Archive and Museum sector to cover the period when an item is taken out of store for digitization or exhibition and when it is returned safely.

[5] For ease of discussion we will employ the term 'object' to refer to all these four categories of material (i.e. objects, artefacts, items and specimens).

References

Alvord, E. and Friedlaender, L. (2012) 'Visual literacy and the art of scientific inquiry: A case study for cross disciplinary institutional collaboration'. In Jandl, S.S. and Gold, M.S. (eds) *A Handbook for Academic Museums: Exhibitions and education*. Edinburgh: MuseumsEtc., 144–65.

Arnold-Forster, K. (2000) '"A developing sense of crisis": A new look at university collections in the United Kingdom'. *Museum International*, 52 (3), 10–14.

Bartlett, D., Meister, N. and Green, W. (2014) 'Employing museum objects in undergraduate liberal arts education.' *Informal Learning Review*, 124 (Jan./Feb.), 3–6.

Bonwell, C.C. and Eison, J.A. (1991) *Active Learning: Creating excitement in the classroom* (ASHE-ERIC Higher Education Report). Washington, DC: George Washington University.

Bowler, K. (2007) 'Zoology is the latest victim of audit culture'. *Times Higher Education*, 16 March. Online. www.timeshighereducation.com/news/zoology-is-the-latest-victim-of-audit-culture/208193.article (accessed 13 March 2018).

Bruchet, L., Malik, A., Collins, S., Beavan, D., Giacometti, A., Volley, J. and Terras, M. (2014) 'The digital curatorial landscape of the Slade Archive Project'. Paper presented at the Archives 2.0 Conference: Saving the Past, Anticipating the Future, University of Leeds, 24–26 November 2014.

Buchli, V. (ed.) (2002) *The Material Culture Reader*. Oxford: Berg.

Bulmer, M. (2003) *Francis Galton: Pioneer of heredity and biometry*. Baltimore, MD: Johns Hopkins University Press.

Challis, D. (2013) *The Archaeology of Race: The eugenic ideas of Francis Galton and Flinders Petrie*. London: Bloomsbury Academic.

Chambers, E. (2008) *UCL Art Collections: An introduction and collections guide*. London: UCL Art Collections.

Chatterjee, H.J. (ed.) (2008) *Touch in Museums: Policy and practice in object handling*. Oxford: Berg.

Chatterjee, H.J. and Hannan, L. (2015) *Engaging the Senses: Object-based learning in higher education*. Farnham, Surrey: Ashgate, 1–20.

Chatterjee, H.J., Hannan, L. and Thomson, L. (2015) 'An introduction to object-based learning and multisensory engagement'. In Chatterjee, H.J. and Hannan, L. (eds) *Engaging the Senses: Object-based learning in higher education*. Farnham: Ashgate, 1–18.

Chatterjee, H. and Noble, G. (2013) *Museums, Health and Well-being*. Farnham: Ashgate.

Cook, T. (1997) 'What is past is prologue: A history of archival ideas since 1898, and the future paradigm shift'. *Archivaria*, 43, 17–63.

Dobrzynski, J.H. (2014) 'Modernizing art history'. *Wall Street Journal*, 28 April. Online. www.wsj.com/articles/a-cultural-conversation-with-james-cuno-modernizing-art-history-1398720987 (accessed 13 March 2018).

ESF (European Science Foundation) (2007) *Standing Committee for the Humanities (SCH) Position Paper 2007*. Strasbourg: European Science Foundation. Online. http://archives.esf.org/fileadmin/Public_documents/Publications/SCH%20Position%20paper_01.pdf (accessed 19 March 2018).

Galton, F. (1884) *Anthropometric Laboratory*. London: William Clowes and Sons.

Galton, F. (1907) *Probability, the Foundation of Eugenics: The Herbert Spencer Lecture delivered on June 5, 1907*. Oxford: Clarendon Press.

Gillham, N.W. (2001) *A Life of Sir Francis Galton: From African exploration to the birth of eugenics*. Oxford: Oxford University Press.

Hide, L., UMG (University Museums Group) and UMIS (University Museums in Scotland) (2013) *Impact and Engagement: University museums for the 21st century*. University Museums Group and University Museums in Scotland. Online. http://universitymuseumsgroup.org/wp-content/uploads/2013/11/UMG-ADVOCACY-single.pdf (accessed 19 March 2018).

Huber, M. and Hutchings, P. (2005) *The Advancement of Learning: Building the teaching commons*. San Francisco: Jossey-Bass.

Kolb, D.A. (1984) *Experiential Learning: Experience as the source of learning and development*. Englewood Cliffs, NJ: Prentice-Hall.

Long, M.P. and Schonfeld, R.C. (2014) *Supporting the Changing Research Practices of Art Historians*. New York: Ithaka S+R.

Lourenço, M.C. (2005) 'Between Two Worlds: The distinct nature and contemporary significance of university museums and collections in Europe'. Unpublished PhD thesis, Conservatoire national des arts et métiers, Paris.

MacGregor, A. (2001) *The Ashmolean Museum: A brief history of the institution and its collections*. Oxford: Ashmolean Museum.

McNeil, M. (2000) 'Techno-triumphalism, techno-tourism, American dreams and feminism'. In Ahmed, S., Kilby, J., Lury, C., McNeil, M. and Skeggs, B. (eds) *Transformations: Thinking through feminism*. London: Routledge, 221–34.

Meyer, J.H.F. and Land, R. (2003) 'Threshold concepts and troublesome knowledge: Linkages to ways of thinking and practising within the disciplines'. In Rust, C. (ed.) *Improving Student Learning Theory and Practice – 10 Years On: Proceedings of the 2002 10th International Symposium*. Oxford: Oxford Centre for Staff and Learning Development, 412–24.

Meyer, J.H.F. and Land, R. (2005) 'Threshold concepts and troublesome knowledge (2): Epistemological considerations and a conceptual framework for teaching and learning'. *Higher Education*, 49 (3), 373–88.

Nyhan, J., Mahony, S. and Terras, M. (2015) 'Digital humanities and integrative learning'. In Blackshields, D., Cronin, J., Higgs, B., Kilcommins, S., McCarthy, M. and Ryan, A. (eds) *Integrative Learning: International research and practice*. London: Routledge, 235–47.

Reeves, C. (2013) 'The importance of being blonde'. In *Conversation Pieces: Inspirational objects in UCL's historic collections*. Oxford: Shire Publications.

Rodríguez, N., Baca, M., Albrezzi, F. and Longaker, R. (2012) 'The Digital Mellini Project: Exploring new tools and methods for art-historical research and publication'. Paper presented at the Digital Humanities Annual Conference, University of Hamburg, 16–22 July 2012. Online. www.dh2012.uni-hamburg.de/conference/programme/abstracts/the-digital-mellini-project-exploring-new-tools-methods-for-art-historical-research-publication/ (accessed 19 March 2018).

Rodríguez, N. (2013) 'Digital art history: An examination of conscience'. *Visual Resources*, 29 (1–2), 129–33.

Roselaar, C.S. (2003) 'An inventory of major European bird collections'. *Bulletin of the British Ornithologists' Club*, 123A, 253–337.

Slade Archive Project (n.d.) Project blog. Online. http://blogs.ucl.ac.uk/slade-archive-project/ (accessed 4 April 2018).

Teitelbaum, M. (1996) 'Notes on the meeting of cultures'. In Watson, S., Hill, T. and White, P. (eds) *Naming a Practice: Curatorial strategies for the future*. Banff: Banff Centre Press, 40–4.

Terras, M., Bruchet, L., Malik, A., Collins, S., Beavan, D., Volley, J. and Giacometti, A. (2015) 'Digital humanities as catalyst for digital art history: The Slade Archive Project'. Paper presented at the Digital Humanities Annual Conference, Sydney, 29 June–3 July 2015. Online. http://dh2015.org/abstracts/xml/TERRAS_Melissa_Digital_Humanities_as_Catalyst_for/TERRAS_Melissa_Digital_Humanities_as_Catalyst_for_Digit.html (accessed 19 March 2018).

Tunbridge, J.E. and Ashworth, G.J. (1996) *Dissonant Heritage: The management of the past as a resource in conflict*. Chichester: Wiley.

UCL Centre for Digital Humanities (2015) 'MA/MSc in Digital Humanities'. Online. www.ucl.ac.uk/dh/courses/mamsc (accessed 10 November 2015).

Von Bismarck, B., Schafaff, J. and Weski, T. (eds) (2012) *Cultures of the Curatorial*. Berlin: Sternberg Press.

Vygotsky, L.S. (1978) *Mind in Society: The development of higher psychological processes*. Ed. Cole, M. Cambridge, MA: Harvard University Press.

Chapter 12

Learning through research: A case study of STEM research-based work placements for post-16 education

Emma Newall and Bahijja Tolulope Raimi-Abraham[1]

Our next study is less concerned with how our graduates turn out than how students can make a transition from school to university life. It documents a project to have A-level-age students discover the world of medical research at UCL: they undertake research-based activities and take part in a joint research project on real issues with global relevance. In other words, they get a chance to see what 'real science' is like. At a time of active encouragement not only to attract students for Science, Technology, Engineering and Mathematics (STEM) subjects, but also to support minorities access what is traditionally a white male preserve, such initiatives can bridge the gap between school and universities, as well as prove that genuine research can be embedded in education even before university.

Overview

The Nuffield Research Placements (NRP) scheme aims to provide young people with the opportunity to work alongside professional scientists, technologists, engineers and mathematicians. UCL School of Pharmacy, in partnership with the Nuffield Foundation, hosted three Year 12 (aged 16–18) school students as part of the NRP scheme. They completed a combined research project in pharmaceutical science that aimed to develop age-appropriate dosage forms for paediatric and geriatric patient groups.

This placement enabled the students to learn through research and enquiry and they were supported in their learning by research, academic and professional staff. The placement was structured to ensure the students both gained research skills and enhanced their personal and professional development. A summative evaluation was carried out after the placement. The placement experience offered the students a unique opportunity to be involved in authentic research and gain important skills. It also provided them with a greater understanding of career options and aimed to contribute to their development as autonomous, independent learners. In addition, the fact the placement was in an authentic research institution gave them the opportunity to experience real-world science and developed their awareness of the global challenges currently being addressed at UCL School of Pharmacy.

Introduction

The Nuffield Foundation is a charitable foundation that supports research and innovation in education and social policy.[2] A key objective of the Foundation is to provide young people with the opportunity to work alongside professional scientists, technologists, engineers and mathematicians through the NRP scheme. This scheme provides research-based work experience placements for more than 1,000 students in the first year of post-16 education across the United Kingdom, in universities, commercial companies, voluntary organizations and research institutions. The placements are between four and six weeks in length and students take part during their summer break before returning to school or college to complete their final year of post-16 education. Participating students have the opportunity to gain insight into real-world research and development, thus supporting university applications and decisions regarding future career choice.

A growing anxiety in Europe and the USA regarding the attitude of school students to Science, Technology, Engineering and Mathematics (STEM) subjects was predominant in the 1990s and the early years of the twenty-first century. Since the 1980s, there had been a decline in students taking STEM subjects beyond the compulsory stage of education (Osborne *et al.*, 2003). Several European reports from 2002 (including the Roberts Report), highlighted the risk to the knowledge economy of the developed world that was raised by a decline in STEM graduates and therefore a skilled workforce to support research and innovation (Roberts, 2002; European Commission, 2015). Although there have been improvements in the uptake of STEM subjects at school and at university level, there remains concern regarding supply and demand of a skilled STEM workforce, with evidence that a significant number of suitably qualified graduates are not choosing careers in STEM industries (Mellors-Bourne *et al.*, 2011). It is with this backdrop that the Nuffield Foundation has sought to inspire students to consider a career in STEM research and development. There is evidence that real-world experience through work-based placements can be highly motivating and highlight opportunities for STEM-based careers: 'if interesting and structured STEM work placements are available to all then a positive impact on the motivation to learn in STEM subjects can be achieved by all' (Centre for Science Education, 2011: 19). Similar schemes offering project-based work experience for school students, such as the British Science Association (BSA) CREST award scheme have demonstrated that these experiences have 'a strong positive impact on its primary target audience towards STEM and aspirations for STEM careers are improved' (Cole, 2009: 14).

There are also concerns that certain groups, such as those from lower socio-economic groups, are particularly under-represented in STEM courses and careers (Archer *et al.*, 2013; DeWitt *et al.*, 2011; Kabacoff *et al.*, 2013; CaSE, 2014). The reasons for this are complex, but there is evidence that collaborative enquiry-based activities have a positive impact on attitudes to learning in STEM and the career aspirations of under-represented groups (Duran *et al.*, 2014). The Nuffield Foundation particularly encourages students who do not have a family history of going to university or who attend schools in less well-off areas to apply for a research placement and the Foundation works to support Widening Participation (WP) through targeted recruitment of students coming under the WP criteria (Department for Business, Innovation and Skills, 2014).

Many investigations into the effectiveness of research-based activities have indicated that undergraduate students derive considerable benefit from conducting their own research projects (Zhan, 2014; Huziak-Clark *et al.*, 2015). A number of reports have emphasized the need for universities to be involved in science education reform at all levels, including compulsory education, to enhance the critical-thinking and problem-solving skills of younger students (Eeds *et al.*, 2014). An innovative research-based education programme for high school students (aged 13–17) at Vanderbilt University in the USA has demonstrated that independent research opportunities can have a very positive impact on both student achievement and the successful promotion of STEM careers. Central to this programme is the concept of a research-based curriculum, giving students the opportunity to conduct their own authentic research projects. Authenticity may be a key factor. Research by Hunter *et al.* (2007) has indicated that the participation in authentic STEM research can improve students' academic confidence and increase their interest in STEM disciplines.

The NRP programme has some similarities with the research-based education programme for high school students at Vanderbilt University, although the timescale for research, at six weeks, is shorter. Students participating in the NRP programme, as is the case with the Vanderbilt students, are of high ability, with a strong potential interest in STEM. NRP students undergo a rigorous selection process and are required to demonstrate some interest in a relevant STEM subject. However, they do not need to have decided on a chosen career path.

Models of student learning through work experience have been demonstrated to have a positive influence on learning and attitude, particularly if the experience is a 'work-based project into an individually designed learning experience' with an academic supervisor giving instruction on research methods (Walsh, 2007: 503). Work-based experiences again offer an authentic experience, as do real-world research opportunities, and provide 'ways to research and develop knowledge, reflect and evaluate situations and think autonomously', thus supporting students' problem-solving and academic reasoning skills (Walsh, 2007: 505). In addition, work-based learning gives students an insight into the priorities and motivations of a particular work context, offering an opportunity to deepen learning by putting it into context (Munby *et al.*, 1999).

Work-based placements are also thought to be particularly beneficial if supported by mentoring with a focus on developing professional behaviours (Kabacoff *et al.*, 2013). These aspects were features of the NRP placement described in this case study and were taken into consideration in the evaluation. The NRP student placements were six weeks in duration. Students attended weekly project meetings and were introduced to the concept of the Principal Investigator (PI), that is, the lead researcher or research group leader. From the fourth week, in order to promote each student's leadership and management skills, the students were each given the opportunity to act as PI for a week in turn. The students were also provided with a weekly timetable (Figure 12.1) for Weeks 1 to 3, but from Week 4 the student acting as PI had the responsibility of producing the timetable for that week (Figure 12.2).

UCL SCHOOL OF PHARMACY

BRUNSWICK SQUARE

WEEK 1 (W/C 21ˢᵀ JULY) (BACKGROUND READING AND TRAINING ON EQUIPMENT

Monday

10am Meet in reception

10-11am Introduction (supervisors, lab etc.)

11:30am Students go to main UCL to pick up their cards

1-2pm Lab B15 induction with safety information etc.

2pm – General safety induction – Adrian

Tuesday

9:45-11am Scanning Electron Microscopy

11-12pm (room 225) Introductory presentation on paediatric and geriatric drug delivery by Dr Mine Orlu-Gul

2pm-3pm Hot stage microscopy – Stefania

3-4pm FTIR training – Stefania

Wednesday

10am UV training – Awis

11am Drug loading (calibration curve etc.) – Bahijja

2-4pm DSC & TGA training (software/hardware and weighing pans) – Fatima

Thursday

09:30am – 12pm Hot melt extraction training – Bahijja & Alison

3-5pm Group meeting (PhD presentations)

Friday

09:30am Dissolution studies - Bhaskar

2pm tableting - Sue & Awis

SUPERVISORS ON ANNUAL LEAVE: NONE

Figure 12.1: Weekly project timetable created by PI for students for Weeks 1–3

Plan for Week Commencing 11/08/14

Monday   **PI: Ramila**

Morning - HME (x1)

- RE-DO UV (Physical Mixture in 10ml Ethanol and 1 Mini Tablet in 10ml Ethanol) Make sure both wavelengths are 316nm (x2)

Afternoon – DSC (x1)

Tuesday   **PI: Anisa**

Tasks for the day

- Hot Stage Microscopy (x1)
- TGA (x1)
- DSC (x1)
-

Wednesday

Morning – Milling (x2)

LUNCH

Afternoon 2pm – Tableting with Awis (x2)

Thursday

All absent today hence, Bahijja will be conducting the XRD

Friday   **PI: Deniz**

Tasks for the day

- Dissolution and UV of HME Naproxen and Soluplus in pH 6.8 (x2 For Dissolution and X1 for UV)

Save all outstanding data onto USB Sticks from DSC, TGA, HSM and XRD

Figure 12.2: Weekly project timetable created by students from Week 4 onwards

The projects were designed to allow the NRP students to learn through research and enquiry and they were supported in their learning by research, academic and professional staff. The objective of the placement was to allow students to develop research skills (e.g. both a practical knowledge and theoretical application of research methods). However, the NRP placements in this case also enabled students to enhance their personal and professional development (e.g. through self-management and team working). The placements also included mentoring to support and develop:

- CV writing
- professional emails
- career options
- presentation skills (to a scientific audience).

Placement and project summary

UCL School of Pharmacy, in partnership with the Nuffield Foundation, hosted three NRP students to work on a joint research project in pharmaceutical science. The project aimed to develop age-appropriate dosage forms for paediatric and geriatric population groups. The joint project allowed the students (aged 16–18) to experience an authentic research project that addressed a real clinical and drug development need. Students were able to learn practical techniques and research methods in the lab, and were also mentored and supported in other areas important for their professional and career development such as CV writing and professional communication. The aims and outcomes of the placements were very much in line with the six dimensions of connectivity outlined in the Connected Curriculum (part of the UCL 2034 strategy).[3]

Connected Curriculum is an institution-wide initiative aiming to ensure that all UCL students are able to learn through participating in research and enquiry at all levels of their programme of study. Connected Curriculum involves the following:

- Educating through dialogue and active, critical enquiry
- Creating an inclusive research and learning community
- Making connections across modules, programmes and beyond the classroom
- Creating assessments that mirror 'public engagement' in research
- Equipping students to address interdisciplinary challenges
- Exploring critically the values and practices of global citizenship
- Engaging students as partners in their education, and as co-producers of knowledge
- Improving the experiences of both students and staff.

The setting of the NRP placement was in a working research laboratory in the Pharmaceutics Department at UCL School of Pharmacy, which allowed the students a unique opportunity to experience authentic research first-hand. The experience also provided the students with exposure to the positives and the challenges of research, thereby broadening their horizons and supporting informed decisions about career pathways.

The students were studying STEM subjects at A-level in their respective schools and all were interested in pursuing STEM courses at university, namely Pharmacy, Medicinal Chemistry and Medicine. Their motivation in applying for an NRP was to find out more about STEM research and develop their skills and experience in order to enhance their university applications. All the students were considered covered by the WP agenda on the grounds of their socio-economic status and had few STEM role models outside school. A summative evaluation given to all Nuffield students allowed an assessment of their attitudes to STEM research and careers following the placement.

Project background

As a direct result of changes in world demographics, there is an increasing need in the pharmaceutical industry to develop age-appropriate dosage forms suitable for paediatric and geriatric patient groups. Paediatric patients can be categorized into five subgroups: preterm new-born infants; term new-born infants (0–27 days); infants and toddlers (28 days–23 months); children (2–11 years) and adolescents (12–18 years). A category for geriatric patients has also been proposed: early old (65–74 years); middle old (75–84 years) and late old (85 years and above).

Mini-tablets are multiple-unit dosage forms that offer the advantages of both tablets and multiparticulates and range in size from 0.05 mm to 2 mm (Tissen *et al.*, 2011). The manufacturing benefits of mini-tablets include the lower production costs and higher production yields (Lopes *et al.*, 2006). Mini-tablets have been developed as a solution to the current need for age-appropriate dosage forms specifically for paediatric and geriatric patients as they have been shown to tackle swallowing difficulty issues experienced by these patients (preventing their ability to take medication). The aim of this study was to apply pharmaceutical processing methods to generate a solid mini-tablet dosage form for paediatric and geriatric patient groups.

The students worked as a team on different areas of the research project. They used two pharmaceutical processing techniques, Hot Melt Extrusion (HME) and tableting to achieve this. HME is a promising processing technique that is used to create solid dispersions (dispersion of poorly water-soluble drugs in a hydrophilic polymer matrix) to improve dissolution rate and in turn enhance oral bio-availability.

All three students were also required to produce a scientific report in the form of a journal-style paper detailing their project. Feedback on drafts and the final report was given by their academic supervisor in order to support their progress in scientific writing. Final feedback and acceptance of their report were given by the Nuffield Research Placement Regional Coordinator.

In summary, through the NRP experience the students addressed real and current pharmaceutical issues. They had the opportunity to experience being a researcher and as such, through literature searching and critical thinking, were able to understand the foundational science, address the problem and develop appropriate research questions. The students were trained on how to use specialized pharmaceutics equipment and then worked independently to conduct experiments and evaluate their chosen method. On a daily basis, they worked as a team to plan their experiments and discussed their work with postgraduate (Master's and PhD) students as well as research staff (i.e. postdoctoral research associates) and academic staff, all present within the research group. They presented (using PowerPoint) a summary of their work to their colleagues and industrial partners at group meetings, produced a report of their findings for the Nuffield Foundation and also presented a poster at the Nuffield Foundation closing event. Overall, this experience differed markedly from the school science they would have experienced. There is very limited access to current real-world problems in school science and far more of a pragmatic need to focus on working towards formal examinations. Practical work is a series of tried-and-tested methods where the answer to any question presented is known. Students also do not have the same level of autonomy or responsibility in school, so this experience was altogether designed to help them develop as novice scientific researchers and go on to become capable of independent working and fruitful collaboration.

Profile of participating students

All three students were female and would be considered candidates for WP based on their eligibility for a bursary and the school or college they attended. Eligibility for a full bursary is principally determined by household income.

Table 12.1: Student demographic data

Gender	Ethnicity (self-identified)	Eligible for full bursary	Preferred subject	School location	School type	Placement length (weeks)
Female	Asian/Asian British – Any other Asian background	Yes	Chemistry	London	Sixth form college/academy	6
Female	Black/Black British – African	Yes	Chemistry	London	Sixth form college	6
Female	Asian/Asian British – Indian	Yes	Biochemistry	London	State-maintained secondary school	5

Post-placement evaluation findings

The placement was structured to ensure the students gained research skills (e.g. both a practical knowledge and theoretical application of research methods) and enhanced their personal and professional development (e.g. through self-management and team working).

All students taking part in the NRP scheme completed a post-placement evaluation. The evaluation was delivered via an online questionnaire that contained a number of statements relating to attitudes to STEM, academic confidence, potential university course/career choices and their perception of their experience in placement.

All three of the students in placement at UCL School of Pharmacy reported high levels of confidence regarding their academic abilities in STEM, but it is not possible to attribute this to the placement experience, as data are not available on their confidence levels before the placement. All three NRP students expressed a strong interest in exploring careers in STEM areas, but Student 2 did express some ambivalence and disagreed with the statement 'I know what scientists do on a day-to-day basis', although this response did not fit the pattern of other responses.

All three students responded that they agreed or strongly agreed that science would be important in their future career and offered many interesting job opportunities. Students 1 and 3 also stated that the placement experience had positively confirmed their initial career choice. In contrast, Student 2 stated that the experience had actively changed their initial career choice to another area of STEM. This is a positive outcome as the scheme aims to help students make informed choices, something that is difficult for students who are still at school to do without relevant experience. The evaluation also provided some evidence of horizon broadening: 'Doing the Nuffield placement has made me realize that there are various fields of chemistry or science in general that I can go into' (Student 3).

The NRP experience made the student participants aware of the global challenges currently being addressed at UCL School of Pharmacy as the statements below indicate. It offered the students a unique opportunity to be involved in real research and gain additional skills, and thereby provided them with a greater understanding of career options and contributed to their development as autonomous, independent learners. Of the experience, one of the students commented that 'the placement helped me understand the challenges that formulation scientists can encounter and the dynamics of working as a part of a team or as the principal investigator [which] has improved my leadership skills' (Student 3). Another student said:

> The NRP was more than I expected it to be as I was able to take part in tackling a genuine pharmaceutical issue, while enjoying every moment of it! Having completed the NRP, I now feel more confident in upcoming independent projects. (Student 1)

When asked what they perceived as the benefits of participating in the placement, the students referred to the opportunity to develop technical skills and an appreciation of the chance to use technical equipment they did not usually have access to:

> ... before my placement I felt intimidated by the notion of working in a laboratory for six weeks. During this placement, I was given the opportunity to build my confidence and independence after intensive and thorough training on the equipment before we conducted our research. (Student 3)

> Working with technical machinery that I would have not otherwise had the chance to do at school. (Student 2)

They also expressed an appreciation of, and a deeper understanding of, scientific research: 'I believe it gave me a great experience and the opportunity to understand scientific research in more depth' (Student 1).

However, the greatest emphasis was on the benefits of working with professional scientists and the opportunity to discuss career or course options. When asked what the main benefits of the placement were, Student 2 included: 'working with experienced seniors such as post docs, PhD students and Master's students'; while Student 3 said: 'The placement helped me decide what I would like to do in the future. Speaking to PhD and Master's students really helped me understand what university life is like.' The exposure to a university research environment was also considered helpful in terms of decision-making regarding courses and careers: 'It also made me consider things from a different perspective such as why looking at a university's research department is just as important as their undergraduate reviews' (Student 3).

One student also highlighted the importance of the mentoring and guidance regarding professional behaviour, which was a key element of the placement: '9–5 Mon to Fri improved my time management skills as this was a professional placement hence being late was not an option' (Student 2).

In terms of suggestions for improvement of the placement, only one student commented (Student 2). They felt that working together was not ideal; that three students was too much. However, this reflects the norm in academia and scientific research, where collaboration and teamwork are important, and the comment may just indicate a personal preference on the part of the student for independent projects.

One project supervisor also gave some summative feedback on the experience of taking part in the NRP scheme:

> As an early-career researcher, I saw the NRP as an excellent learning opportunity, offering me the chance to develop my supervision skills as well as gain experience in conducting independent work, which was essential for my professional and career development as an academic.

> It was important to us that we gave the students a unique opportunity to be involved in a *real* research project, providing them with career options in science which they may not have otherwise considered for their future.

> Hosting an NRP student could provide an additional platform for an institute to promote ongoing research as well as promote undergraduate courses offered by the department. (Project supervisor, NRP scheme)

Conclusions and future directions

Overall, the students reported having a very positive experience and the evaluation feedback provides some evidence of increased confidence, positive impact on decision-making regarding career direction, and a greater insight into research generally and into pharmaceutical science specifically. The evaluation indicated impacts on career choice both in terms of confirming and reassessing choices. This is a positive outcome in both instances and supports the aims of the NRP scheme as the objective is to allow informed decision-making.

This was a small-scale evaluation of three NRP placements and can offer limited insight into the outcomes of participants. Future research could include:

- a larger-scale evaluation of a number of placements in different STEM research settings
- comparison of student outcomes in placements with varying levels of academic and professional mentoring.

All three students were female in this instance. Ideally, further research would look at the outcomes by gender, looking in particular at STEM settings that traditionally have a gender imbalance. For instance, Pharmaceutical Science has traditionally had a greater number of female students, and it would be valuable to assess the experiences of male students in this setting and explore barriers to participation (Collender, 2009).

Acknowledgements

We would like to thank the Nuffield Foundation for funding and coordinating the student placements. We would like to thank the students who took part in UCL School of Pharmacy placements for agreeing to give their personal feedback. We would also like to thank BASF[4] for their support of the project and donation of samples. The invaluable support of UCL School of Pharmacy library staff, Dr Awis Mohmad Sabere, Dr Alison Keating, Dr Susan Barker and Dr Mine Orlu-Gul, and members of Professor Duncan Craig's Research Group should also be recognized.

Notes

[1] Addresses for correspondence: e.newall@ucl.ac.uk; bahijja.raimi-abraham@kcl.ac.uk
[2] www.nuffieldfoundation.org
[3] www.ucl.ac.uk/2034
[4] www.basf.com/gb/en.html

References

Archer, L., DeWitt, J., Osborne, J., Dillon, J., Willis, B. and Wong, B. (2013) '"Not girly, not sexy, not glamorous": Primary school girls' and parents' constructions of science aspirations'. *Pedagogy, Culture and Society*, 21 (1), 171–94.

CaSE (Campaign for Science and Engineering) (2014) *Improving Diversity in STEM: A report by the Campaign for Science and Engineering (CaSE)*. London: Campaign for Science and Engineering. Online. http://sciencecampaign.org.uk/ CaSEDiversityinSTEMreport2014.pdf (accessed 19 March 2018).

Centre for Science Education (2011) *STEM Subject Choice and Careers: Lessons learned (Part 1)*. Sheffield: Sheffield Hallam University. Online. www4.shu. ac.uk/_assets/pdf/cse-stem-lessons-learned-report.pdf (accessed 30 March 2018).

Cole, J. (2009) 'A framework for STEM-based work experience accreditation: CREST awards'. *Education in Science*, 233, 14–15.

Collender, G. (2009) 'Pharmacy education and workforce planning important to improve health'. *London International Development Centre News*, 6 August. Online. www.lidc.org.uk/news/pharmacy-education-and-workforce-planning-important-improve-health (accessed 19 March 2018).

Department for Business, Innovation and Skills (2014) *National Strategy for Access and Student Success*. Online. www.offa.org.uk/publications/national-strategy-for-access-and-student-success/ (accessed 30 March 2018).

DeWitt, J., Archer, L., Osborne, J., Dillon, J., Willis, B. and Wong, B. (2011) 'High aspirations but low progression: The science aspirations–careers paradox amongst minority ethnic students'. *International Journal of Science and Mathematics Education*, 9 (2), 243–71.

Duran, M., Höft, M., Lawson, D.B., Medjahed, B. and Orady, E.A. (2014) 'Urban high school students' IT/STEM learning: Findings from a collaborative inquiry- and design-based afterschool program'. *Journal of Science Education and Technology*, 23 (1), 116–37.

Eeds, A., Vanags, C., Creamer, J., Loveless, M., Dixon, A., Sperling, H., McCombs, G., Robinson, D. and Shepherd, V.L. (2014) 'The School for Science and Math at Vanderbilt: An innovative research-based program for high school students'. *CBE Life Sciences Education*, 13 (2), 297–310.

European Commission (2015) *Does the EU need more STEM graduates? Final report*. Directorate-General for Education and Culture. Luxembourg: Publications Office of the European Union. Online. https://goo.gl/ZUHRXj (accessed 6 April 2018).

Hunter, A.-B., Laursen, S.L. and Seymour, E. (2007) 'Becoming a scientist: The role of undergraduate research in students' cognitive, personal, and professional development'. *Science Education*, 91 (1), 36–74.

Huziak-Clark, T., Sondergeld, T., van Staaden, M., Knaggs, C. and Bullerjahn, A. (2015) 'Assessing the impact of a research-based STEM program on STEM majors' attitudes and beliefs'. *School Science and Mathematics*, 115 (5), 226–36.

Kabacoff, C., Srivastava, V. and Robinson, D.N. (2013) 'A summer academic research experience for disadvantaged youth'. *CBE Life Sciences Education*, 12 (3), 410–18.

Lopes, C.M., Sousa Lobo, J.M., Pinto, J.F. and Costa, P. (2006) 'Compressed mini-tablets as a biphasic delivery system', *International Journal of Pharmaceutics*, 323 (1–2), 93–100.

Mellors-Bourne, R., Connor, H. and Jackson, C. (2011) *STEM Graduates in Non STEM Jobs* (BIS Research Paper 30). London: Department for Business, Innovation and Skills. Online. www.gov.uk/government/uploads/system/uploads/attachment_data/file/32379/11-771-stem-graduates-in-non-stem-jobs.pdf (accessed 19 March 2018).

Munby, H., Chin, P., Hutchinson, N.L. and Young, J. (1999) 'Co-operative education: Studies of learning from workplace experience'. Paper presented at the American Educational Research Association (AERA) Annual Meeting, Montreal, 19–23 April 1999.

Osborne, J., Simon, S. and Collins, S. (2003) 'Attitudes towards science: A review of the literature and its implications'. *International Journal of Science Education*, 25 (9), 1049–79.

Roberts, G.G. (2002) *SET for Success: The supply of people with science, technology, engineering and mathematics skills: The report of Sir Gareth Roberts' review*. London: HM Treasury.

Tissen, C., Woertz, K., Breitkreutz, J. and Kleinebudde, P. (2011) 'Development of mini-tablets with 1mm and 2mm diameter'. *International Journal of Pharmaceutics*, 416 (1), 164–70.

Walsh, A. (2007) 'Engendering debate: Credit recognition of project-based workplace research'. *Journal of Workplace Learning*, 19 (8), 497–510.

Zhan, W. (2014) 'Research experience for undergraduate students and its impact on STEM education'. *Journal of STEM Education*, 15 (1), 32–8.

Chapter 13

Learning from 'front-line' research and research-based learning

Amanda Cain, Paul Bartlett and Andrew Wills[1]

The next set of case studies are reflections by UCL staff from three different subject areas about how degree courses as a whole can have research-based education embedded in them. Traditionally, in science (in particular) the approach was that students could not possibly do research until they had learnt 'the basics', which took virtually the whole degree. Here, three scientists think through and experiment with how the process of transforming the curriculum can be done, such that students face forward, building for a professional life instead of being caught in a trap of merely looking back at how they've done in the last test. In Life Sciences, ways for students to encounter research are explored, for instance through students engaging directly with researchers about *their* research; in Physics, volunteers get the opportunity to be involved, with the notable advantage that they and their peers benefited from the experience; in Chemistry, we encounter possibilities of structuring the curriculum so that students' own 'intrinsic' motivation can be supported – but not supplanted – by 'extrinsic' factors, such as a leaderboard for different clearly marked stages of learning and accomplishment.

Life Sciences solutions

Implementation of research-based learning has many challenges, particularly in a very practical-based subject like Life Sciences. When our new Provost, Michael Arthur, took office he published his UCL2034 vision for UCL, which included a desire for all our undergraduates to be involved in the research process as early as possible. Initial reaction within the department was that there was no way that we could have first-year students in the research laboratories. There are clear barriers to this in terms of both their practical skill base and physical space in the laboratories. It is often a challenge to find sufficient laboratory bench space for final-year project students, so the idea of opening this opportunity up to first or second years direct looked very unlikely.

Shortly after Professor Arthur's address, UCL held its annual Teaching and Learning conference at which the keynote speaker was Etienne Wenger-Trayner who, with Jean Lave, proposed the concept of communities of practice. One of the many concepts that he introduced explained that we should use the research activities that we all partake in as an inspiration to our incoming students. During the three or four years of their undergraduate career they will face increasingly difficult intellectual challenges and for some these will feel like insurmountable obstacles. Wenger-Trayner used an analogy of taking our students on a helicopter ride up the mountain to show them the type of activities that they can aspire to. If they understand how the basic concepts are put into practice and the type of exciting outcome that this can lead to, it should help them work through the subject areas they find difficult and give them an insight into the potential future career that could await them.

We have therefore used this analogy as the basis for introducing more research-based activities into our first-year curriculum, and beyond. While it may not be practical to have Year 1 students working at the research bench there are no such barriers when it comes to introducing them to the main themes of departmental research. An induction week session on key skills clearly showed that as they join UCL, most students have little or no idea of the areas in which their lecturers are carrying out research. One way to address this is to use relevant local examples to illustrate teaching points within lectures, but not all subjects are amenable to this method. Another approach we undertook was to initiate a new seminar series aimed specifically at first-year students. Post-doctoral researchers, from labs where the work is less easily linked to Year 1 lecture content, were asked to present specific aspects of their bench work and framed at an appropriate level. While the seminars were well received by the students and interesting questions and discussion followed at the closure, attendance levels were disappointing. When asked, students commented that they had not realized the potential benefit to their studies by attending as it was not made clear that these sessions were linked to their curriculum.

Engaging students in connecting current research to the academic curriculum at the earliest stages of the university career is, I believe, of upmost importance, so we have developed additional activities to engage them with the research we are undertaking. One of the first of these is the opportunity for students to meet front-line researchers and find out about their work. We set this in the context of our departmental tutorial system but many other departments at UCL engage in similar 'Meet the Researcher' activities. We task our tutorial groups with carrying out an investigation into their tutors' main topics of research and presenting this as their first written assignment. This is then discussed as a group to delve further into the topic and discuss possible future outcomes and developments, and is followed by a tour of the research laboratories. One striking point of note is that most students will not have set foot inside a research facility previously and, in my experience, are quite surprised by the range of equipment required for basic lab work. Their previous experience of laboratories has mostly been based around school or college settings, perhaps with a glimpse of technical preparatory areas, but which are both visually very different to a research facility.

A final important example that we use specifically in Year 1 is our post-exam key skills module. At UCL the examination period runs for most of May and term finishes in mid-June. After their examinations there are few activities planned for the younger year groups, so we decided to exploit this time to reaffirm the importance of transferable skills. These are embedded in a week-long programme of varied activities. This includes a research project where students get much more freedom to design and implement their experiment than is usual in class practicals. They are required to make up their own solutions, including carrying out the required calculations to determine quantities of reagents, which is a skill that is key to successful laboratory research but impractical to include in class practical sessions due to problems of scale. In some instances, students find this sense of freedom liberating, but others are much less confident in their own abilities. Setting these skills into a non-assessed module means they have a non-threatening opportunity to explore their practical understanding and develop the necessary skills required in a research setting.

As students progress into Year 2, the focus of all our modules starts to shift further from 'textbook learning' and more towards understanding how the concepts and theories that they learnt about in Year 1 are used in research. To complement the lecture series, our practical classes now shift from individual stand-alone experiments to focus on a suite of techniques as would be required in the research laboratories. A specific example of this is where students are challenged to clone and identify a fragment of DNA. This takes place over a period of four weeks: the students have to carry out multiple different techniques and work on parallel aspects of the experiment at the same time. They need to be made aware of the requirement to keep accurate working notes in the laboratory and to think ahead so they are fully prepared for the next stages. To emphasize the change in style of their practical learning, we now refer to the laboratory sessions as a mini research project rather than a class practical and all results are presented as a research paper rather than being written up in a standard laboratory report format. We have found that just shifting the language we use to introduce the experiments in this research-focused manner has inspired students to take the experimental work more seriously and to think more deeply about what they are being asked to do and why.

The links between research and teaching have always been much more explicit by the time students reach their third and fourth year of study, so less focus has been placed on emphasizing connecting the curriculum in this area. One beneficial activity that we have introduced, however, has been the concept of an undergraduate research symposium. Oral presentation of their research findings has been a long-standing component of our project modules, and the traditional format had these taking place over a period of several days, with relatively low levels of attendance due to the extended time frame. Our more recent approach has been to model the presentations in the format that would be seen at a conference. Students are required to submit an abstract in advance, which is published before the symposium. Parallel themed sessions take place over an afternoon, with students and staff moving between events followed by a poster session and a closing reception. Sponsorship of prizes has been arranged and relevant societies and companies have presented stands to add to the overall impression of a conference. As this takes place towards the end of the final teaching term, it provides an excellent environment for staff and students to meet in a professional setting. The students excel in their presentation skills, and the setting gives a sense of gravitas to their achievements over the course of their studies. Just changing the setting of these research talks has given benefits to both staff and students and makes a landmark event to finish the teaching in each academic year.

Physics solutions

Individual researchers

UCL's Physics and Astronomy Department has encountered similar difficulties to our Life Sciences colleagues. How can we integrate real research experience into the undergraduate curriculum? For a number of years, we have been investigating how some students can gain this experience. The following describes work in progress rather than a complete solution, but it does raise some important questions regarding how we view undergraduates as potential researchers.

In the past, it was commonly believed that undergraduates could not contribute to research programmes because of their lack of knowledge and experience. In some cases this may have been an accurate description. However, for the last four years it has been possible to place first-year students who request to be volunteer researchers within our research groups. This has had pleasing results. Why do this? From the 'person development' point of view, giving keen undergraduates a chance to do real research can help them to develop as scientists, give them a context for their studies and can help them decide if this is a career path they want to follow. In addition, it helps them to establish a record of achievement prior to seeking employment or further study opportunities when they complete their degrees. In today's employment or academic environments, this is a significant competitive edge for them.

When it comes to the research groups, it is possible that they can obtain a willing volunteer researcher who can develop skills that are useful to the research group. In addition, good students can be encouraged to stay within the discipline. Indeed, if a good student chooses to stay in the field to undertake a PhD, the potential academic supervisor would, already, have significant knowledge of the applicant and their skill set. This can enhance the quality of a research team without the potential risks associated with new, unknown, PhD student applicants.

An example might be useful here: in 2012, a first-year student came to me, in the physics laboratories where I teach, and asked if there were opportunities for him to undertake research work in the department. Initially, I was unsure if this was possible because of the usual hesitations regarding very junior students, but I said I would approach a research group leader to see what he thought. To our mutual pleasure, this research group leader was willing to take on a first-year volunteer, and he was integrated into the team.

One year later, this student and another of his year who joined him were co-authors on a scientific paper that they had directly contributed to Wickenbrock *et al.*, 2014, which was a significant achievement. This resulted in a growing group of undergraduate volunteers (now around 20) choosing to spend their spare time contributing to real research projects.

How the teaching laboratories helped was by allocating space and facilities, if needed, to those students who were taking part in these research programmes. The students were regarded as working for the research groups, but this was part of their undergraduate training, so it was appropriate to give them space in the teaching laboratories. In addition, using our teaching laboratories as a 'hub' meant that volunteers who were working in different research groups (as more students and academic staff became involved) could organize themselves into a virtual undergraduate research community that spanned all study years. This is something that I think is important to achieve, as it:

- helps the undergraduate research students to be a research community
- makes them responsible for their work
- allows them to become autonomous professionals
- helps them to help other students (researchers and non-researchers).

We have now created a 'Nexus Laboratory' within the teaching laboratories where students, academics, teaching fellows and industrial researchers can join together to work on research programmes.

It is considered important to bring students into the 'research world' as it helps to erode any perceived borders between them and the research the university is undertaking. It makes them feel as if they belong to a community that they can contribute to, where they are helped and can help others.

Indeed, some 'non-research' undergraduate students were struggling with a practical exercise that involved an area that one of the student researchers was working in (magnetic imaging tomography). I suggested that they contact him so he could help them to resolve the problem. Within ten minutes he was at the laboratory bench helping the students to come up with a solution that would work for them.

It must be said that this kind of activity need not be restricted to subject discipline research areas. It is also possible to have students conduct tasks that contribute to the teaching of a subject. In my case, I have had students investigate the feasibility of new 'teaching experiments' and develop new, more open-ended, activities within our laboratories. This can help to show that teaching is as important a research activity as the core subject work.

It is clear that the 'volunteer researcher' route may not touch every undergraduate student. However, it does offer those who are interested a means to develop their knowledge, skills and attributes in the field that they wish to contribute to in the future. Indeed, some students may not wish to get involved in research and may only see a physics-based degree as a means to obtain a position in another discipline. For example, in UCL, it is not unusual for students to undertake this degree as part of their plan to gain employment in the financial sector. They are more likely to focus their attention on experiences that will help them on this path. However, this approach does seem to give those who are keen to explore what it is like to be part of a university research group a means to do so.

Group researchers

For twenty years, third-year physics students of all sub-disciplines (Theoretical, Applied, Astro- and Medical Physics) have been grouped together to undertake a team-based research project. Typically, the number of students in such a group is around eight people. They are given a task by an academic member of staff (the Board Member) and the group must produce a solution to this task. This is to teach them about such things as:

- team dynamics
- leadership and management
- programme planning
- systems engineering.

All of this is done within a physics or engineering context, but can range from purely theoretical to purely applied in nature. However, in practice, there is a balance between these two extremes so that everyone can contribute to the team effort. The group projects last for one academic term.

In the past, the students would only conduct group projects that were supplied by university academics. However, there has been an increase in the number of projects that are supplied by external organizations. These Industrial Group Projects (IGPs) add an extra dimension to the work that the students undertake as they seem to view professionals from outside the university family as being, in some way, more 'real' and not just a simulation of a set of project requirements.

Examples of IGPs are:

- Magnetic imaging tomography for medical applications: this is where students design a magnetic imaging system to investigate if it is possible to image, say, bones inside flesh (industrially supported)
- The creation of a Lego-based 'Watt Balance' that could measure fundamental physical quantities such as Planck's Constant
- A physical analysis and mathematical modelling of prototype pre-stressed mechanical structures for use in deep-sea habitation structures (industrially supported).

When IGPs were first introduced, they were much like the academic group projects: they were only active for the duration of the group project. Once the project finished, a report was supplied to the industrial sponsor and that was that. However, we have been working with one industrial sponsor for four years and this has created a new way of engaging with students in the group projects and beyond.

Working with one long-term industrial sponsor meant that there was a natural continuity in the yearly IGPs. The sponsor has specific interests, which were reflected in the work packages. Quite quickly, the industrial sponsor helped us to create a PhD programme that would investigate some of these interests in more detail. This was a delightful spin-off from that IGP programme, which has so far resulted in three PhD students.

As the continuity continued, so did the ability for the IGP students to interact with the related research group (including these PhD students) and, more importantly in some ways, previous IGP students in this field. Third-year students would actively seek the advice and assistance of their fourth-year predecessors. In addition, student volunteer researchers would continue with the work they started in the IGPs, thereby becoming associated with the general research group efforts. This experience would be used by a subsequent IGP team, which would take up the reins of the research project.

What is clear is that by having an ongoing student research programme (it need not be industrially focused), it is possible to create a complex interaction between students and other students, students and academics/ industrialists, and also students and research students. In addition, it enables students from different years, in a degree programme, to interact to solve problems. It helps more experienced students to lead and guide more junior ones. This creates a situation where all students can be exposed to research-based learning that is not, purely, a research professional–undergraduate student exchange dynamic but is something much more rich and complex. It creates a community of interconnectivity.

Looking at the individual and group research work outlined above, it seems that something interesting is evolving here in UCL's Physics and Astronomy Department. It is in the early stages and the process is not applied to all students at the time of writing. However, there is something in this that needs to be explored further. What it suggests is that we need not have this separation between research and teaching if it is handled well. Undergraduates can be part of the whole and can contribute to the generation of knowledge as well as its consumption.

Amanda Cain, Paul Bartlett and Andrew Wills

Chemistry solutions

Introducing gamification and working towards professionalism
The current drives to research-based education are well summarized by Brew:

> For the students who are the professionals of the future, developing the ability to investigate problems, make judgments on the basis of sound evidence, take decisions on a rational basis, and understand what they are doing and why is vital. Research and inquiry is not just for those who choose to pursue an academic career. It is central to professional life in the twenty-first century. (Brew, 2007)

Teachers of science recognize a validation of the importance of delivery of the scientific method in this. It also reiterates the initial goal of a university education in the sciences to supply the professionals of the future – educated people, able to function as professional scientists and create knowledge. In modern times, expansion of the student base, accompanied by sectoral shifts from manufacturing to services, has resulted in a minority of science graduates continuing to work in science or research. The motivations of students have changed in response, from those based on intrinsic desires to learn about a topic that is of great interest to them, to an extrinsically motivated and points-based ambition to succeed in summative assessment of modularized courses. The primary quest for many students is commonly the attainment of degree class, consigning the acquisition of knowledge and skills to the status of a minor goal.

In considering the educational journey of our students, it is useful to relate their developments towards being the professionals of the twenty-first century that are championed by Brew. We find that the reference point of being a professional scientist can help greatly in designing and focusing our activities, and reinvigorate our feedback structures and assessments. For emphasis, we employ a contrived distinction between feedback and 'feedforward', based on feedforward being part of an ongoing process of immediate skills reuse and development, while feedback is a commentary on mistakes or suggestions of improvements for deferred applications.

The goal of this brief text is to explore how the role of a professional scientist can be applied to provide perspectives on the different levels of student ability, and how they resonate with gamification constructs that can be embedded within our learning activities. The laboratory-based education that characterizes many of the sciences also provides a useful architecture within which we can engineer and manage closely how this is done. The techniques introduced are able to support student learning and develop an intrinsic motivation that can assist in improving student engagement. They work directly to meet the psychological and educational needs of students, and as a consequence also have the potential to improve the levels of satisfaction expressed within the assessment and feedback components of the National Student Survey (NSS).

Gamification in teaching laboratories: Engineering motivation

Modern education is just starting on a journey to understand how motivation can be enhanced by the application of techniques originally developed for computer games. The massive success of games such as *FarmVille* and *Minecraft* relies on enticing and retaining high levels of user motivation: millions of users choose to spend many hours within these virtual realms and to exchange real money for game objects or opportunities. They choose to because they want to: the games have tools that tap into the psychological needs and desires of the player. The success of the games is testament to the power of the tools they use. These game-based motivators are most clearly seen in the Massive Open Online Courses (MOOCs), such as the Khan Academy, where they are used to reduce the drop-off in student engagement.

The field of gamification has developed rapidly since its large-scale entry into software engineering in 2010 and much of higher education is behind on its practice. Techniques such as points, checkboxes, rewards, badges and leaderboards are common and strongly evangelized. They are simple to apply but we argue that they operate at the wrong level. They are extrinsic motivators that trigger drives based on attainment or possession, and reinforce the points-based ambition that we want to move away from. The key characteristic of modern gamification, and the great potential for it to support our students in higher education, is the incorporation of devices that support intrinsic motivation. Working to encourage intrinsic motivation is extremely important as an overemphasis on extrinsic motivators can lead to the subsumption of intrinsic drives, and subsequent removal of the extrinsic motivators often causes the motivation to collapse to a level that is below that when the extrinsic motivators were first applied. For this reason, the author proposes that the effective movement from feedback and summative assessment to feedforward and the strengthening of professional skills must be supported by a structure where extrinsic motivation, embodied by the ownership of grades, is counterbalanced by intrinsic motivations aimed at encouraging students to operate at the required level. We cannot negate the extrinsic motivations, and indeed they can operate as effective drives, but we can utilize them in a more constructive manner. The challenge in higher education is to engineer motivationally balanced learning activities and structures.

Teaching laboratories are rich with opportunities that can be used to develop motivation and help students on their journey to becoming professionals through gamification, and some examples of intrinsic motivations are given below:

- **To perform experiments that they design.** A natural strength of experimental work is the ability to be creative, to come up with a hypothesis that will be tested, to interpret results, and to make deductions. This is tremendously empowering and motivating. While a free rein is rarely possible in a teaching laboratory due to resources and safety, choices and options can be built into experiments at levels that match the knowledge and skills of the students. Indeed, well-constructed rules of limited resources and possibilities can combine with problems that may be solved in a variety of ways, to fuel creativity by empowering students to make decisions and to **become co-creators.** In turn, this encourages intrinsic motivation. They also receive the powerful **immediate feedback** from the experiment itself, rather than from a person, of whether their decision was good and led to success.

- **To work in subjects relevant to the real world.** Structures where students collect samples from the real world, and perhaps also connect with societal issues, **help them to connect with meaning** and is intrinsic motivation. It would also be likely that these experiments would involve student choice and gain a degree of unpredictability that would also increase motivation.

- **Give a measured level of instruction.** An important aspect of motivation is allowing students to have the space to think about a course of action, and to call on their own experience and skills. For example, the final experiment of a lab course could directly build upon aspects of the experiments that the students have already covered, and the level of instruction reduced to encourage deep reflection of these past activities. This structure builds intrinsic motivation as the students **see the connections in what they do.** It also engenders senses of ownership (extrinsic) and co-creation (intrinsic).

- **Leverage peers.** Many laboratory experiments involve group activities, but the analysis and write-ups are to be done separately by the students. Changing to a feedforward structure where activities and initial milestones are formative allows the write-ups and analysis to become

group-based. Scheduling regular write-up sessions helps encourage
peer support structures and strengthen intrinsic motivation through
social influence, such as friendship and demonstration of prowess. The
social aspects of these sessions would also allow students to learn about
different viewpoints and backgrounds, potentially aiding the student
transition to university as well as strengthening their motivation for
undertaking the practicals.

- **Orchestrated failure.** Effective growth requires students to become
  comfortable with failure, gain the confidence that they will succeed,
  and understand that they will be supported. This can be incorporated
  into experiments with relative ease. Situations where aspects of an
  experiment fail can be contrived and matched by learning goals centred
  on the discussion of the reasons behind the failure and an appropriate
  response, rather than the gaining of a 'correct' answer. These events
  teach about consequences and need to be matched by frameworks that
  provide the students with support and guidance. Allowing safe failure
  is potentially a powerful tool in the **movement away from extrinsic
  motivation** based on the possession of grades.

As mentioned earlier, extrinsic motivators also have a place in a balanced
motivational structure: bringing several into play can help weaken the
predominance of grade ownership and so round the student drives and
experience. Some examples relevant to teaching laboratories are:

- **Completing stages quickly and leaving early.** The speed with which
  a student accomplishes the required work is effectively a **leaderboard**
  and acts as an extrinsic motivator. Importantly, it shows accessible
  outcomes – students are able to complete stages quickly and to
  finish early. Care must be taken to prevent those who fall behind
  from becoming demotivated. Additional coaching from the (senior)
  demonstrator can be effective in turning a potentially demoralizing
  situation into one where the student feels supported and gains a sense
  of achievement.

- **Increasing the challenge – levelling up.** Making laboratory experiments
  harder and more complicated increases the **sense of accomplishment**,
  which is an **extrinsic motivator**. This often occurs in great leaps,
  such as in going from Year 1 to Year 2, which students can find
  very demoralizing. A better scenario is to engineer an increase in
  performance that is accessible but still challenging, such as by raising
  the workload by 20 per cent once a particular skill set (level) has been
  attained. Experiments that are done in different orders by different

groups could have additional activities if they build upon practicals that have already been completed.

- **Making it personal.** As introduced above, the act of selecting directions within an experiment can create the sense of co-creation. It also imparts **ownership**, which is an extrinsic motivator. Care must be taken to avoid possible negative consequences from scarcity and the student not getting what is desired.

E-learning tools are able to play many roles in supporting these structures and enabling learning analytics to be created, though it must be recognized that a tension can exist between the ideal of supplementing intrinsic drives and the more easily programmed extrinsic motivators based on accomplishment and ownership that characterized early gamification examples, such as completion boxes, rewards, badges and leaderboards.

Towards professionalism and an end to feedback?
The movement from feedback to feedforward occurs naturally within the working environment of an early-career professional where coaching structures are used to support the development of skills and abilities – employees are shown where they have made mistakes or underperformed and how they can improve. This behaviour lies in the best interest of the employer as it is focused on the rapid improvement of an employee's performance. In education terms, this can be classed as a feedforward mechanism where the goal is to help improve abilities and knowledge for the next activity. The coaching structure is key to this process as it intrinsically allows failure to occur, to become accepted as part of the role, and for employees to start building a network that provides them with the help and support that they need. It also makes clear the level of performance that they are expected to operate at.

In many UK chemistry degree programmes, this structure is most effectively mirrored by the final-year research project, the pinnacle of any research-based learning programme. For undergraduate students to operate effectively, they need to report frequently on progress and problems, and to receive guidance on how they should proceed. The primary coaching role may be held by an academic or another member of the group. It is expected that experiments will not always work and that there will be problems that the student will need to overcome by the application of rational analysis and hypotheses. Experience quickly allows the coach to define the student's performance with respect to the norms of the research group and this understanding can be swiftly passed on to the student during informal conversations. Again, the drive of this feedforward discussion is improvement of the student's performance and, ideally, increases in their confidence, self-motivation and productivity.

It is interesting to consider how effectively this coaching structure can be translated to earlier on in a degree. In UCL's own chemistry laboratories it most effectively begins in the third-year practical modules that aid students make the transition from teaching labs to working in the research environment. A baseline practical module, where students gain the lab skills necessary to complete the more specialized experiments, is used to support synthetic organic and inorganic chemistry. Importantly, no feedback is made on the milestone submissions from the students. Instead, feedforward is provided within a coaching structure of one-to-one discussions with academic staff. This is timely as it helps students improve their performance in the following practical. The milestones are assessed by comparison against the standard of a professional, which reinforces the role of extrinsic expectations and the level that the students should aim to meet. The face-to-face nature humanizes the processes and strengthens the effectiveness of the coaching.

Moving to the earlier years, conventional laboratory write-up and feedback types still dominate as vestiges of the rule of summative assessment. Possible feedforward coaching structures are being introduced. The importance of the face-to-face contact effectively pushes this towards the postgraduate demonstrators. They are able to translate guidelines and operational standards for the students in their charge, imprint expectations, provide the frequent feedforward that best helps correct mistakes, and build skills and confidence. Professionalism can be reinforced by replacing classical and highly directed laboratory write-ups with the report-style write-ups of a practising chemist. A coaching discussion with the demonstrator or a senior academic again allows the identification of problems and actions that would improve them. Summative assessment can then be based on the quality of the student's milestones or their ability to work with the information that they have themselves generated and collated.

As well as helping restructure feedback, working with a framework of professionalism can also make clear the connection between the learning activity and what it is to be a professional. Its perspective traverses the potential division between being a student within higher education and the application of its knowledge and skills within employment, while also connecting with an intrinsic motivation to find meaning in what we do.

Notes
[1] Addresses for correspondence: amanda.cain@ucl.ac.uk; paul.bartlett@ucl.ac.uk; a.s.wills@ucl.ac.uk

References
Brew, A. (2007) 'Research and teaching from the students' perspective'. Keynote address at 'International policies and practices for academic enquiry: An international colloquium' held at Marwell Conference Centre, Winchester, 19–21 April.

Wickenbrock, A., Jurgilas, S., Dow, A., Marmugi, L. and Renzoni, F. (2014) 'Magnetic induction tomography using an all-optical ^{87}Rb atomic magnetometer'. *Optics Letters*, 39 (22), 6367–70.

Chapter 14

Teaching chemistry in a virtual laboratory

Chris Blackman, Caroline Pelletier and Keith Turner[1]

Staying with chemistry, Blackman *et al.* distil a decade of thinking and redesigning the curriculum to have students get the chance to consider the principles underlying the chemistry they are learning through experiments. The constraints on laboratory time mean that there is little thinking space, and students can end up 'recipe following' to ensure they get the experiment completed safely. What seemed a good way to get them used to lab procedures in a virtual world led them to an insight not unlike Dewey's, mentioned in the first chapter: it is the artificiality of a learning environment that, if judged well, underpins learning. The virtual world has turned out to have its own rules, which has led to an exploration of how these differences can form part of the learning.

The laboratory is a unique environment in which to understand chemistry. The subject comes alive as theory is put to the test in the real world. Teaching chemistry can take the form of giving students an equation and then demonstrating how theory can be used to predict that the reaction will take place because it is energetically favourable (i.e. gives out heat), what the products will be and what we should expect the reaction to look like. Students can then carry out the practical and see first-hand whether their observations are consistent with those theories. A good laboratory experience involves seeing for oneself how different aspects of a chemical process are connected, such as colour changes, heat transfer (i.e. things heating up or cooling down) and the formation of gas bubbles from solution. Concrete understanding of abstract constructs, such as chemical equations, thermodynamics and standard states of elements and compounds, is thereby achieved through observation. In this way, laboratory work helps students develop a practical understanding of chemistry as a conceptually organized subject area. However, let's consider an extract from a typical laboratory practical:

---

1. The effect of various ligands on the magnitude of Δ_0 in homoleptic chromium(III) complexes

1.1 Preparation of $[Cr(en)_3]Cl_3.3H_2O$
Place between 0.5 and 1.0 g of granular zinc and 2.66 g (10.0 mmol) of $CrCl_3.6H_2O$ in a 50 cm³ Quickfit conical flask containing a magnetic stirring bar. Add 10 cm³ (0.15 mol) of ethylenediamine (en), followed by 10 cm³ methanol. Attach a water condenser fitted with a drying tube containing $CaCl_2$. Place the assembly on a hot plate stirrer and heat the mixture, with stirring, at reflux for at least 1 hour.

Cool the solution to room temperature. Collect the grey-green product by suction filtration using a Buchner funnel. Remove any unreacted zinc using forceps. Wash the filter cake with 5 cm³ portions of 10% ethylenediamine in methanol (v/v) until the washings are colourless.

Purify by recrystallisation by stirring the crude product in a **minimum** quantity (< 15 cm³) of warm water to which 1 drop of conc. HCl has been added (**Note:** not all the solid will dissolve), filtering, and adding approximately 100 cm³ ethanol until a heavy yellow precipitate is formed.

A crystalline sample can sometimes be obtained by warming the solution until most of the precipitate just redissolves followed by cooling in an ice bath. Filter the bright yellow crystals, wash with 2 x 10 cm³ of cold methylated spirit and air dry. A second crop of crystals may be obtained by adding more ethanol to the filtrate and cooling.

Dry the product in a dessicator at least over night. Record the melting point and yield.

Figure 14.1: An extract from a second-year laboratory practical in inorganic chemistry

Source: University College London, 2014

The extract represents only about 15 per cent of a typical practical procedure. Doing laboratory work, therefore, typically requires students to get to grips with a large amount of information at the same time as developing complex handling and other practical skills necessary for using pieces of apparatus. Unsurprisingly, students can become overwhelmed and struggle to differentiate between what is more or less important. Consequently, conceptual understanding can sometimes be hampered by undue concern with following instructions to the letter, a phenomenon colloquially referred to as 'recipe following' by chemistry teachers, who contrast this with understanding the underlying theory.

Since laboratory work is so fundamental to the subject area, students are traditionally asked to prepare for it beforehand, and thereby obtain best 'value' from this precious and scarce resource. They are told to read and familiarize themselves with an experiment before performing it, to mitigate the risk of not understanding what to do or being overwhelmed by what is involved. This strategy is not always very successful. Students can ignore the recommendation to prepare, not least because its realization remains vague: it is difficult to know what counts as being adequately prepared for laboratory work before actually carrying it out.

Improving pre-lab preparation using digital resources

In order to address all of these issues, which are widely recognized by those teaching chemistry in higher education institutions, Chris decided from the start of his appointment at University College London (UCL) in 2007 to explore what might make pre-lab preparation more effective. To this end, he endeavoured to increase use of UCL's virtual learning environment (VLE) – Moodle – in undergraduate provision. With funding provided by UCL (e-learning Development, CALT Secondment, UCL Advances), he developed online guided pre-laboratory tutorials, consisting of written instructions, video and interactive software resources, to help students familiarize themselves with both the practical and theoretical elements of the experiment before undertaking it. These resources proved extremely popular with students, and provided a valuable resource that was reused in subsequent years.

Using interactive software to support chemistry teaching is not new: for example, LabSkills[2] have created a 'virtual laboratory' for use at different levels of education. It is available commercially, although it was initially developed with funding from the Higher Education Funding Council for England's Bristol ChemLabS project.[3] However, Labskills' software, like most examples of 'virtual laboratories', are relatively simple 'point and click' two-dimensional interactive animations. These can be valuable for teaching concepts, but they do not simulate a laboratory environment, or experimental conditions consisting of multiple variables. They can only make a limited contribution, therefore, to helping students prepare for laboratory work in which they will be expected not only to understand the underlying concepts, but also to master practical skills and negotiate unfamiliar, and potentially dangerous, environments.

With a view to exploring the scope of more 'immersive' virtual laboratories, Chris entered into discussions with Solvexx Solutions Ltd, a software company that has developed the most advanced platform to date.[4] Screen shots of Solvexx's virtual laboratory – Learnexx 3D – are shown in Figures 14.2 and 14.3.

Figure 14.2: The Solvexx virtual laboratory
Source: http://learnexx.com; copyright Keith Turner

Figure 14.3: A sample procedure for filling a well plate with a pipette
Source: http://learnexx.com; copyright Keith Turner

Chris identified the potential advantages of this platform as follows:

- The platform can automatically assess whether the lab procedure has been followed correctly and the correct result achieved. This means that feedback is based on student performance.
- The lab equipment is typically based on real models and not simplified or stylized versions, and as such the equipment control interface is intended to provide familiarity and develop competence with the salient aspects of 'real' equipment.
- Because it is based on games technology similar to that used on consoles and tablets, Learnexx 3D can be explored and interacted with using controls that many students will already be familiar with. This also helps to address some of the problems associated with other 3D virtual world environments (e.g. Second Life/OpenSim) that require a long induction period. Other existing 3D environments do not support the type of user interactions needed to teach lab skills and can only support low resolutions and limited amounts of equipment.

On the basis of his discussions about the platform with its developers, Chris identified an opportunity for UCL to develop, in partnership with Solvexx, a number of simulated experiments for use in undergraduate chemistry teaching. A development project was therefore set up with Solvexx, and co-funded by UCL, to investigate the use of 3D virtual environments for teaching chemistry – the first project of its kind in the UK. The aim of this project was to develop an online teaching resource that would enable students to rehearse techniques and experiments as well as develop conceptual understanding, in order to maximize the pedagogic benefit of 'real' laboratory time. It is worth emphasizing that the aim was not to replace 'real' laboratories but to make better use of these expensive and limited teaching facilities through more effective prior learning.

Designing experiments in a 3D lab: Phase 1

The project team's starting point in creating these simulations was to generate an environment as close as possible to the environment the student would encounter in the laboratory. The rationale was that a student would most effectively prepare for an experiment in a 'real' laboratory by rehearsing it in a realistic environment. This guided several key design principles. For example, the project team decided that users of the simulation should have to navigate the laboratory space in order to locate and collect the necessary chemicals and equipment. Furthermore, the team wanted to make sure that the environment did not become *too* 'game-like', so feedback on success or failure appeared as it would during the real-world practical procedure, i.e. typically through analysis of data obtained at the end of the procedure. The team also wanted the simulations to take the same amount of time to work through as the 'real' ones they represented, to map as closely to the actual procedure as possible.

Because of the complexities that these design principles imposed, there was time and funding available only for a subset of the practicals that a first-year undergraduate student is expected to complete.[5] Chris did not make the simulations a compulsory element of the teaching programme, since this was a pilot project. However, this decision had implications for how the students engaged with the software, as discussed below.

Evaluating the 3D lab

The project team planned to obtain student feedback in the first couple of years of use, to inform both software and curriculum development. In the second year of use, the team involved Caroline Pelletier in evaluating its usage. This was because of her previous experience with researching the use of simulations in education. We wanted the evaluation to examine students' experience of the virtual laboratory in depth, so that it could be more centrally integrated into undergraduate chemistry and natural sciences teaching at UCL. Beyond this, we also wanted to examine the benefits of virtual laboratories/facilities in science education, and through engagement with a range of users explore how such facilities can contribute to post-compulsory education more generally. The evaluation involved asking ten students individually to work through a procedure in the virtual laboratory while talking to them about their decisions, thoughts and experiences as they did so. These interviews were videoed for subsequent analysis. This method for evaluating software is widely used in approaches that practise participatory and iterative design.

The student feedback proved extremely interesting. Much of it focused on the issue of realism. Despite the project team's initial expectations, students found navigating the environment challenging, even those procedures that, in the 'real' world, are relatively straightforward, such as moving chemicals and equipment between locations. In addition, students felt that the laboratory had been designed to support a specific way and order for doing the experiment, and that they had to second guess this order with no guidance, or that this order did not reflect the realities of a laboratory. In other words, they felt that they had to work out how the procedure had been designed to work in the virtual laboratory specifically, independently of the 'real' world. These challenges highlight that although the simulation was designed to be realistic, acting within it to effect explicit intentions involved learning a whole new set of skills specific to the software environment, which were different from those needed in a real laboratory.

Student feedback indicated that the difficulty was not that the software was not realistic enough, but rather that students did not know the ways in which it was or was not realistic: they could not deduce the conventions according to which the virtual world operated. For example, if too much iron was put into the weighing boat, did this require re-launching the experiment from the beginning, since iron could not then be removed? Should the beaker be weighed or not: in a virtual world, did it have any weight? Did the bottle of acid have a lid, and if so, did this need to be taken off using a specific control, or was the lid symbolic and pouring happened simply by using the control for 'pouring'? Does the visual representation of liquid or powder relate to the approximate amount or weight of the substance, or it is completely unrelated? Were there specific controls for using two hands, and if so, how could they be activated to perform two simultaneous actions, such as pouring liquid into a funnel? Students could not deduce answers to these questions from the software itself, since one of its design principles was to delay feedback on performance until the experiment's completion – a principle justified in terms of realism, but which actually appeared to impede usage.

Rethinking realism and immersion

On the basis of this feedback, we recommended that the priority for the project team was to provide further guidance on how to interact with objects in the virtual laboratory. Although guidance was available, in a separate dedicated tutorial on how to use the virtual laboratory, the evaluation showed that students did not work through or consult this before starting a practical procedure. The team therefore decided that it would be better to embed guidance within each procedure, rather than separate it off in a simulation of its own. This would make the environment less 'realistic', since pop-up texts would appear within the 'immersive' environment, but such texts were deemed necessary to help users understand the specificities of the 3D lab.

The evaluation highlighted several other ways in which the virtual laboratory's 'realism' hindered, rather than helped, student learning. Delaying all feedback on the success or failure of the procedure until its completion proved to be a source of frustration rather than support for immersion. Although this had been intended to make the virtual laboratory function like a real laboratory, it made it impossible for students to assess whether they were making sense of the virtual laboratory appropriately. The project team decided that a more game-like system of feedback would be more helpful, with users receiving information on their performance sufficiently frequently to be able to adjust it, in the light of the effect they were aiming to achieve in the virtual environment. Similarly, the evaluation highlighted the value of automating certain basic operations or simplifying them. For example, the use of biuret: in the 'real' world, this involves altering the view height to be able to observe the liquid meniscus correctly and concurrently control the volume added by constantly manipulating the flow rate; in the virtual laboratory, this operation defeated most students because of the complexity of the controls required to pour, zoom in and change viewing height. This detracted from, rather than supported, learning of the simulation's substantive learning objectives.

Designing experiments in a 3D lab: Phase 2

The evaluation was used to review how the simulation software could be improved and also more generally how this type of tool could best be implemented in a teaching environment. Some of the issues that the evaluation identified arose because of the way in which the virtual lab had been implemented, i.e. as a 'value-added' element to some practical procedures rather than as a required, and thus planned, element for all practicals. This meant there had been little teaching support, and no requirement, to learn the software's functionality or learn to work through its procedures: the virtual laboratory's intended purpose and benefits consequently remained mysterious to students – a distraction from their learning rather than an aid to it.

This led Chris to review how a 3D simulated lab could be effectively integrated into a curriculum, rather than added to its margins, and specifically, how it could be integrated into his own field of study, Inorganic Chemistry. He concluded that even if the virtual laboratory incorporated the design changes suggested by the evaluation, this would still not address the non-handling skills required of Inorganic Chemistry as a research practice. Such skills do not consist of competence in techniques or procedures, but rather capability in experimental design, and specifically the design–test–interpret–redesign cycle. Teaching this kind of research-based capability is key to UCL's concept of a Connected Curriculum.[6] It was therefore also central to Inorganic Chemistry as a curricular area at UCL.

Chris therefore revised his initial aims in using a virtual laboratory: rather than simply *preparing* students for 'real' laboratory work, he decided that he also wanted it to provide sufficient flexibility and scope such that it could be used at several levels of undergraduate study, from a basic early-years 'follow the procedure' approach to higher-level study, in which students can be posed research-like questions involving genuine experimentation.

From following recipes to designing experiments: Assembling a progressive curriculum

In the light of the evaluation, then, the project team re-conceptualized the purpose for using the 3D laboratory, or more precisely, differentiated between different ways of using it. A progressive curriculum was imagined, stretching from the early years of the chemistry syllabus, to higher levels of study.

In the early years, the project team envisaged that the virtual laboratory could be used to provide pre-lab training for the specific procedure to be carried out in the laboratory. Students would be asked to follow the real-world procedure as written using the simulated laboratory, to characterize the (virtual) products and then rationalize the results. This level of use would be similar to the current available simulations.

For teaching during intermediate years of a degree programme, specific parts of *the same* procedure could be opened up to provide variability beyond that which is 'realistic' – in other words, in ways that cannot be done within the confines of the real-world laboratory environment, not least in an undergraduate context. The purpose of using the 3D lab at this juncture would be to have students build a hypothesis about what they expect to happen at various steps in the procedure before attempting the procedure, modified to use these variables. This would require students to understand the chemistry behind the reactions through a process of experimentation, rather than simply following a procedure and then trying to post-rationalize the results. Also at this level, the team envisaged providing additional, but related, procedures to go beyond the basic procedure: the rationale for this is that the 3D lab could then be used to carry out procedures that could not be done in the real lab, due to limits on its availability, or potentially also, to rehearse more advanced procedures for those students who could tackle these in the real lab. Such additional procedures could also include the use of compounds that would not be utilized in an undergraduate context, because of their toxicity and the hazards of their preparation.

For the highest level of use in an undergraduate context, the purpose of using the lab could be imagined in terms of supporting students develop research capacities. Research in chemistry involves modelling and predicting outcomes, and devising procedures to test these. At this level, then, the

3D lab could be equipped with various solvents and reagents, with students assigned a design task such as, for example, devising a successful target synthesis. Students would be expected to model and predict outcomes of each of the procedural steps and determine the outcomes of their experiment overall. Using the 3D lab in this way would require extensive tutor support, to help students interpret results and guide them in their efforts. However, the benefit of using the 3D lab in this way is that students would then be asking themselves the types of questions required to tackle research problems, i.e. why something works, or does not work; how it could be improved, etc.

Concluding thoughts: Reviewing the use of virtual laboratories in chemistry teaching

When the use of virtual laboratories was first considered in UCL's Chemistry Department, the aim was to provide an additional, and optional, resource to improve the effectiveness of pre-lab preparation. Through implementation, evaluation and re-design, this aim has been modified. We take two main lessons from this experience.

First, although the 3D lab was initially valued for its degree of realism and propensity to 'immerse' students in a lab environment, the project team now recognizes that the value of the 3D lab also lies in its difference from real laboratories, for example in the possibility it offers to enable students to design and rehearse their own experiments and thereby develop research skills, rather than follow set procedures. Although this possibility is theoretically possible in real labs, it is limited by cost, health and safety management, and the availability of lab time in an already packed teaching timetable. This difference – between a real and virtual lab – was initially problematic in this project, partly because it was denied: the 3D lab is, after all, highly 'realistic'. But problems arose precisely because of this realism: in trying to stick as closely as possible to 'real lab' behaviour, the project team neglected to identify, and teach, the specificities of the software, and how to follow a procedure within it. Phase 2 of the implementation process represents an effort to transform this problem into a strength of the 3D lab.

Second, although the 3D lab was initially envisaged as an optional enhancement, the project team is now making efforts to integrate its use into the curriculum fully. This is in recognition of the need to support the use of such a tool, not only through instructions on its use, but also more comprehensively, by linking its use to core teaching, such as existing materials on Moodle, teaching activities and lectures, formative and/or summative assessment, and modular learning objectives. It became clear during the evaluation that the pedagogic purpose of the virtual laboratory needed clarification in order to make it usable: for example, students needed greater clarity on whether the software was intended to develop understanding of generic techniques or particular practicals, or both. In addition, integrating the 3D lab into the curriculum requires planning for progression from year to year. Supporting progression does not simply take the form of additional procedures, but more fundamentally, a re-conceptualization of what doing chemistry involves: from following procedures to designing them. At the moment, the procedures in the 3D lab are independent of one another and are not ordered in any sequence. This is because of restrictions on time and funding, but more fundamentally, because the lab was initially understood to support teaching by being realistic – like a real lab. But in considering how the laboratory could be integrated into teaching, and therefore support progression, the project team has been led to a different conclusion: that the software itself should support development towards increasing complexity, in conceptual, technical and functional terms. In other words, progression should happen at three inter-related levels: the chemistry concepts, the technical requirements of an experiment, and, crucially, the functionality of the software.

Notes

[1] Addresses for correspondence: c.blackman@ucl.ac.uk; c.pelletier@ucl.ac.uk; k.turner@solvexx.com

[2] www.labskills.co.uk

[3] www.chemlabs.bris.ac.uk/DLM.html

[4] http://learnexx.com

[5] These can be viewed and accessed at http://learnexx.com/Universities.html

[6] www.ucl.ac.uk/teaching-learning/education-initiatives/connected-curriculum

Chapter 15

Teaching interdisciplinarity

Carl Gombrich[1]

UCL's deliberate combination of the BA and BSc, the BASc, throws up issues such as those raised in Chapter 8 about interdisciplinarity. Students explore fundamental concepts such as truth and knowledge: they see how discipline-based ideas confront assumptions and find an ever-richer understanding in disciplinary difference. Critical thinking and creativity characterize the learning (and assessed tasks). Carl Gombrich's honest reflection on the difficulties of running an interdisciplinary course across such a wide range brings to life the issues raised by nearly all the position pieces in Part One, but also shows that these seas can be navigated.

Introduction

This chapter addresses some of the points regarding interdisciplinary education raised in Jason Davies' chapter on that theme. It attempts to answer some questions raised there and will no doubt pose others. Specifically, we ask: can we teach interdisciplinarity as a subject to undergraduates?[2] If so, how? What are our ambitions and what are the pitfalls? And to motivate these questions we should perhaps ask a preliminary question: why should we try to teach interdisciplinarity to undergraduates at all?

We will not answer these questions in a strict succession, but the answers will become clear as the chapter progresses and will be summarized at the end. The vehicle we will ride in search of answers is a first-year undergraduate module called Approaches to Knowledge: An Introduction to Interdisciplinarity (ATK), which is a core module for undergraduates studying on UCL's Arts and Sciences BASc.

The Bachelor of Arts and Sciences (BASc) degree at UCL

A prototype of the Bachelor of Arts and Sciences (BASc) degree was originally conceived by Malcolm (now Sir Malcolm) Grant, the then-Provost of UCL, and the Vice Provost International and Education, Professor Michael Worton, in the 2000s. It is, roughly, UCL's 'liberal arts and sciences' degree but, unlike many related programmes, it is also explicit about the intention to foster interdisciplinarity. Development of the curriculum began in earnest in 2010 and the degree accepted its first undergraduates in 2012. There are two versions of the programme: a four-year, 'study abroad' version, in which students spend their third year studying overseas at a partner university, and a more standard three-year version. The programme has now graduated more than 150 students and welcomes 120 students per year in steady state.

The degree is structured around a core (50 per cent of student study time) and four 'pathways' (50 per cent of student study time). The pathways organize UCL's entire academic offer into four bands of broadly cognate disciplines:

- Cultures (Humanities and Arts)
- Societies (Social Sciences, Law)
- Health and Environment (Health and Environmental Sciences)
- Sciences and Engineering (Hard Sciences, Maths and Computer Sciences).

Students 'major' in one of the four pathways. If they major in one of the science pathways (Health and Environment or Sciences and Engineering) they must 'minor' in a non-science pathway (Cultures or Societies), and vice versa. The core contains explicitly inter-, cross-, post- and trans-disciplinary modules as seen in Table 15.1 below.

Table 15.1: The core of Arts and Sciences BASc

CORE	
(students spend 50% of their study time on these courses)	
Compulsory core modules	**Interdisciplinary electives**
Approaches to Knowledge: An Introduction to Interdisciplinarity	Data Visualization
Exploring Complexity: Quantitative Methods	Evolution and the Human Condition
Interdisciplinary Research Methods	Qualitative Thinking
The Knowledge Economy (a 'real-world' consultancy project, in the final year of the degree, on which all students work in small teams to assist a local business)	Technology, Heritage and Material Culture
	Migration and Health
	Object-based Learning: Museum Stories
Final-year (capstone) interdisciplinary dissertation	Psychology and the Real World
Foreign language (students choose their own language to study)	Understanding Cities
	Environmental Sociology
	Citizen Science for Multiple Knowledges
	Interdisciplinarity and Art

The first core course: Approaches to Knowledge: An Introduction to Interdisciplinarity

BASc students meet their first core module, ATK, in their first week at UCL.[3] The edited overview of the module given to students is:

> This course is an introduction to interdisciplinarity. It is divided into two halves.

> **First Half – Weeks 1–5**

> Here the overall 'lens' through which we will be looking at the material is 'Interdisciplinarity and the Disciplines'.

> Each week we will look at a different theme associated with interdisciplinarity and the disciplines.

Week 1. Introduction. Why is there is a renewed interest in interdisciplinarity today?

Week 2. Evidence and the Disciplines. We look at what constitutes evidence in different disciplines.

Week 3. Truth and the Disciplines. We look at how different disciplines across the academic spectrum approach the idea of truth. Why does this matter?

Week 4. Imperialism and the Disciplining of Knowledge. Many of the categories of knowledge we take for granted in academia today were created during times of Western empire. Does this affect how we think about them?

Weeks 4 and 5. The Future of Knowledge and the Disciplines.

Second Half – Weeks 6–10

In the second half of the course we look at interdisciplinary 'superconcepts'. These are ideas that have arisen in one discipline but have come to have wide-ranging and fruitful applications in other disciplines. Examples include:

- Complexity
- Evolution
- Structuralism
- Fiction.

Loosely, I call the experience of this course a more epistemological encountering with interdisciplinarity. There are more references to 'knowledge' than 'methods' here – though, of course, methods are never far away, e.g. in talking about evidence and the evidential requirements of different disciplines. Naturally, the methods angle is also immensely important in teaching interdisciplinarity (highlighted by Davies, Chapter 8, this volume). The BASc addresses this methods aspect in two further first-year courses (see Table 15.1), but these further courses are designed to teach different methodological techniques (and where different methods may be more appropriate or yield more revealing results) rather than dwell on knowledge claims associated with a given method.

The ATK module, like any worthwhile educational experience, is difficult to summarize in a few words, but let us look at just one lecture in more detail before zooming out again to address the questions posed at the beginning of this chapter.

A lecture on 'Truth and the Disciplines'

This lecture occurs in the third week of ATK – see the schedule above. The lecture begins by asking students to vote (with clickers) on the question: 'On balance, do you think there is such a thing as objective truth?' The students are asked to vote *by pathway*, i.e. all Cultures majors vote first, then Societies majors, and so on. The results (aggregated over two years here) are given in Figure 15.1.

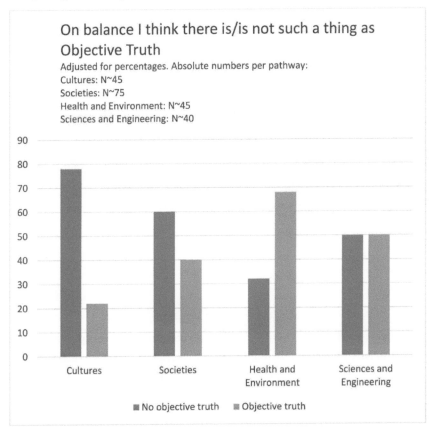

Figure 15.1: Students' beliefs about objective truth, by BASc study pathway

It is pointed out to students that this is far from a scientific experiment. There are numerous possible errors: 1) human mechanical error (pressing the wrong button on the clicker); 2) deliberate subterfuge (students may choose to deliberately click at the wrong time); 3) poor attendance in class, and so on. However, the rise in the belief in objective truth – upwards, from a low base with humanities students, to higher in social scientists and health and life scientists – as well as the slight anomaly of the reverse of the trend for physics, maths and engineering students,[4] is used as a basis for class discussion.

One interesting point raised is whether an individual ends up studying one type of discipline or another because they already have certain attitudes towards truth. Or do they come to have certain attitudes towards truth because of the disciplines they are studying?

The lecture then proceeds to give exemplars of scholars' attitudes towards truth from different disciplinary perspectives. For example, we read the entire abstract of a paper by UCL anthropologist, Martin Holbraad, manifesting what I judge to be an attitude that many anthropologists would be sympathetic to:

> This article holds that deeply entrenched assumptions about the nature, provenance, and value of truth can be brought into view and examined critically when set against the backdrop of a radically different set of concepts and practices that are associated with truth seeking in contemporary Afro-Cuban divination. Drawing briefly on an ethnographic analysis of the ways in which Cuban cult practitioners use oracles, the article seeks to formulate a radically alternative concept of truth. This viewpoint eschews common premises about the role of 'representation' in the pursuit of truth in favor of a notion of truth as 'conceptual redefinition'. If the ethnography of divination in Cuba forces the analyst radically to reformulate the concept of truth, what effect might this new approach have on the project of anthropology itself? (Holbraad, 2009)

Contrast this with science as 'an objective, knowledge-seeking discipline' (Turnbull, 2010: 34) or with this perspective on truth in psychiatry from a recent BASc alumna:

> I think modern faith and belief in science leads to perception of prominent scientific advances as truth. In mental health for example, it's interesting how ready different generations have been to embrace new categories of illness and modes of treatment (some of which have later been dismissed). Western society seems accepting of the myriad new disease categories presented to us, and prepared to view these as truth. We readily see our own minds through the lens of recent scientific 'truth', I think. And readily apply our categories to other cultures, because our categories have their roots in science and progress ... So that's just one example of what I see as the sometimes problematic association of science and truth ... I think critical psychiatry could therefore

> be a good starting point for research that does openly question
> and discuss ideas of science, health and truth (Kirk-Smith, 2014)

There is much to tease apart here, not least the differences between objectivity, truth and knowledge. These issues are, in fact, briefly acknowledged and addressed in the lecture, but this is not a philosophy class. Indeed, we specifically examine philosophy *as a discipline* here and try not to allow too much philosophical hegemony over the analysis of truth. We are trying to understand different disciplinary attitudes towards truth, not to give a first-year course in Truth and Logic.

Through these examples from different disciplines, and after a short introduction to the Sokal scandal and postmodernism,[5] the lecture gradually builds a 'typology' of truth as shown in the slide on Figure 15.2.

Build up a Rough Typology of Truth and the Disciplines...

One side: Science, (normal) Economics, Engineering, some Maths.	Other side: Humanities, Arts, (heterodox) Economics, Social Science (e.g. Anthropology, Sociology), some Maths
• Objective	• Subjective
• Positive	• Normative
• Science	• Non-Science
• Absolute	• Relative

Figure 15.2: A rough typology of Truth and the Disciplines

The lecture concludes with instructions for an assessment that asks students to write a blog relating one or other of these aspects of truth to one of their pathway disciplines.

It can be seen that this lecture asks students to take a 'high level' view of the disciplines. This is something explicitly stated throughout ATK: good interdisciplinary practitioners often need to toggle between zooming in and zooming out. Zoom in when you need to work within a discipline – usually the discipline where you have most expertise, zoom out when you need to work with or in other disciplines (see Galway *et al.*, 2016: 395 for a recent example from interdisciplinary work in public health). Thus, from a higher vantage point, you may begin to understand other disciplinary perspectives, assumptions, preoccupations, etc.

In other words, in this lecture (and in much of ATK) we are attempting to view the disciplines 'from above', without committing to any particular one. We are starting a process of trying to think from different disciplinary perspectives. This occurs at the same time as students start studying on more conventional courses within their pathways. The students' learning is therefore not a linear process (this, too, is emphasized). Coming from a Level 1 class in Anatomy or Engineering, it may be challenging to consider more philosophical or sociological aspects of your discipline, but this interleaving of the particular with the universal, the detail with the big picture, is what we hope to educate in sophisticated interdisciplinary practitioners.

Having examined this one lecture from the ATK course in more detail, let us return as promised to ask:

Why should we teach interdisciplinarity to undergraduates?

For those involved in the BASc there was a local reason, amounting to something of a moral imperative: if you offer a major new interdisciplinary degree, and while doing so make claims about the importance and value of interdisciplinarity, you should take interdisciplinarity and its teaching seriously. A comparison with disciplinary courses makes this clear. It would be strange to offer new courses in, say, economics or history, or even much newer disciplines such as digital humanities or synthetic biology, without any foundational courses relating to the concepts, methods, assumptions and foci of those disciplines.

However, although these local reasons were the immediate concern of UCL, they are, of course, just a manifestation of wider, more global reasons – those behind the offering of the BASc course in the first place: the belief that interdisciplinary learning has an important place in contemporary higher education.

As Davies mentions in the context of *disciplinary* education, university is about 'a transformation of one's thinking' (Chapter 8, this volume) not just 'more [disciplinary] knowledge'. In this light, an interdisciplinary education should be about a *particular* transformation of one's thinking, parallel to, but also somehow superseding (or at least matching in some sense), any transformations resulting from disciplinary training.

Apart from the problematic idea of superseding, in the sense of 'rising above' any given discipline, and the flavour of arrogance with which this is infused (more on this in the section on the role of the teacher below), there is an obvious and immediate paradox here: interdisciplinarity, by this process, is turned somehow into a super-discipline, with its own parameters, rules, ways of measuring success, and so on (Boix Mansilla, *et al.*, 2009). In Becher and Trowler's phraseology (Becher and Trowler, 2001), while attempting to avoid disciplinary 'tribalism', we risk setting up our own tribe of supra-disciplinary über-scholars. I think a certain amount of this criticism is fair and unavoidable. We must take it on the chin: we *are* seeking some distinct gains that arise from studying more than one discipline. However, we can certainly mitigate any charges of arrogance by being humble (and, indeed, realistic) about the costs as well as the benefits of studying more than one discipline (Davies, Chapter 8, this volume).

So, what might the broader rationale for teaching interdisciplinarity be? Gombrich and Hogan (2017) identify two sets of reasons:

1. To foster better ability to engage with multiple disciplines in due course on the programme. Call this a more practical aim – even if the 'practical' element here means simply learning how to relate to and engage in the practice of different academic disciplines
2. To foster 'metacognitive' and broader intellectual gains, for example perspective-taking, creativity and bridging.

Both sets of reasons improve on what Davies calls the 'incidental' aspects of interdisciplinarity learning (Chapter 8, this volume) – which I take to mean what happens more or less by accident when students study more than one discipline contemporaneously.

To expand a little on each of these sets in turn:

1.a. The practical aspects – how to write an essay, how to reference, teamwork in different disciplines, etc. – are immensely important but not so difficult to impart. It should further be acknowledged that some of these gains are not *solely* practical in the sense that a richer understanding of any culture (including any disciplinary culture) is best achieved by immersing yourself in it and going with its practical flows. Why do political scientists encourage more use of the first person in student essays than lawyers? What does this tell us about the respective epistemological assumptions of each discipline? And the monotonous passive tense of the lab report ... what does this reveal about science's positivist claims? There are as many examples of such differences as there are disciplines themselves. Immersion in different disciplinary practices invites immediate questions about differences between disciplinary cultures.

2.a. Undoubtedly, the metacognitive gains have the potential to be more exciting than simply learning different disciplinary writing conventions or referencing styles. Many of these gains form part of what are widely known as twenty-first century skills (Van Damme, 2016), which are explicitly sought after by many stakeholders in education (for example, see DfES, 2003; Suto, 2013; Neumeier, 2013). Although the nomenclature around these skills is still widely criticized and the possibility of their very existence is ridiculed in some parts of the education world (Bennett, 2016), the evidence for their existence is in fact well established (Hogan *et al.*, 2015). Current studies linking interdisciplinary education to the fostering and learning of such skills is still at the level of small-scale, qualitative studies, but we are watching the evidence base with interest. It is certainly plausible – call it a research hypothesis – that by teaching students about different epistemological positions as espoused by different disciplines, and then asking a student really to enter into the spirit of such positions, or to approach a given problem using the knowledge assumptions and methodological techniques of more than one discipline, the student will gain an ability to take multiple perspectives on a problem or learn a habit of scanning widely for creative solutions.

Deep Critical Thinking

The teaching of these different disciplinary epistemological viewpoints is what I dub 'Deep Critical Thinking' (DCT). What we might call Surface Critical Thinking (the more usual examination of premises, assumptions, logical progression of argument, etc.) is also, of course, important, especially for less experienced learners. But DCT aims for something different. By looking at what different disciplines count as truth, evidence, their history, etc., we try to understand why people who trained in certain disciplines take different perspectives on these matters. What is it about studying a discipline that might make you more likely to think that knowledge is subjective? Do certain disciplines discount all qualitative evidence? If so, why? How might this affect what assumptions an academic makes and what arguments they think are acceptable? What do these positions tell us about the knowledge claims emerging from a discipline? Given a better understanding of these matters, how should a student choose to interact with various disciplinary claims? The stance here is that these questions are worthy of consideration before one looks at any texts or any utterances of the academically disciplined.

In short, we recognize that there is no view from an Academic Nowhere. This point is made to students. We are not claiming supra-disciplinary omniscience. But it is just as important not to dive down disciplinary rabbit holes before you are fully aware that there are many other tunnels, thickets and, indeed, wider landscapes to scan and explore.

The role of the teacher on inter- or non-disciplinary courses

There are unique challenges for a teacher or module lead on an inter- or non-disciplinary course. Just three are commented on below.

First, as Davies (Chapter 8, this volume) notes: 'Put simply, a university teacher's role is to induct students into their "tribe"'. We have already noted above the paradoxical notion that there should be an 'interdisciplinary tribe' for those on interdisciplinary courses. The interdisciplinary teacher must somehow create boundaries for the essentially boundary-breaking or boundary-less.

Second, 'The more interdisciplinary the situation, the less likely it will be that our guest lecturer understands other aspects of what the students are studying. Their ability to guide the students on these kinds of questions will be limited and unpredictable' (Chapter 8, this volume).

A successful module leader will therefore have some genuine expertise in more than one discipline and must remain non-partisan. The more 'inter-' or 'non'-disciplinary the course is, the harder this is to achieve. Academics who have genuine expertise in more than one discipline are rare, but expertise in three or four disciplines? It would be exciting indeed to have Herbert Simon or Michael Polanyi to lecture on our programmes, but these sorts of people only come along once or twice in a generation and may not be released by their heads of department for much undergraduate teaching. One can (and usually does) get around this situation of limited expertise in each area by delivering team-taught courses, but such courses still benefit from a strong module leader acting as an intellectual lens through whom the students can engage with the course. For what is teaching if not some kind of inter-subjective transfer of meaning? This is likely to be especially important in complex interdisciplinary courses involving several teachers.

I cannot avoid a little personal biography here. Over the last five years of teaching ATK, I have used my position on the module to make a virtue of the generalism required to lead it. Perhaps at the beginning of the course in 2012 this was less convincing. Although I was qualified as someone with postgraduate degrees in both humanities and science, and professional knowledge of music and languages, I did not have a research career and so did not fit the usual template of a modern academic. To my mind, this was an advantage. I was not academically 'disciplined' in the now usual way. What better starting point from which to launch an excitingly new high-profile interdisciplinary degree!

However, my stance no doubt caused tensions. In an original version of ATK (called 'Foundations of Knowledge') there was a much stronger pull towards what I would call a more sociological position, in which, broadly speaking, social construction of all knowledge was assumed. I understood enough science to realize that we would have to take BASc students who were primarily scientists or engineers along with us on the programme's journey. So I was uneasy about such a stance, with its strong hues of relativism and 'problematization' of science. This could well have alienated half our student cohort from the start. It is not that I am opposed to constructivist or even postmodern views – far from it – and there are infinitely better scientists (for example, the particle-physicist-turned-philosopher, Andrew Pickering) who are more postmodern than I am. However, my hunch is that many young scientists, even interdisciplinary ones, have a belief in and love of the apparent objective truth of much science, and it is important that they can flourish within the BASc. My goal therefore was to try to be as respectful to each disciplinary stance as possible, using evidence (e.g. in the examples from ATK above) to show exemplars of disciplinary approaches to truth, evidence, and so on, and then to allow the students, through their assignments and personal research and reading, to further their understanding of what it means to be a scholar in one discipline or another. I call this approach a fostering of 'academic empathy' (Gombrich, 2013) and this idea makes its way onto ATK as part of the idea that to be a good interdisciplinary practitioner you should endeavour to enter into the spirit of more than one discipline.

To return to the idea of generalism, my experience of leading this module, and the BASc in general, has led me to research further into conceptions of generalism. There is now a growing body of literature (Burke, 2010; Mikkelsen and Martin, 2016) on the need to return to historical intellectual values of polymathy and generalism as goals for education. There are arguments to support both the inherent and instrumental value of such goals. From the instrumental perspective, what, really, is the purpose of narrow disciplinary training at university when around 99 per cent of graduates will not be academics and the modern workplace (changing so rapidly in the technological revolution) has almost no use at all for disciplinary training as such (Gombrich, 2016)?

The work on generalism and polymathy attempts to build an evidence base for the somewhat out-of-favour ideas of breadth and wider learning. This, in turn, allows me to lead a course with a very broad remit in a way that is intellectually honest. However, the intellectual honesty can best be maintained by remaining avowedly outside any specific disciplinary programme within the university. And almost by definition, this approach must remain an anomaly. So how scalable can it be? I am lucky that UCL has supported me in this venture. Would other universities do the same with their 'generalist' teachers?

Although I pose these questions with a slightly negative spin, I am in fact optimistic that institutions can adapt to allow more flourishing of younger, highly interdisciplinary, polymathic scholars.[6] The graduates from the BASc itself, some now moving into PhDs in such areas as Environmental Change Management and Computational, Cognitive Neuroscience, would make excellent leaders of the BASc in due course. And the British Academy has noted recently the importance of institutions adapting in order to support vital interdisciplinary research of young academics (British Academy, 2016). Universities must meet these challenges if they are to remain places of intellectual excitement and relevance to wider society.

Third, on such a broad course, each lecture topic will most probably only appeal to, at best, 70 per cent of the cohort. At least, this is what the free comments in the student evaluations reveal. If you have joined the BASc as a student intending to focus broadly on economics and social sciences, but also taking courses in coding and data handling, it is unlikely that a lecture on 'Truth in Art' will be closest to your interests. Conversely, those who come to study art, design and their applications in engineering may find too much focus on the social sciences tedious. Or many may find several of the lectures simply 'too philosophical'. There is no substitute in these cases for frequent framing and sign-posting from the teacher, and frequent reassurances to individuals that something they are likely to be interested in will be coming up in the next week or two.

Measuring the success of teaching interdisciplinarity

When we ask 'Can we teach interdisciplinarity to undergraduates?' we should seek some metrics that allow us to answer this question precisely. These metrics are hard to find. On the one hand, we might look hopefully at the overall, big picture metrics for the BASc degree; on the other, we have small-scale student evaluations for courses such as ATK. But it is not clear exactly how either of these relate to 'teaching interdisciplinarity'. The big metrics for the BASc programme are very positive: 97–98 per cent retention rate, excellent graduate employment statistics, very many students progressing to prestigious Master's courses and PhDs at Oxford, Cambridge, UCL, Imperial College, LSE, etc.

We might wave our hands enthusiastically at this and say, 'See, teaching interdisciplinarity works!', but this is unlikely to appease sceptics. On the other hand, student evaluations for the ATK course (and, indeed, its sister course in interdisciplinary research methods) remain somewhat resolutely stuck at around 3.5/5 on a Likert scale measuring overall satisfaction. This is an acceptable number, but not brilliant. And it is perhaps striking that this ratio has not changed much over the past four years despite responding every year to student feedback and delivering considerable improvements in structure, assessments and clarity of delivery.

To try to improve our metrics, we recently conducted a small-scale research project inviting students 'who did not enjoy ATK in Year 1 but who have subsequently – in later years of the degree – come to appreciate the value in its approach and themes' to participate. This has yielded some interesting extended feedback and qualitative data that highlight very positively the part these broader, more conceptual interdisciplinary courses have played in the learning journeys of these students, but, of course, this sample is manifestly self-selecting. Would it be possible to find a similar number of students who in retrospect considered ATK to have been more of a waste of time than when they undertook the course?

We don't know the answer to this question and we are still working out how best to measure the learning gains of teaching interdisciplinarity. There are many serious conceptual and operational challenges. For example: how can we define clearly what we mean by interdisciplinary education (as opposed, say, to 'joint honours degrees' or 'single honours degrees with electives')?; how can we filter out metacognitive gains due to educational programmes from those that may simply be due to the natural cognitive development of our students?; how can we find and follow large enough comparative cohorts to measure differences between interdisciplinary and non-interdisciplinary students? Some of these problems are common to many large-scale educational research projects, but they remain problems. However, there is no cause for any major changes to the current BASc project. The overall success of the degree means that we are very positive about our core courses and the degree as a whole. There is certainly room for more hard-edged research into the gains made by explicitly teaching interdisciplinarity, but there is also cause for cautious celebration of the results so far, and encouragement for continuing to innovate along some of the lines already explored.

Conclusion

We have answered the question of why we should teach interdisciplinarity by looking at both practical and metacognitive gains. We have shown that it is possible to teach interdisciplinarity, using a 'high level', conceptual course like ATK on the Arts and Sciences BASc programme. We have concluded that it is certainly possible to do this but that it remains challenging to provide clear metrics regarding how teaching interdisciplinarity leads to benefits distinct from the learning gains of any sophisticated introductory course in, for example, history or engineering. We would like to see more research into possible metacognitive outcomes, such as improvements in bridging, creativity and perspective-taking.

Recently, at a 'future of work' debate at UCL organized by *The Economist* magazine, a final-year BASc student, speaking positively about the programme, nevertheless cautioned, 'talk of "imaginative, cross-disciplinary thinking" is admittedly an uncomfortably abstract, hard-to-grasp concept; and an even harder one to teach. No degree course can claim to have this mastered' (Devine, 2016). This is true. But perhaps we can be content with Davies' idea that interdisciplinary courses will always require students and teachers to 'puzzl[e] things out together' (Chapter 8, this volume). This, surely, is appropriate for our rapidly changing world, our increasingly complex environment and the need for our universities to adapt in an age of technological and social change. The 'unique kind of creativity' (Chapter 8, this volume) that teaching interdisciplinarity brings is worth the challenges it presents.

Notes

1 Address for correspondence: c.gombrich@ucl.ac.uk

2 It is worth mentioning that the idea of 'teaching interdisciplinarity' may also require some background and explanation. It is reasonable to ask whether 'interdisciplinarity' is something one can really study like mechanics, sociology or French. In other words: does it have anything like the ontological status of a discipline, or at least some subject matter? This is a good question. However, we assume here that interdisciplinarity has, in fact, now been sufficiently *reified* – has become enough of a 'thing' – in the intellectual consciousness that it has sufficient ontological status to be approached as an object of study.

3 There is immense value in the community-building aspects of having a major core course for all students on a Liberal Arts and Sciences programme. Such a degree can otherwise easily become fractured and dissipated for the student body, whereas studying core courses together fosters a healthy community of practice (Lave and Wenger, 1991; see also Davies, Chapter 8 in this volume). However, we will not explore this positive aspect of large core courses here.

4 I have a hunch that mathematicians are more inclined to be 'mystical' than some other scientists. (Take Cantor, Gödel and Gröthendieck as three random, but not insignificant, examples.) Whether this means they would therefore believe more in

objective truth or not, I cannot say, but they would certainly query more mundane scientific attitudes towards truth. A serious interdisciplinary work of scientific history remains to be written on this.

[5] Alan Sokal is an American physicist who, in 1996, 'hoaxed' a humanities journal by submitting a fake article on 'quantum gravity and hermeneutics', which the journal accepted and published (see https://en.wikipedia.org/wiki/Sokal_affair). His intention was to expose charlatanism in parts of the humanities – especially those associated with postmodernism – and the revelation that the article was a hoax led to much debate between practitioners of different disciplines. This event is considered to be part of the 'Science Wars' of the 1990s in which such notions as the objectivity of science truth claims, the social construction of knowledge, etc. were widely discussed (see https://en.wikipedia.org/wiki/Science_wars).

[6] There are subtleties to be addressed here regarding the interplay between generalism, polymathy and interdisciplinarity. For example, I am careful to stress to students that interdisciplinary study can, even at undergraduate level, lead to highly specialized outcomes, not just generalist ones. For example, our prize-winning graduate who, in 2016, wrote her capstone dissertation on the feasibility of installing small-scale anaerobic digestion plants at inner-city sites, using analyses from engineering, economics and sociology, is now a budding expert in this highly specialized field. My view, now copiously evidenced by graduate outcomes, is that the BASc degree can lead to the graduation of both generalists and specialized interdisciplinarians, and that both outcomes are valuable. This requires far more analysis than we have space for here.

References

Becher, T. and Trowler, P.R. (2001) *Academic Tribes and Territories: Intellectual enquiry and the culture of disciplines.* 2nd ed. Buckingham: Society for Research into Higher Education and Open University Press.

Bennett, T. (2016) 'Problem with 21st century skills …' [Tweet], 3 November. Online. https://twitter.com/tombennett71/status/794104232907575296 (accessed 28 January 2017).

Boix Mansilla, V., Dawes Duraisingh, E., Wolfe, C.R. and Haynes, C. (2009) 'Targeted assessment rubric: An empirically grounded rubric for interdisciplinary writing'. *Journal of Higher Education*, 80 (3), 334–53.

British Academy (2016) *Crossing Paths: Interdisciplinary institutions, careers, education and applications.* London: British Academy. Online. www.britac. ac.uk/sites/default/files/Crossing%20Paths%20-%20Full%20Report.pdf (accessed 28 January 2017).

Burke, P. (2010) 'The polymath: A cultural and social history of an intellectual species'. In Smith, D.F. and Philsooph, H. (eds) *Explorations in Cultural History: Essays for Peter Gabriel McCaffery.* Aberdeen: Centre for Cultural History, 67–79.

Devine, K. (2016). 'Full Economist Future of Work Talk' [sic]. [Video]. Online. www.youtube.com/watch?v=mGUjYy4b2r0 (accessed 28 January 2017).

DfES (Department for Education and Skills) (2003) *21st Century Skills: Realising our potential: Individuals, employers, nation.* Norwich: The Stationery Office. Online. www.gov.uk/government/uploads/system/uploads/attachment_data/file/336816/21st_Century_Skills_Realising_Our_Potential.pdf (accessed 28 January 2017).

Galway, L.P., Parkes, M.W., Allen, D. and Takaro, T.K. (2016) 'Building interdisciplinary research capacity: A key challenge for ecological approaches in public health'. *AIMS Public Health*, 3 (2), 389–406.

Gombrich, C. (2013) 'Academic empathy'. Blog, 8 December. Online. www.carlgombrich.org/academic-empathy/ (accessed 28 January 2017).

Gombrich, C. (2016) 'Polymathy, new generalism, and the future of work: A little theory and some practice from UCL's arts and sciences degree'. In Kirby, W.C. and van der Wende, M. (eds) *Experiences in Liberal Arts and Science Education from America, Europe, and Asia: A dialogue across continents*. New York: Palgrave Macmillan, 75–89.

Gombrich, C. and Hogan, M. (2017) 'Interdisciplinarity and the student voice'. In Frodeman, R., Klein, J.T. and Pacheco, R.C.S. (eds) *The Oxford Handbook of Interdisciplinarity*. 2nd ed. Oxford: Oxford University Press, 544–57.

Hogan, M.J., Dwyer, C.P., Harney, O.M., Noone, C. and Conway, R J. (2015) 'Metacognitive skill development and applied systems science: A framework of metacognitive skills, self-regulatory functions and real-world applications'. In Peña-Ayala, A. (ed.) *Metacognition: Fundaments, Applications, and Trends*. Cham: Springer, 75–106.

Holbraad, M. (2009) 'Ontography and alterity: Defining anthropological truth'. *Social Analysis*, 53 (2), 80–93.

Kirk-Smith, A. (2014) Email to author [personal communication].

Lave, J. and Wenger, E. (1991) *Situated Learning: Legitimate peripheral participation*. Cambridge: Cambridge University Press.

Mikkelsen, K. and Martin, R. (2016) *The Neo-Generalist: Where you go is who you are*. London: LID Publishing.

Neumeier, M. (2013) *Metaskills: Five talents for the robotic age*. San Francisco: New Riders.

Turnbull, J. (2010) 'The context and nature of engineering design'. In *Philosophy of Engineering*. Vol. 1. London: Royal Academy of Engineering. Online. www.raeng.org.uk/publications/reports/philosophy-of-engineering-volume-1 (accessed 25 March 2018).

Suto, I. (2013) *21st Century Skills: Ancient, ubiquitous, enigmatic?* Cambridge: Cambridge Assessment. Online. www.cambridgeassessment.org.uk/Images/130437-21st-century-skills-ancient-ubiquitous-enigmatic-.pdf (accessed 28 January 2017).

Van Damme, D. (2016) 'Transcending boundaries: Educational trajectories, subject domains, and skills demands'. In Kirby, W.C. and van der Wende, M. (eds) *Experiences in Liberal Arts and Science Education from America, Europe, and Asia: A dialogue across continents*. New York: Palgrave Macmillan, 127–42.

Wikipedia (2018) 'Sokal affair'. Online. https://en.wikipedia.org/wiki/Sokal_affair (accessed 13 March 2018).

Chapter 16

Forensic science: Interdisciplinary, emerging, contested

Ruth Morgan[1]

In creating a degree course for forensic science, Ruth Morgan faces similar hurdles and possibilities to the previous case study. She is tackling a subject that in its application makes sense in the world, but is far more difficult to bring together as a coherent single subject than it might at first appear. Making education coherent, broad *and* expert in potentially high-stakes environments (involving judicial process, guilt, innocence and sentencing) requires that she tailor the learning, like so many other examples here of research-based learning, around scenarios and real-life situations that help the students understand the relevance of the learning they must draw on to address the situation before them. As with other interdisciplinary courses, the lack of an existing 'rulebook' invites a great deal of creativity and persistent application as the tutors and the students work together to discover ways forward in a field full of genuine uncertainty. A situation where no one has the right answers is the perfect environment for research-based education.

Forensic science, the application of scientific knowledge and methods to legal issues and criminal investigations, is an emerging interdisciplinary subject. The forensic science process addresses the identification of clues at a crime scene and other pertinent locations, the analysis of those materials, interpreting their meaning to develop a forensic reconstruction of events, and then presenting those findings as intelligence to an ongoing investigation and/or as evidence in court. Forensic science has many of the hallmarks of a 'subject' (Becher and Trowler, 2001; Strand, 2007). It has a broadly understood name (there are job titles and building names that include 'forensic science'), a large number of university courses, a published literature and a professional society. However, forensic science is still developing and its scope is yet to be fully articulated. Forensic science as a subject and approach has methodological underpinnings and it has developed a critical mass in addressing applied problems. However, the philosophical frameworks underpinning forensic science are contested, and forensic science is arguably yet to realize its potential fully in the production of new knowledge.

In this context the UCL MSc Crime and Forensic Science was developed. It was designed to be distinctive from other well-established programmes in forensic science in the UK in terms of content, and also to challenge students to develop critical interdisciplinary thinking and research skills. The programme focuses on forensic science as it stands at the intersection of science and the law, and addresses the scope of forensic science in the context of the influences from society, politics and economics. We have a strong emphasis on the interpretation of evidence, on the role of research in the production of new knowledge, and in developing approaches to articulate and apply generalizable theory in context-sensitive scenarios. An example of this is the Understanding and Interpreting Forensic Evidence core module. The focus of the module is to raise the question 'how do we know what forensic evidence means when it is identified, analysed and classified?' In addressing this question, the module highlights where there are currently gaps in the evidence base, and engages students with the fundamental issue of how can we interpret evidence robustly and transparently, and what approaches may offer solutions in the context of forensic reconstructions. We have a commitment to developing a synergy between research and the challenges identified in the practice of forensic science, with the aim of producing the foundations for evidence-based practice that is implementable.

There have been a number of challenges. The most significant one has been crafting a programme in forensic science (a term generally understood to equate with the traditionally applied, practical focus of professional forensic science provision) that addresses and develops our students' critical thinking and engagement with the philosophical and theoretical underpinnings of forensic science, some of which are only just in the process of being articulated. It has required considerable thought to develop a programme that challenges students to make links across traditional disciplinary boundaries (for example, interpreting DNA profiles for forensic reconstruction requires agility in making links between genetics, psychology and the law), and to engage with a subject where there are still significant questions being posed that have yet to be answered, which will be critical in refining the scope of the subject. One area that has highlighted this has been in the development of assessments that encourage students to make arguments and justify their stance or approach where there are few 'right' answers.

Managing student expectations of a course that incorporates a familiar term ('forensic') is a constant challenge at every stage of both recruitment and enrolment. Consistently and coherently throughout every part of the course seeking to articulate and define this developing subject has been an interesting exercise and one that we have refined each year in response to each cohort. It is recognized that the term 'forensics' has become the dominant model of understanding the forensic science, in contrast to 'forensic science' (Roux *et al.*, 2012; Roux *et al.*, 2015). Within 'forensics' the focus is predominantly on how the parent disciplines (such as chemistry, biology, computer science, geology) can assist in the exploitation of evidence within the criminal justice system. The crime scene is considered to be a distinct activity generally addressed by the police in an operational and processing capacity (Roux *et al.*, 2012). Our approach within the MSc is to reflect the research we are undertaking that is part of a movement calling for a return to 'forensic science'. Research in 'forensic science' in contrast to 'forensics' enables the discipline to use science in problem-solving endeavours rather than solely establishing a series of mechanical and standard technical operations that can be followed in a laboratory or crime scene setting (Morgan, 2017). Conveying this subtle, yet fundamental, difference to prospective and current students remains a challenge. We actively seek prospective students from diverse backgrounds to ensure that each cohort comprises students from different original disciplines from across the sciences, social sciences and humanities. We consistently use a number of 'sound bites' to convey the essence of 'forensic science' that we engage with in our online and course materials, such as '… our ability to analyse may outstrip our ability to interpret' (Walport, 2015: 6). We have developed our online presence to make the distinctive nature of our approach a unique selling point and to ensure this is as upfront and clear as possible. More recently we have been able to highlight the types of employment our graduates go on to (very few go into traditional 'forensics' jobs such as 'forensic scientist', with more going into problem-solving, research and management roles within policy and consultancy groups and government organizations).

It is in this context that maintaining supple teaching approaches that can incorporate a disciplinary gaze, but also instil a curiosity within a field that is yet to be fully defined, is so critical. The MSc course is designed to enable students to explore forensic science issues, concepts and challenges from different disciplinary points of view, and it is hoped that this is a model that is also present in our research because it is critical to the development of this interdisciplinary subject. Our hope is that by setting out the puzzles and challenges forensic science is facing, the dialogue between students, researchers and practitioners is part of the learning experience, and the learning experience fuels new pathways for research. An example of this was in one of the MSc modules where part of the assessment of the Practices of Crime Scene Investigation and Expert Testimony module was to present the findings of a crime scene examination in a court setting. In other modules on the programme we deal with the theoretical approaches to interpreting evidence and the importance of multiple lines of evidence and evidence bases being used to assess the weight and significance of evidence to build a forensic reconstruction. In particular one case example had been utilized illustrating that it was not possible to build an entire case on the basis of one line of evidence (in that particular case, a DNA profile). During the 'crime scene investigation' assessment, one student outlined how she had identified, collected, packaged and labelled a pertinent exhibit. She was cross-examined and asked why she had not requested DNA analysis to be undertaken on the item. In the 'courtroom', the student explained that given the type of crime scene and given the lack of other evidence, DNA analysis had not been requested as it would only have provided one line of evidence, which would not be sufficient to progress the case. There was a pause and hush in the 'courtroom'. The professional crime scene investigator undertaking the cross-examination outlined that it was quite usual to progress a case with just DNA evidence. There was a mutual realization that the casework experience of the investigator, and the understanding of the published (theoretical) literature of the student, had resulted in answers that, while not mutually compatible, were both 'right'. The students, and the academics and professionals who had collaborated to deliver the course, were able to see first-hand in this moment an example of the mismatch that occurs in interdisciplinary fields between theory and real-world practice in a most powerful and palpable way. The fuel this provided for the reading group that took place the following week was dynamite. The MSc course seeks to enable as much of this interaction between the different actors and the different contexts within forensic science as possible to equip our graduates for their future roles.

Forensic science is familiar with the frustrating and often disorientating process of 'critical interdisciplinary'. There are benefits of having outside agencies such as the criminal justice system, the police and the professional forensic science providers identifying the priorities and articulating the sought-for solutions within forensic science. However, there are also distinct challenges. The currently dominant focus on 'forensics' is perhaps due to the preference for the more explicit (codified) nature of the knowledge that can be applied to developing rigorous procedures and protocols to establish good practices (such as fingermark development, or the analysis of a substance by mass spectrometry methods). The development of such procedures enables quality assurance to be codified and easily measured and identified. As such the resources made available within forensic science are often restricted to addressing questions of process or evidence capture. However, the real-world and applied nature of 'forensic science' requires both explicit and tacit forms of knowledge, and it is challenging to get these questions on the agenda in a context of very limited resources. Herein lies a challenge but also the potential for significant creativity. Our students are exposed to this landscape and encouraged to foster a spirit of curiosity, to ask questions that are not yet being asked and to develop elegant approaches to finding solutions. For example, we have developed a relationship with a company that produces analytical tools for crime scene examination to run a number of MSc research projects each year to test the capacity of new and emerging technologies within the context of evidence interpretation and forensic reconstruction (as opposed to the identification and characterization of a trace). The students gain exposure to the real-world consideration of a competitive marketplace within which forensic science resides, and the industry partner is able to use the research to illustrate the wider value of their technologies to customers within the forensic science stakeholder community.

Our vision for this interdisciplinary degree is to create an environment that fosters creativity and strategic thinking. We are endeavouring to equip our graduates with a way of thinking that can see the context within which a problem is situated, and then be willing and able to provide an expert perspective. Along with this we are training our students to have the skills to be able to offer a problem-solving approach that identifies where the knowledge gaps are and the disciplines that may be able to offer insights to fill those gaps. These are the skills that are in great demand within an applied subject. Graduates with those skills will be among those who contribute to the development of the subject in both theory and practice.

Notes

[1] Address for correspondence: ruth.morgan@ucl.ac.uk

References

Becher, T. and Trowler, P.R. (2001) *Academic Tribes and Territories: Intellectual enquiry and the culture of disciplines*. 2nd ed. Buckingham: Society for Research into Higher Education and Open University Press.

Morgan, R.M. (2017) 'Conceptualising forensic science and forensic reconstruction – Part I: A conceptual model'. *Science and Justice*, 57 (6), 455–9.

Roux, C., Crispino, F. and Ribaux, O. (2012) 'From forensics to forensic science'. *Current Issues in Criminal Justice*, 24 (1), 7–24.

Roux, C., Talbot-Wright, B., Robertson, J., Crispino, F. and Ribaux, O. (2015) 'The end of the (forensic science) world as we know it? The example of trace evidence'. *Philosophical Transactions of the Royal Society B: Biological Sciences*, 370 (1674), Article 20140260, 1–8.

Strand, T. (2007) 'The discipline of education in a world of change'. *Nordisk Pedagogik*, 27 (3), 265–76.

Walport, M. (2015) *Forensic Science and Beyond: Authenticity, provenance and assurance: Evidence and case studies*. London: Government Office for Science. Online. www.gov.uk/government/uploads/system/uploads/attachment_data/file/506462/gs-15-37b-forensic-science-beyond-evidence.pdf (accessed 13 March 2018).

Index

Index

Index

Index